THE
Luminaries

THE
Luminaries

THE PSYCHOLOGY OF THE SUN AND MOON IN THE HOROSCOPE

SEMINARS IN PSYCHOLOGICAL ASTROLOGY, VOLUME 3

——by——

Liz Greene & Howard Sasportas

WEISER BOOKS
Boston, MA/York Beach, ME

First published in 1992 by
Red Wheel/Weiser, LLC
P. O. Box 612
York Beach, ME 03910-0612

08 07 06 05 04 03 02 01
10 9 8 7 6 5

Library of Congress Cataloging-in-Publication Data

Greene, Liz.
     The Luminaries / Liz Greene & Howard Sasportas
           p.   cm. -(Seminars in psychological astrology : v.3)
      1. Astrology. 2. Moon-Miscellanea.   3. Sun-Miscellanea
    I. Sasportas, Howard.   II. Title.   III. Series.
    BF1723.G74   1992
    133.5'3—dc20   91-43968

ISBN 0-87728-750-3
TCP

Cover illustration copyright © 1992 Liz Greene

Typeset in 10 point Palatino

Printed in Canada

The paper used in this publication meets the minimum requirements of
the American National Standard for Information Sciences—Permanence
of Paper for Printed Library Materials Z39.48-1992(R1997).

CONTENTS

To Alois and Elisabeth

and to their twin daughters, Artemis and Lilith,
who were conceived at the time this seminar was given

INTRODUCTION

The word *luminary*, according to the *Chambers Twentieth Century Dictionary*, means, very simply, a source of light. It also describes "one who illustrates any subject or instructs mankind." Thus a luminary in the world of literature or the theatre is someone with a great talent—an actor like Laurence Olivier or a writer like Thomas Mann—who through his or her excellence defines the standard toward which we aspire. A luminary is one who sets an example, embodying the best of what might be achieved.

In an earlier and more poetic astrology, the Sun and Moon were called the Luminaries—or, alternatively, the Lights. What are these luminaries, these exemplary "instructors" within us which define in their separate domains the internal standard toward which we aspire as individuals? In the past, astrology has interpreted planetary placements as a kind of immovable given—the way we are made. The Sun and Moon are therefore said to represent essential characteristics which irrevocably define the individual personality. But any astrological factor is also a process, for when the human being is seen through the lens of psychological insight, he or she is not static, but moves through life in an unending process of change and development. An astrological placement describes an arrow which points somewhere, a creative energy which gradually layers flesh onto the bare bones of archetypal patterning, an intelligent movement which, over time, fills in the stark black-and-white outlines of the essential life-myth with the subtle colours of experience and individual choice. The luminaries in the horoscope are truly instructors, reflecting what we could one day become, portraying in symbolic form the best of what might be achieved.

Human beings are born unfinished. Compared to other animal species, we come into the world prematurely, depending for many years on others who can ensure our physical and psychological survival. A baby crocodile, newly emerged from the egg, has teeth which can bite, a fully coordinated body which can run and swim, and a rampant aggressive instinct which allows it to hunt for food and which protects it from other predators. But we, the *magnum miraculum* of nature, whom Shakespeare described as "mewling and puking in the nurse's arms"—toothless, weak, uncoordinated and incapable of feeding ourselves—are born potential victims; for unless there is someone out there who can look after us, we will die. Cast from the Eden of the womb without those basic essentials of our own car, our own flat and our own American Express card, we need a mother or a mother-surrogate upon whom we can depend, and this immediate and absolute physical dependency gives rise to a profound and binding emotional attachment to the primal life-source which is counterbalanced only by our later struggles to separate from her. And because, in the beginning, mother is our whole world, we begin to perceive the world in the light of our earliest experience of her, and learn to mother ourselves according to the example given. If mother is a safe container who can sufficiently meet our basic needs—Winicott's "good enough mother"—then we become adults who trust life and believe that the world is essentially a kind and supportive place because we have learned by example how to be kind and supportive to ourselves. But if our needs are denigrated, manipulated or simply denied, then we grow into adults who believe that the world is full of predators of superhuman strength and cunning, and that life itself does not favour our survival, for we do not favour it ourselves. Mother gives us our first concrete model of the Moon's instructive self-nurturing—our earliest example of what might be achieved. But the Moon, the luminary which teaches us how to care for ourselves according to our own unique needs, is ultimately within us, and can show us—if our early containment was not "good enough"—how to heal the wounds, so that life can be trusted after all.

Differentiating ourselves as entities in our own right, related to but not the same as mother, heralds our psychological birth. There is something within us which struggles against the utter dependency and fusion of infancy, and which propels us on the long and thorny road toward becoming independent beings with power over our own lives. This is not merely a matter of growing teeth and learning to bite other crocodiles. The Sun, the luminary which instructs us in the rites and rituals of separation, beckons us on with the great mystery of "I," the shimmering promise of a distinct and authentic personality which is different from others and which possesses not only the wit to survive, but also the capacity to fill life with meaning, purpose and joy. The passage from dependency on mother to independent existence, inner and outer, is, as the archetypal hero's journey portrays, fraught with fear and danger. Oneness with mother is bliss—the timeless and eternal cocoon of the Paradise Garden where there is no conflict, no loneliness, no pain and no death. But autonomy and authenticity are lonely, for what if no one loves us? And what is the point of all the struggle and anxiety if one day, like all living creatures, we must die? Our inner instructors, like the Babylonian fire-god Marduk and his oceanic mother Tiamat, appear to be locked in nothing less than mortal combat. Or, in the words of the poet Richard Wilbur, "The plant would like to grow/ And yet be embryo,/ Increase and yet escape/ The doom of taking shape . . ."[1]

It has been said that history is the story of the unfolding of consciousness. Just as our personal history begins with the emergence of the infant out of the waters of the womb, so too does the mythological history of the universe begin with the solar god or hero emerging triumphant out of the body of the primal Great Mother. The hero's battle with the mother-dragon and eventual apotheosis in the arms of his divine father is not, of course, the end of the story; for he must ultimately return from the Olympian heights and unite as a human being with his feminine counterpart, transformed through the hero's struggles from dragon into beloved. But the solar hero within us, embattled for a time (and sometimes a lifetime), is that inner luminary which guides the emancipation of the ego from the blind instinctual compulsions of nature into the initially lonely but truly indestructible light of "me."

---

[1]Richard Wilbur, "Seed Leaves," from *The Norton Anthology of Poetry*, 3rd edition, Alexander W. Allison et al. eds. (New York: W. W. Norton, 1986) pp. 1201–1202.

The Sun and Moon symbolise two very basic but very different psychological processes which operate within all of us. The lunar light which lures us back toward regressive fusion with mother and the safety of the uroboric container is also the light which teaches us how to relate, to care for ourselves and others, to belong, to feel compassion. The solar light which leads us into anxiety, danger and loneliness is also the light which instructs us in our hidden divinity and—as Pico della Mirandola put it in the 15th century—our right to be proud co-creators of God's universe. To find a viable balance between these two, an alchemical *coniunctio* which honours both, is the work of a lifetime. The differentiation of the self from fusion with the world of mother, nature and collective allows us to develop reason, will, power and choice—and in historical terms, this has generated the remarkable social and technological advances of our 20th century Western culture. We may glamourise the distant past of the more "natural" matriarchal world, but when we consider what was then on offer—an average life-span of 25 years, a total helplessness in the face of disease and the forces of nature, and an utter disregard for the value of an individual life—we might better appreciate what kind of gift our solar instructor has given us during the long sweep of our evolution out of the mother-cave. Yet perhaps we have gone too far, at the expense of heart and instinct; and our blind brutalisation of mother earth has led us to the brink of an ecological abyss. With our eyes on the brilliance of the solar light, we have mythically dissociated, rather than differentiated from, mother; and where we were once at her mercy, now she is at ours—and so too are our bodies and our planet. In our personal lives, too, it seems that we are still struggling toward that rhythmic balance reflected by the cyclical dance of the Sun and Moon in the heavens. Jung said that if there is something wrong with society, there is something wrong with the individual; and if there is something wrong with the individual, there is something wrong with me. "Me" is both Sun and Moon—two inner instructors which, because of their unique placements in every birth chart, provide us with our personal standards of excellence in body, heart and mind, and our personal models of the best that might be achieved for the unfoldment of the spirit and the soul. However powerful the heavier planets might be in the birth chart, it is ultimately the Sun and Moon which must channel and embody these energies and fashion them into individual experience and expression. Understanding the Sun and Moon as descriptions of character traits is only the beginning of understanding astrology; yet developing what the luminaries symbolise so that we are fitting vessels for what lies within us may be the most challenging and the best of what we can achieve in an individual life.

Note: The lectures in this volume form the first part of a week-long seminar called *The Inner Planets*, which was given in Zürich in June, 1990. The remaining lectures from this seminar, on Mercury, Venus and Mars, will appear in a subsequent volume.

Liz Greene
Howard Sasportas
London, November, 1991

PART ONE

THE MOON

AVdANCA
565 th   aus 320   Quent
                    to
                  Sean Sula
                    then
                      to John
                         ok

ply 408
    312
    800 Am
         142   10 2017

      John Ry

MOTHERS AND MATRIARCHY

THE MYTHOLOGY AND PSYCHOLOGY OF THE MOON

BY LIZ GREENE

In this session we will explore the Moon, mothers and matriarchy. I want to say a word first about the illustration you have been given (see figure 1 on p. 4). We will work with these mythological maps for both the Sun and the Moon throughout week. This particular diagram is meant to help you find your way around an interconnected group of lunar mythic images, but it is not a definitive compilation, as there are obviously a great many figures and themes I have not included. The ones I shall refer to this afternoon are intended as imaginative triggers which might help deepen your insight into the astrological symbol of the Moon. Mythic images are self-portrayals by the psyche of its own processes. If we explore these images and see how they operate within people on an everyday personal level, we can begin to grasp the multidimensional symbol of the Moon much more profoundly and subtly than if we tried to list simple definitions.

I would like you to first put to one side all the astrological knowledge you have acquired about the Moon in the horoscope, and think about your direct experience of the actual physical Moon in the heavens. Have you ever observed it regularly over its monthly cycle? I think every astrological student should have a telescope and a good astronomical map. The lunar cycle is quite miraculous to watch, and it can provoke strong imaginative and emotional reactions in us, as it has done in human beings for millennia. The full Moon is very magical and hypnotic, and can sometimes even seem sinister, as if it were a mysterious eye watching us from the darkness of the night sky. How many of you have ever played the old childhood game, and tried to find a face in the full Moon? All of you? Well, you are proving my point. It's almost

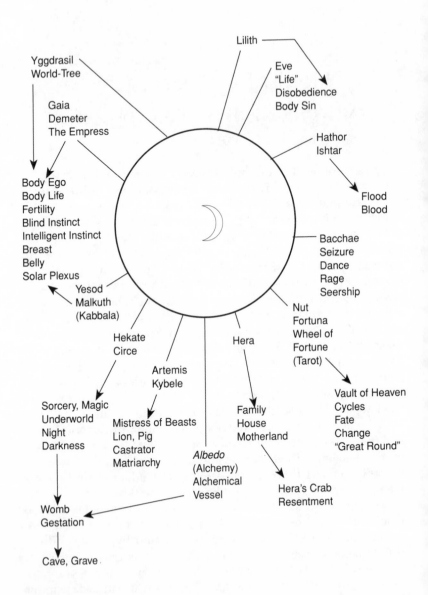

Figure 1. The mythology of the Moon.

impossible, if we are with someone and the Moon is full overhead, to avoid pointing at it—"Oh, look at the Moon!" we say, although one could scarcely miss it. And have you ever admired one of those elegant, slender crescent Moons? There is something so terribly fragile and delicate and even poignant about this phase of the Moon. It never appears sinister in the way the full Moon sometimes does. Have any of you ever watched a lunar eclipse? This is a strange and rather baleful phenomenon, because the Moon darkens, turning blood red or brown; in ancient and medieval times this was interpreted as the herald of some dreadful event.

Imagine what it might have been like to watch the Moon in ancient times, without any knowledge of the material universe, and you will begin to realise how very powerful a symbol it has always been, and how splendid a hook for our psychic projections. If you were a Neolithic cave-dweller, the first obvious fact about the physical Moon which you would notice is that it is always changing, yet it repeats its cycle in an unchanging way. From one night to the next the Moon's shape is different, yet you can always be sure it will repeat its pattern in a month's time. The Moon is a paradox: It is unreliable at the same time that its cycle is utterly reliable. Sometimes it gives light, but not quite enough to clarify anything, while at other times the light vanishes altogether and the night is black. So if you were an ancient traveller relying on the Moon's light at night, you would have fallen into trouble very soon, because of the inexorable shrinking of the light. Thus the Moon was viewed as treacherous, and the earliest lunar goddesses who personified it are paradoxical and ambiguous in character.

It might be useful to remember that in built-up areas in Western countries we are accustomed to seeing the night lights of towns and cities reflected against cloud banks; and this reflection can extend for many, many miles. We live in an age of electricity, and have no recollection of times when houses were lit by hearth fires or candles or oil lamps. Thus the night sky is never really totally dark, but we do not realise it. Many city-dwellers have never seen a truly black night. Unless we are on board a ship in the middle of the Atlantic, or in relatively uninhabited countryside such as the Australian Outback or the Sahara Desert, we almost never experience the absolute darkness of the new Moon which our ancestors did. And when there is lunar light, it is a very peculiar light, which bleaches the colour from everything. Ordinary landscapes and objects look strange and otherworldly under the full Moon. If one is romantically occupied, then this light is enchanting. But if one is alone, it can be very disturbing.

Nursery rhymes are full of the magic of the Moon—the Man in the Moon, and the Moon being made of green cheese, and the cow jumping over the Moon. Pop songs and romantic tunes address the Moon—"Blue Moon," "Fly Me to the Moon," and so on. The Moon makes us think of lovers, but also of lunatics, the latter word deriving from the Latin *luna*. There are fairy and folk tales about people turning into wolves or vampires when the Moon is full, and about people going mad if the light of the full Moon shines through the window on one's face during sleep—hence the association with lunacy. Even before we begin to look at the mythic figures who cluster around the different lunar phases, we can see that the Moon has invoked the most extraordinary fantasies and projections from the human imagination over the centuries. These fantasies invariably concern the night world of human emotions—love, madness and sorcery.

The perpetually changing yet constant lunar cycle has gathered to itself a characteristic body of myth, with which many of you will be familiar. The lunar deities, who are usually female (although there are exceptions) most often appear in a triad, or with three aspects which reflect the three distinct phases of the full, new and crescent Moon. If we play about with the images which these three phases invoke, we can see how the new Moon, the treacherous black Moon, was associated with death, gestation, sorcery, and the Greek goddess Hekate who presided over birth and black magic. After the dark of the Moon, the crescent Moon appears with its virginal delicacy and promise, looking as though it is ready to be impregnated by something. It is shaped like a bowl, open to that which may penetrate it from outside. The crescent Moon was linked with the virgin goddess Persephone, who was abducted by Hades. It was also said to be the emblem of Artemis, the virgin huntress and mistress of wild beasts, whom we will look at more closely later. The full Moon in contrast has a pregnant look; it is round and juicy, lush and ripe, and might give birth at any moment. This is the Moon at its maximum power, the apex of the lunar cycle, and it was associated with the fertility goddess Demeter, mother of all living things. Then the Moon begins to wane, growing thinner and darker, and then suddenly it is not there any more. Hekate, the old crone, is now in power once again, hidden in the underworld weaving her spells and spinning the future in the darkness.

The triad of lunar deities which has always been associated with the Moon reflects an archetypal human experience, projected onto the physical Moon in the heavens. One important dimension of this experience is the body itself, which reflects in its own cyclical development and mortality the phases of the Moon. The lunar deities presided over the yearly cycle of vegetation, and also over the human cycle of birth and death. Thus the Moon in myth governs the organic realm of the body and the instincts, which is why these deities are usually female—it is out of the female body that we are all born and receive our first food. The lunar cycle was called the Great Round, reflecting its connection with fate and with things always coming back again, endlessly repeating. All things which are mortal have their cycle, and it is a universal rather than an individual cycle, since individuals die but the species continues to regenerate itself.

From the solar perspective, the body is only of value as a symbol. Solar consciousness is concerned with that which is eternal, and it does not give value to birth, fruition, disintegration and death. The world of the body is transcended in the light of day, and we are offered instead the promise of immortality and of ultimate meaning. If we identify exclusively with this day-world, we disconnect from the Moon, at least for a time, for the Moon is a "distraction," part of the web of Maya, as they might say in Hindu circles. If we view and experience things through the Moon, life is not constant and eternal, for we are viewing a play in which the ordinary person incarnated in life has the lead role. Everything is in a state of flux, bound to the wheel of Fortune and Time.

Now, there are individuals who are more attuned to viewing through the lunar lens because of the Moon's importance in their birth charts, and it is the changeability and cyclical nature of reality which seem the dominant characteristic of life to them. Safety and security and the warmth of human contact thus become much more important than any abstract quest for meaning, because life is so full of flux and must be coped with from day to day. These people are especially gifted at keeping their feet on the ground and dealing with events and people in a sensible, reassuring and compassionate way. Because we all have the Moon in the horoscope, all of us are capable of experiencing the world and ourselves through the Moon's eye. Some of us get stuck there and cannot look beyond our immediate personal circumstances. Equally, some of us don't look sufficiently at the cyclical nature of reality, and consequently cannot cope very well with ordinary life, because we are addicted to eternity and have forgotten how to trust the instincts and work intelligently with time.

The Moon was associated in medieval times with the goddess Fortuna, whom some of you will recognise in the card of the Wheel of Fortune in the Tarot deck. You may also know the opening verses of Orff's *Carmina Burana*:

O Fortune, changeable as the Moon!
You always wax or wane;
Hateful life is one moment hard
And the next moment favours the gambler.
Poverty, power,
All melt like ice.

Whenever we reach a peak moment in life, a full Moon moment when things are coming to fruition, we can be sure that there is a past which has led to this moment, a hidden beginning when the seed was sown at the dark of the Moon and a time of promise and development when the Moon was in its crescent phase. And we can also be sure that there is a future when decay sets in, and the cycle must continue to its inevitable end, because nothing in mortal life remains the same. Then, as the Moon wanes and the moment passes, we look back to the past when things seemed so full of promise. When we view life through the eye of the Moon, there is always a looking back to the past, and the feeling of the body growing older reflects this looking back to the youth of the crescent Moon with its unlived potentials. We can always remember a time when we had more energy and fewer wrinkles, even if we are only 20. Once upon a time, in childhood, the body was young and unfinished. Once upon a time, one was naive and innocent and open, before experience intruded like the Serpent in the Garden and shaped one's perceptions and values. So you can see that there is a deep poignancy and melancholy attached to the Moon. The Moon sings in a minor key, because everything passes. We cannot stay anywhere forever, because we will outgrow it one day, and must face the dark of the Moon before a new birth and new potentials can emerge. And if one is identified with the lunar landscape, death is the inevitable end of the cycle. Under the light of the Moon, everything in life follows the Great Round. Relationships have their cycles. Creativity has its cycles, as any artist can tell you. Family life has cycles, and so do financial affairs (Fortuna rules the stock market), and so too does history. Everything comes back round again, and there is nothing new under the Sun because the Moon has done it all before. Now it is interesting to look at the positive and negative dimensions of this cyclical experience of life, which is really a psychological state of being. We might call it matriarchal, because it is a vision of life which is essentially female and organic, reflecting the processes of conception, pregnancy, birth, puberty, maturation, ageing and dying. Mythically, matriarchal consciousness is concerned with natural cycles, giving priority to harmony with the Great Round rather than to a human will or spirit which can transcend it.

We can easily idealise matriarchal consciousness, voicing a perhaps necessary counterbalance to the destructive power of too much rationality and will. This is rather in vogue in certain circles at the moment. But it is possible to have too much of a good thing, which is the case with every planet. Because the Moon governs the realm of nature, a purely matriarchal consciousness dispenses with the value of the individual, giving absolute importance to family and to tribe, justifying the suppression or destruction of individual self-expression if the security of the group is threatened. There are no ethics or principles in this domain, nor any disciplined use of the will. All is justified by instinctual need and preservation of the species. Many women are angered at having projected on them by men the darker lunar qualities of manipulativeness, treacherousness, unreliability, moodiness and emotional voracity. I have heard numerous men complain of how difficult it is to work with or discuss things objectively with women, because reasonableness and cooperation fly out of the window in the face of personal feelings. But these qualities will often be very pronounced in any person, male or female, where the Moon dominates the horoscope.

You can begin to see what an extreme lunar consciousness is all about, which is why the lunar deities were seen not only as nourishers and child protectors, but also as child swallowers and castrators.

Equally, it is not difficult to see what happens if we remain unrelated to the Moon. We may lose our sense of connection with and care for the body, which on a more global level means disconnection with and lack of care for nature and the living earth. It is the body which reminds us that we are mortal. Our bodies experience pain, sickness and ageing as well as pleasure and delight. We also have body moods, for our emotional states are intimately connected with our bodies. It is impossible to say which comes first. Low blood sugar and a poorly functioning thyroid gland reflect depression, and depression affects the immune system, so we get a cold, which depresses us even more. Sometimes we get up in the morning just feeling rotten, with puffy faces, and the weather is also rotten, but how can we say that one causes the other? Or might our bodies, being part of an interconnected world organism, simply move in harmony with climatic changes more than we realise? What we eat has a profound effect on our moods, but our moods in turn affect what we eat. If we are unhappy or stressed, we grab for "comfort food" like chocolate, which in turn makes us feel unhappy and stressed because the blood sugar level crashes afterward, which makes us depressed. And so on. If we cannot sleep, we feel pretty rough; but if we are feeling rough, we cannot sleep. You can see how circular it all is. It is the body, the domain of the Moon, which keeps us in touch with life in the moment, whether it is the dark or the light face of experience we are encountering. Without sufficient expression of the Moon, it is not only the body which suffers. It is our capacity to experience life in the present. Then it comes as a horrible shock when we discover that life has somehow flown by without our really knowing we have lived it. The container remains empty, so there is no memory, no feeling of continuity, and no sense of a fruitful past.

We might consider more closely two of the figures in the diagram, Gaia and Demeter. Both of these are very ancient earth goddesses, of which Gaia is the elder, the original female principle with whom the heaven god Ouranos mates to create the manifest cosmos. Demeter is a later, more humanised version of the same figure. The earth goddess or earth mother is really an image of the animating principle in nature itself, the intelligent and purposeful life force within the material universe, which has been associated since earliest times with the Moon. She not only embodies the world of nature as a unified life-form, but also the human body, which is our primary direct experience of her. The earth mother is thus a mythic portrayal of our experience of our body life, which is beyond our control and therefore seems numinous or divine.

Because the body runs itself—we don't think about breathing, or making our hearts beat, or digesting lunch—it appeared magical to the primitive mind. It is still magical, for although we have considerable knowledge of how the various organs in the body work, we are no closer to really comprehending the nature of the animating life principle than we were six millennia ago. It is still a great mystery. The complexity and intelligence of the body are extraordinary. When something goes wrong, there is a great wisdom within the body which, with very little encouragement, will heal itself. Many approaches under the umbrella of alternative medicine might therefore be considered matriarchal or lunar, since they aim to encourage this wise self-healing within the body rather than intervening forcibly with drugs and instruments. Before our enlightened era, the village "wise woman" (who was often burned as a witch) dispensed natural remedies which are only now being medically recognised as valid or even superior methods of healing. In mythic language, the actual substance and tissues of the body are made of earth, but the intelligent life principle operating within those tissues is symbolised by the Moon.

So the earth mother is an image of the power of nature to sustain and perpetuate itself. Gaia and Demeter, as well as Artemis and Hekate, are portrayed as goddesses of conception and birth in myth, since they represent the intelligent principle which creates and animates the vessels needed for the continuity of the physical life of the world. The Old Testament image for this is Eve, the first woman, whose name in Hebrew means "life." When we are babies, we do not have any ego which can say, "I am myself first, and happen to be incarnated in a body." The sense of an "inner" self, independent of the body, is reflected in astrology by the Sun, and it unfolds as we mature. But the Moon is there from the beginning. A child's first experience is of the body, for in the early weeks of life there is nothing but sensation and body need. We are hungry, we need to sleep, we need to be held and touched, we need to be safe. If these basic instinctual needs are satisfied, then we are content, and life is a safe place. Being able to express the Moon means being able to experience and express the body's survival needs and appetites, without having to justify these through the reasoning capacity or self-awareness of the solar ego.

Therefore, when we consider the psychological principle symbolised by the Moon, we need first of all to consider our basic need for safety and survival. If this need is not sufficiently met, the result is anxiety—a state which everyone experiences at some time in life, but which afflicts some people all the time. Anxiety is really a feeling that life out there is not safe, that we will be obliterated or that something awful will happen to us. Different people have different triggers for anxiety, but I believe that most anxiety states (and I am differentiating between anxiety and common or garden-variety worry, which usually has an immediate and realistic basis) are rooted in very early experiences of feeling unsafe, regardless of the trigger which activates them in adult life.

For some people, it is the threat of rejection or abandonment which triggers anxiety. For others, it is a change in the environment, the threat of being uprooted from one's job or one's home. When we are anxious and need to feel safe again, we turn to the Moon, for this is the earth mother inside us, the instinctual principle which knows how to nourish and sustain life. The Moon's natal sign and house offer a very precise description of what kind of things give us a feeling of safety. Although our lunar hunger is a basic human requirement, the ways in which we express and nourish it are different, and these differences are evident even in early childhood. If we do not know how to receive and act on our innate lunar wisdom, then the Moon cannot operate directly through the personality, and must therefore express itself indirectly. The blind mechanisms which we adopt when we are unconsciously anxious and need safety comprise a huge range of what are called compulsive behaviour patterns. We are all a little compulsive in some way, because life is sometimes unsafe, and no one is so completely secure that he or she will never feel fear. That would be rather stupid, after all, since there are many things which we would be wise to fear, including things within ourselves. But sometimes these compulsions take us over, or dominate our behaviour for many years, often without our realising it. These are what we might call lunar malfunctions. We do not recognise that some primal anxiety has been activated, and we do not know how to nourish ourselves to re-create the feeling of safety which is so necessary for a sense of freedom and fulfilment.

An obvious example of a lunar malfunction is compulsive eating. There is quite a wide spectrum of what are known as "eating disorders," including anorexia, bulimia, and so-called food "allergies"—although many people would not consider the latter an "eating disorder." Most of us experience some kind of compulsion around food at some time in life, even if this is a brief period when we reach for the crisps or the chocolates because we are temporarily under stress. I am inclined to relate these food cravings to the Moon (which in ancient astrology was said to rule the stomach), although usually other planets will be involved in difficult configurations with the Moon when such eating problems are chronic. Our earliest experience of food and safety, and our first encounter with the lunar principle after birth, is mother's breast. Although the Moon is really inside us, we first meet it exteriorised in the person who has given birth to us, feeds us and protects us. If mother goes away, then the dark of the Moon has come, and we are overcome with terror of the abyss of extinction.

Because the human psyche is so wonderfully versatile and creative, unconscious lunar needs do not always express themselves through such a concrete medium as food. A lot of things can be food surrogates, just as food itself is a mother surrogate on the personal as well as the archetypal level. Rather than devouring an entire box of After Eights, we might hoard money instead, since money can also be equated with safety. This is often the case when the Moon is in the 2nd house in the natal chart, or in the 10th, or strongly aspected to Saturn. As long as we own our house, or have a particular sum in savings, or have topped up our pension fund, or can keep that particular car or that particular outfit or that particular piece of jewelry, then we feel safe. You can tell the difference between a common-sense attitude toward money and possessions and a compulsive one, because with the latter there is usually an irrational fear attached to loss. In other words, there is anxiety rather than sensible concern. Often what people call their "lucky charm," their talisman, is an object upon which the Moon has been projected. This kind of magical thinking is typical of the primitive, the child, and the archaic layer of the adult psyche. But of course the object is not really lucky. It has somehow taken on a symbolic value and has become the 20th-century embodiment of the lunar goddess, alienated from consciousness and reduced to translating herself into a chocolate biscuit or a string of worry beads.

For some, other people constitute lunar food. It might be a lover or spouse, children or grandchildren, or even a social circle or a professional or ideological group. Some of us simply enjoy the company of friends or family, while others are dependent upon them in a compulsive way, and react with great anxiety to any threat of expulsion from the group or any change of roles within the family. I have met people who are so identified with the family, so accustomed to unconsciously turning to the family unit for their lunar food, that in their terror they will emotionally brutalise any family member who threatens to go his or her own way and follow an individual path. This is often referred to as "love" or "concern," but lunar hunger, as we shall see when we explore some of the other images in our diagram, can at times be utterly ruthless and destructive. Whole families can suffer from a lack of lunar connection amongst the individual members, since each of us learns how to express the inner planets from the parents who are our models. Then anxiety permeates the entire family organism, and the members unconsciously feed off each other for safety.

At the end of this session, I would like each of you to go away and think about what constitutes food for you. What do you reach for when you are anxious? There is no way that human beings can avoid anxiety, because life is a changeable and unpredictable business. A good relationship with the Moon will not spare us anxiety. But it may offer a capacity to feed ourselves with the right kind of nourishment, which in turn allows us to cope with anxiety in a reasonably creative way. No one else can tell us how to do that because it is such a highly personal business, dependent upon where the Moon is placed in an individual chart, and also where it has arrived in the progressed chart at a particular juncture in life.

I think now we should have a closer look at Artemis, the Anatolian goddess of the Moon who was adopted by the Greeks. She is a highly ambivalent goddess, and can tell us a lot about the darker face of the Moon. I should say again, as we explore each of these lunar figures, that everyone is different, and each of us will have more affinity with one figure than with another in our inner and outer lives. Perhaps on a deep collective level we all have access to the whole spectrum of lunar images, but these will be biased according to what the Moon is doing in the birth chart. If your Moon is in Scorpio, for example, or in strong aspect to Pluto, you might have more empathy with Hekate and the dark face of the Moon, appreciating rather than fearing its depth and mystery. But Hekate's realm might be very disturbing to someone with the Moon in Gemini. The Moon in Taurus might have great affinity with the image of Demeter and the world of nature, but Demeter, the earth mother, might not resonate terribly well with the Moon in Aquarius or in strong aspect to Uranus. Usually we will find a combination of aspects and images in any chart, and of course sooner or later the progressed Moon will contact every natal planet. So the opportunity to experience each of these figures is always offered during a lifetime. But people are made differently, after all. Since in this seminar we are working primarily with life as viewed through a lunar lens, the issue is to learn to appreciate what we need as individuals, rather than attempting to become some ideal vision of complete wholeness.

Artemis, whose roots stretch back much further than the nubile huntress in the gym slip, was known as the Lady of the Beasts. The earliest images of her come from central Anatolia, where a 7000-year-old terra cotta statue was unearthed at Catalhöyük portraying an extremely fat woman giving birth, flanked by lions on either side. These lions are her most ancient emblems. As she developed over the centuries, she became known as Kybele, Mother of All, and is portrayed standing in a chariot drawn by lions. Her centre of worship was Ephesus in southwest Turkey, where you can see in the local museum an extraordinarily beautiful marble statue of her, carved in the late Roman period, once again surrounded by her lions and other beasts who adorn her robes. This marble figure in the Ephesus Museum has rows of what might be breasts or eggs or even testicles lined up across the front of her body from the shoulders to the abdomen. Archaeologists are forever arguing about what these appendages represent. Around her neck is carved the zodiac, indicating her rulership over the Great Round of fate written in the heavens. Kybele-Artemis was associated with a youthful son-lover, Attis, who castrated himself to remain faithful to her. Although she is a fertility goddess, this most ancient lunar deity is an image of the dark heart of wild nature, and in this form she is not altogether pleasant.

Now what dimension of the Moon is this? Artemis seems to embody the untamed, savage face of the instincts. She is a strong statement against our traditional astrological assumptions that the lunar or Cancerian nature is all about fresh-baked bread and cuddly babies and domestic bliss. There is an ecstatic, raging quality to this goddess which brings us closer to understanding the connection between *luna* and lunatic. Here the lionesses (they have no manes) are lunar, not solar, beasts. If you know anything about lions, you will know that it is the female who does all the real work. She goes out and hunts, while the male lies about preening himself and looking wonderful, waiting for his dinner to be brought back. The lioness is a matriarch, and her mates are essentially toy-boys, although they would eat you rather than admit it.

This face of the Moon is often what emerges when we get drunk, or lose control of solar consciousness. One can find a glimpse of Artemis in one's own emotional savagery, if the instinctual needs are violated or threatened. The wolf is also her creature, and the myth of the lycanthrope or werewolf, which was originally Greek before it worked its way into eastern European folklore, also belongs to her. The werewolf appears when the Moon is full, and it is said to destroy only those it loves. Any of you who have ever seen the old Universal Pictures film *The Wolf Man*, which starred Lon Chaney, Jr., as the werewolf, might remember the gypsy's warning:

> Even a man who is pure at heart
> And says his prayers at night
> May become a wolf when the wolfbane blooms
> And the Moon is full and bright.

Lycanthropy in folklore is a state of possession by a supernatural bestial force which turns savagely against those upon whom the person is emotionally dependent. The werewolf can only be destroyed by a weapon made of silver, the Moon's traditional metal—as though only nature itself can tame or contain nature.

Although we have had to endure even sillier werewolf films than Lon Chaney's (such as Oliver Reed appearing as a Spanish aristocrat with a shiny black nose, furry hands and little tufts of hair on his ears), we have also had some beautiful cinematic portrayals such as *The Company of Wolves* and *Wolfen*, starring Albert Finney. The eternal attraction of werewolf films tells us how very potent and enduring an image it is.

We do not often meet this face of the Moon in astrological textbooks. Yet it is a dimension of the full rather than the new Moon, when the lunar light is at its most powerful and the matriarchy rules. It is matriarchy at its most dangerous, because the carrier of the seed is faceless and dispensable, ritually slaughtered to fertilise the earth and ensure the continuity of the crops or the family or the group. I have sometimes heard women give voice to this archaic matriarchal feeling—"Oh well, I'm not very happy with him, but all cats are grey at night after all, and he's no worse than someone else would have been, and anyway all I really wanted was to settle down and have a family." For such a woman, the individual relationship with the partner is not paramount; it is the family which matters, and which justifies any amount of martyrdom or destructiveness. The implication is that any old sperm would have done just as well, so long as the family is secure. In myth the Amazons, who worshipped Artemis, ritually mated once a year with men whose names they did not know and whose faces they never saw, for the purpose of becoming pregnant; the male children of these unions were destroyed, while the females were raised as members of the tribe.

This is a very archaic facet of the full Moon, and when we are identified with it, individual relationship becomes irrelevant. It is the power of gestation and birth and nurturing which are most important. This is the natural state of most women during pregnancy, and it is a potent protector of the newborn child. In the animal kingdom, the female often must protect her young from the male, who is occasionally liable to eat his own progeny. This is actually sometimes the case with lions and other big cats. So you can see both the positive and negative dimensions of this matriarchal consciousness, which protects and preserves life but also destroys with great ruthlessness.

You will also see a reference to the Bacchae or Bacchantes in the diagram. They are also called *maenads*, a word related to mania. The Bacchae were women who worshipped Dionysos, the youthful vegetation god whose earlier forms are Adonis, Tammuz and Attis, the boyish son-lovers of the Mistress of Beasts. These women, when possessed, would climb the hillsides in their lunar mania or ecstatic trance, and tear apart wild animals. You should all read Euripides' *Bacchae*, which is a chilling portrayal of their ecstatic power. In archaic times, they did not limit themselves to wild animals, but ritually dismembered the year-king who was then ploughed into the earth with the sowing of the crops. The most primitive form of matriarchy goes hand in hand with king sacrifice, for the male is only relevant for the seed required for the continuity of life. This is the other side of the bread-baking.

Now, it is worth thinking about what outlets, collective and individual, we have in the 20th century for this dimension of the Moon. Where has the Mistress of the Beasts gone? In any mob frenzy, where a scapegoat is metaphorically or literally torn to pieces, we can glimpse her savagery. But we have few rituals to contain her, other than stag parties, the World Cup, and political rallies. There are no religious cults such as that of Dionysos where we can lose ourselves in lunar ecstasy while remaining within the framework of the law. Even if we release Artemis through alcohol, we have lost our religious connection with her, and all we are left with is the hangover without the rebirth. Sexual ecstasy has also lost its religious connection for many people, so the satisfaction remains physical but does not touch the soul. When the lunar deities are not lived out with honour, they are condemned to express themselves unconsciously and compulsively. Can any of you think of appropriate expressions for the Mistress of the Beasts?

Audience: What about dance?

Liz: Yes, dance can be one of her vehicles, particularly where there is an insistent pounding rhythm and one can work oneself up into a kind of trance state. Instead of Dionysos we have discos. The ancient lunar goddesses were worshipped with music and dance. The Amazons, whom I mentioned earlier, were said to go into such a profound trance during the sacred dance that they could pierce themselves with weapons and not bleed. We would now call this a hypnotic trance, and it is a medical fact that one can slow down or stop bleeding when in a state of hypnosis. The insistent rhythm of tribal as well as disco music can induce a kind of hypnotic state. We forget that we were tired, all the old aches and pains go away, and the body is at one with some deeper force or power. Many so-called religious miracles occur in this state, and there are strange connections between miracle cures and the state of ecstasy induced by chanting, music and dance.

When this face of the Moon is too violently denied, one result can be hysteria. We usually use the word "hysterical" to describe overemotional behaviour, where one screeches and smashes plates and weeps and goes temporarily over the top. But this sort of behaviour can also be chronic and a serious clinical condition, which in psychiatry is known as hysterical personality disorder. It is a kind of ongoing and compulsive Moon madness, where no real solar individuality or consciousness has formed. There may be a well-trained persona but it can easily shatter to reveal the maenad within. Hysteria is a deeply manipulative and often violently destructive disorder, producing all kinds of inexplicable bodily symptoms as well as a virtual revelling in emotional excess; and its ambience is truly matriarchal. Clinically, it is related to severe damage in the early mother-child relationship, and an independent personality never fully develops. Although superficially adapted and often charming and appealing to acquaintances, the person remains primarily infantile and utterly lunar, demanding emotional food through a kind of helpless dependency which exerts absolute control over the family. It is one of the most disturbing ways in which a stifled or injured Moon can find an outlet through the personality.

Now we should look at the figure of Circe in the diagram, for the Moon is also a sorceress. Hekate, whom we have met already, is the dark lunar goddess who presides over sorcery and enchantment. The more humanised figure of Circe, who appears in Homer's *Odyssey*, tells us about this lunar power of enchantment in greater detail. Circe rules a magical island onto which Odysseus and his men stumble on their wandering way back from the Trojan War; and she turns all his crew into swine. These poor men are stuck for a time in pig bodies, still able to think rationally but unable to control their appearance or their behaviour. The instinctual nature, taking the form of a pig (another animal associated with the Great Mother), has taken over, rendering the conscious personality inarticulate and impotent.

I do not really need to elaborate on what it might mean to behave like a pig or a swine — we use both words in a perjorative way to describe boorish, offensive behaviour. The motif of being turned into an animal by a powerful sorceress or fairy is common in folklore, and appears also in Shakespeare's *A Midsummer Night's Dream*, where poor Bottom acquires an ass's head to confirm the fact that he is an ass anyway. The deity who performs these spells is nearly always female (excepting Shakespeare), and she is most commonly found transforming princes into toads. Under the spell of the Moon, one is reduced to the level of a beast. Often in these tales there is a moral issue involved — the person needs to learn to respect the outraged lunar power which has previously been ignored, dishonoured or repressed. Sometimes it is sheer malevolence or caprice, of which the lunar deities are perfectly capable; their morality is not that of the solar realm. In other words, nature may simply be wantonly cruel, or else revenges herself on us when we become too disconnected or arrogant by pitching us into brutish or asinine behaviour which teaches us that we are mortal after all. We are reduced to our body natures by that instinctual power which we have neglected in our heroic climb toward the Sun. Perhaps sometimes, like Bottom, we need to wear an ass's head.

Finally, we can explore the figure of Hera before we leave the diagram and move on to an example chart. This Greek goddess who presides over family life can give us further insight into the nature of the Moon. She embodies the stability and sanctity of marriage and the family unit, and because of her sharply defined morality she may seem Saturnian as much as lunar. But the Moon also has laws and structures, which exist for the protection of the species rather than for the efficient functioning of society. If one breaks these lunar laws, Hera takes vengeance. She describes our need to belong somewhere, to define ourselves in terms of the roots from which we come. The lunar side of us says, "This is my name, this is my family, these are my children, this is my patch of land, this is my country. This is where I belong." Such things provide us with a collective identity and a sense of security within the group. Many people have a tremendously powerful need to identify with their historical roots, and suffer great anxiety if they are torn away from their place of origin. They would rather risk pain and even death than pack their bags and move somewhere else. Often we cannot understand why people persist in living on the slopes of active volcanoes which are guaranteed to erupt periodically, or remain entrenched in zones of obvious danger such as Germany during the 1930's. For the same reason, many people will remain in miserable marriages, or cling to destructive families. The terror of being alone, a wanderer in the world, is deemed worse than the suffering and claustrophobia of their situation. The Moon cannot bear isolation, and will often cling to a familiar family demon rather than pursuing an unfamiliar independent angel. This is Hera at work within, placing the value of roots and tradition before the fulfilment of an individual life.

We can see both the positive and negative aspects of this archetypal need. Without a sense of relationship to roots and family and nation, any society falls into anarchy and chaos, for overwhelming anxiety drives the collective into regressive and often destructive behaviour. Sometimes it unleashes the hunt for a scapegoat; sometimes it paves the way for a tyrant-parent to take over and bring order back. Both are characteristic reactions to severe anxiety. This has been the case historically when nations have been stripped of their traditions or their pride in nationhood, such as France after the Revolution, or Germany after the First World War. The bloodbath of the French Revolution led inexorably to Napoleon; the debacle of the First World War left in the German people an overwhelming need for both a scapegoat and a Messiah who would restore their lost dignity and sense of roots. One presented himself fairly quickly. On the other hand, if there is too much lunar law, the individual suffocates, for we are back once again to matriarchal rule. No act or thought or emotion or creative effort is permissible which might threaten the security of the collective, and the individual must either turn outlaw or slide into the living death of chronic depression.

Sometimes a person may feel that they have successfully detached themselves from their roots. "Ah well, I'm a citizen of the world," says the Sagittarian or the Aquarian, "and my family are those with whom I share intellectual and spiritual values." This may be true of the conscious personality, especially when Jupiter and Uranus are strong in the birth chart. But there is a deeper level where we do not escape Hera so easily. This facet of the Moon can also create compulsive behaviour patterns if it is not acknowledged. Our need to belong may unconsciously seek root surrogates if we reject such values on the conscious level. Even the most enlightened and nonattached of souls can turn clannish, bigoted and vengeful if their root surrogate is threatened, although it may be in the name of an apparently freethinking ideology. Instead of the family or the nation, the surrogate might be a spiritual or political philosophy, which then takes on a curiously emotional and compulsive cast. A good example is Marxism in Russia and Eastern Europe, espoused, in theory, to bring enlightenment and freedom to the archaic Hera-like world of the Czar, the Orthodox Church and the rigid Russian social hierarchy. However, Marxism rapidly became a root surrogate of the most suffocating and ruthless kind. The Party unconsciously metamorphosed into the Family, and the prodigal children, whether individual dissidents or recalcitrant countries such as Hungary and Czechoslovakia, were whipped into submission. Psychological dynamics of this kind—what Jung called *enantiodromia*—occur in both collectives and individuals who utterly reject this facet of the Moon. It may be very necessary for one's psychic (or even physical) survival to part ways with one's racial, religious and social roots, if these roots strangle rather than nourish. But we cannot dismiss the ancestral bedrock with mere intellectual sleight of hand. Until the conflict and its pain are made conscious, someone or something will inevitably replace the lost sense of roots and continuity, and we merely recreate the original dilemma somewhere else.

It might be interesting to ask yourselves what, in your own lives, provides a sense of family, roots and connection with the past. This may be especially relevant if you have rejected these things on ideological grounds, or if your own family choked rather than nourished you. Often the frustrated Moon inside us tries to create a safe and indestructible family in some other way, through blind clinging to our partners and children, or through equally blind clinging to a job or company. If we lack a feeling of lunar roots inside, we will seek them outside. If this is unconscious, then it may be addictive and imprisoning, and then we cannot understand why we are still stuck in the boring job or the destructive marriage after thirty years when so many other potentials are being stifled. Perhaps we need to develop a genuine appreciation of the positive aspects of our ancestral past and how they might be expressed in our present lives, so that Hera can find a place to be at home.

Audience: I would like to ask about what you called a matriarchal attitude in women—overvaluing the family and feeling the husband is dispensable except as a breadwinner or a sperm donor. Why do some people feel like this? It might be fine for the woman, but I wouldn't like to be the husband.

Liz: Nor would I; and many men leave such marriages later in life. But often the man is as identified with the matriarchal world as his wife, and he needs to be mothered rather than related to as an individual. This is an archetypal attitude, which I associate with the Moon at its most primitive level. It is intrinsically neither "good" nor "bad." Some degree of it is healthy and necessary in both men and women, in order to cope with the complexities of family and social life. We must sometimes put the collective before our own self-gratification, which is the very powerful message of environmentalists at the moment. But if one has a bit of an individual self, it can be very lonely and frustrating being the husband of a matriarchal woman or the wife of a matriarchal man (and they do indeed exist), because one's individual value is constantly being undermined and ground down. It is rather like those James Thurber cartoons with giant house-sized women pulling little spindly husbands after them on leads. Nor is it pleasant to be a child in such a matriarchal world; the child is inevitably idealised because the mythic background of the matriarchy is the parthenogenic or self-fertilising goddess. This means that the child is divine, magically engendered, and destined to be its mother's heroic redeemer. That is quite an expectation for a child to live up to, and can lead to many emotional difficulties in adulthood.

I think there are many reasons why any individual woman would fall into such an archaic identification at the expense of other, equally important facets of her personality. Usually the causes lie in her own family background. If a woman has been severely emotionally undernourished in childhood, and is consequently full of anxiety, she may seek her emotional food by unconsciously identifying with the archetypal lunar goddess. Many women try to find the security of the lunar mother inside by embodying her outside. If we feel bereft of something, there are two characteristic human ways of trying to find it: hoping someone else will give it to us, or becoming an exaggerated version of it ourselves.

This is only one possible factor. Often there is great anger toward men because of unrequited love for the father, or a feeling that one's mother has been too powerful and has denied her daughter any feminine potency. Where we feel inadequate, we may try to borrow the magical power of the archetype to compensate for what we experience as a personal lack. The problem is that archetypal power is a fraud, because it is not one's own. If we have not worked to process these energies through the lens of our own individuality, they take us over, and we abdicate all choice and sense of personal responsibility. Hence a woman who is unconsciously identified with the lunar goddess may be deeply voracious and destructive without realising it. If we identify with the gods, we get the whole package, not just the nice bits.

Audience: Can you say something about which Moon signs and aspects Hera might have affinity with?

Liz: The Moon in Capricorn, as well as in Cancer, seems to have affinity with Hera, as does the Moon strongly aspected to Saturn. The Moon in Taurus can also resonate nicely with Hera, because of Taurus's appreciation of stability and traditional values. The Moon placed in all these signs has a well-known resistance to divorce and the breakup of families, and the person will often endure considerable personal unhappiness in order to keep the family structure intact. Anxiety is usually related to the Moon's needs being threatened or frustrated, and the Moon in Capricorn can become very moralistic and controlling in order to cope with the spectre of uprooting. The Moon in Taurus can become stubborn, acquisitive and mean (what Freud called "anal"), and the Moon in Cancer can turn manipulative and pathetic and a bit hysterical. These are all defensive reactions against the loss of roots. When the Moon's needs are being met sufficiently, the best qualities of these signs show themselves – Capricorn's deep sense of responsibility and care for others, Cancer's profound compassion and emotional empathy, Taurus's serenity and gentleness and patience. This is Hera as a beneficent deity, protector of women and young children and guardian of the home.

Audience: You mentioned other planets in strong aspect to the Moon showing an affinity with different mythic figures. Can you say something about the outer planets in conjunction with the Moon? Are the personal needs of the Moon less important for someone in that case?

Liz: I would like to leave a detailed analysis of the Moon's aspects to Howard as he will be interpreting them in depth later. But in general, the Moon does not lose its importance for us, regardless of what natal aspects from other planets are involved. Another planet introduces additional and sometimes conflicting components to the Moon's basic needs and mode of expression. But the Moon remains the Moon, the primal substance on which the personality is built, because it describes our capacity to mother ourselves.

The outer planets may challenge the Moon's more mundane ways of expressing itself. This is particularly true of Uranus. If you have Uranus in aspect to the Moon, you will need to include Uranian values in your lunar expression; and if it is a hard aspect, this may complicate matters when it comes to feeling content within a traditional family structure, or identifying with life as portrayed in *Coronation Street*. But there are many Uranian spheres of life where the Moon can still find its sense of belonging and continuity. For example, aspects between the Moon and Uranus are traditionally associated with the study of astrology and other New Age subjects. The feeling of connection with an orderly and predictable cosmos, and the recognition of common needs which link all human beings, might provide the sort of "family" which is not desirable or possible on the more ordinary level. In effect, astrology, with its long history and absolute dependability, becomes a kind of heavenly Great Mother. Remember the statue of Artemis of Ephesus, with the zodiac carved around her neck? With Moon-Uranus, a sense of roots and family can be found in the safety of the Great Round, which might explain why these studies are so fulfilling for Moon-Uranus people.

Audience: Could a certain kind of partnership affect the way the Moon is expressed in one's own chart?

Liz: Certainly. If your partner has planets strongly aspecting your Moon, then he or she will activate your lunar side very powerfully. This may not always be comfortable, but it can always be productive in some way, since it can help you to become more conscious of just what your Moon needs. For example, you might have the Moon in Leo opposed to Saturn in Aquarius and embedded in a very rational and self-controlled earth-air type of chart. This fiery Moon, the playful divine child who needs regular doses of joy and drama, may have been sadly ignored or repressed. Or maybe that Leo Moon is tucked away in the 12th house, and the family has covertly communicated the message that it is wrong to be selfish and individualistic. Then someone comes along with Venus in Leo conjuncting your Moon, and you feel as if for the first time in your life you can be yourself. He or she validates your need for fun and romance and self-expression, and on the emotional level you feel supported and nourished and valued.

Equally, if someone else enters your life with Saturn in Taurus in square to your Moon, you will also become much more aware of your Leonine emotional needs. But you may discover them through being constantly criticised for your selfishness and irresponsibility. Even if you have repressed your Leonine side, your partner's Saturn will be sure to spot it anyway, and remind you of it *ad nauseam*. Being told you should not be what you are is one sure way of discovering how important it is to you. You may have to fight for your Moon in such a case, or even ultimately let go of the relationship, but it will teach you what you require as essential food, through having that food denied you. We all learn a great deal about the Moon from our interaction with others. The cross-aspects to the Moon between two charts produce "gut" responses within a relationship which are not always conscious but which determine whether we feel contented and secure with that person. If the Moon is not strongly aspected by another person's planets, or is badly blocked by them, the relationship may be very valid and important, but it may not feed us on the instinctual level. We must then either find other outlets for the Moon, or find another partner. Most relationships can take a lot of pounding from other difficult planetary cross-aspects if the two Moons are mutually supported to some extent. If not, there may be deep feelings of discontent and unease, and if there is no consciousness of the problem, the stifled Moon may generate very destructive emotional situations within the relationship.

Audience: Then is it inevitable that a relationship where there are bad cross-aspects to your Moon will go wrong?

Liz: No, it is not inevitable that it will go wrong. It is inevitable that one's Moon cannot be repressed without consequences. Some conscious understanding is needed of what the difficulty is really about. The more we know how to nourish ourselves, the less resentful we are likely to be when someone else is not doing the feeding in exactly the way we might like. Because the Moon is a reflection of the instinctual nature, it is essentially inarticulate, and one often does not know that one is unhappy, or why. The Moon tends to produce moods and vapours and little illnesses if we are not conscious of our needs. Moods and vapours and compulsive behaviour are not a lot of help to an ailing relationship. It is ultimately up to each of us to form some basis of connection with our own Moon, so that we can articulate to a partner why we are unhappy, or find other outlets which compensate for what the partner might not be able to provide.

Now I would like to leave our mythic diagram behind and look at the issue of the personal mother in relation to the Moon; then we can begin to explore the Moon in the different signs and houses of the chart. The Moon tells us a great deal about the earliest weeks and months of childhood, because it is the personal mother who first mediates the archetype of the lunar Great Mother for us, and embodies or incarnates particular dimensions of that archetype. We "internalise" these particular characteristics as part of our own developing psychic structure because the personal mother not only enacts them; she also carries the projection of something within ourselves. So this primal relationship will set the tone for how we later relate to the Moon inwardly. No lunar configuration describes a "bad" mother. But some configurations describe energies which might inevitably be difficult for any mother to express in her role as mother—energies which are, in effect, innately incompatible with the needs of the Moon—and she might not have handled it very well. Then it is up to us to do something more constructive with the same archetypal issue. Astrology has a strange way of describing things which are both objective and subjective, inner and outer; and the Moon is not just a subjective picture of our image of mother. It also describes important qualities which the mother actually possesses, albeit sometimes repressed, so it is a kind of shared substance which describes both mother and child as well as the dynamic of the early relationship.

For example, your Moon might be in Gemini, and this could reflect qualities of intellectual curiosity, restlessness, aesthetic appreciation, and a need for constant social interchange. These qualities might apply to both your mother and yourself. So far, so good—your Moon in Gemini is best nourished by having these particular needs met, and in an ideal world your mother will be just the right person to do it because she shares this aspect of your nature. One might imagine a lively, sparkling mother reading fairy tales and telling stories to her lively, sparkling child, taking the child on exciting journeys, encouraging the best schooling, and so on. Maybe such a mother is not the most domestic of creatures, but a child with the Moon in Gemini doesn't need a cordon bleu cook and resident nurse anyway. This child needs someone who will offer lunar safety and security through listening and communicating.

But what if your mother could not express her own Mercurial qualities, or could only enact them in a negative way? What if she did not even know she had such potentials? In that case she is hardly going to respond warmly to her Mercurial child's lunar needs, and may even become resentful and impatient with the child's natural inquisitiveness and restlessness because of her own frustration. You might find a configuration in your chart such as Saturn in Virgo in square to that Moon in Gemini. This could suggest that an overdeveloped sense of duty, a horror of losing her security, and a fear of what the Great They might think, combined to stifle your mother's natural sparkle, because she was too afraid of appearing flighty or callous or a "bad" mother, or too burdened with responsibilities to have time for Geminian play. Inevitably you will internalise this dilemma, and experience a conflict between your lunar needs and what you think the world expects of you. The Moon square Saturn is a problem which you share with your mother, and it is not very helpful to blame her for being critical, duty-bound and uninterested in your emotional requirements. Probably she *was* emotionally rejecting in some fundamental way, despite her conscious efforts. But the chances are that, as an adult, it is you who are failing to find a workable internal balance between self-nourishment and collective demands, because you have internalised her conflict and are now treating yourself as she once treated herself and you.

Thus the Moon-Saturn aspect tells you something important about your mother, and what might have been a prime source of her own depression or frustration. It also tells you that there was probably an early climate of emotional coolness and alienation in your relationship with her, even if her outward behaviour seemed dutiful and self-sacrificing. But most importantly, it tells you that you might be beating up your own Moon with your own Saturn in adult life. Or the reverse might be the case—perhaps you are wallowing in the Moon's dependency and hunger at the expense of Saturnian self-sufficiency. Recognising the inner conflict permits the possibility of change and freedom from the harsher effects of this configuration, because you can work toward a better balance if you can take responsibility for your feelings of emotional deprivation. No one else can do it for you now.

The mythic images which we explored earlier belong both to our mothers and ourselves. These images can help us to understand the particular archetypal background to our emotional needs, and also the mythic themes operating within the early mother-child relationship. Lunar aspects offer incredibly rich insights about our infancy, and from the psychological point of view they can be of great help in shedding light on problems such as chronic anxiety and compulsive behaviour. The Moon can be read as a history book, telling us about important physical and emotional experiences in the earliest months of life according to the timing of applying and separating lunar aspects. But I think we must look at both the mundane and the mythic levels of the mother-child relationship when we interpret the Moon, so that we can understand its creative possibilities as well as its record of past hurts.

The mythic tale described by lunar signs and aspects is one which has been embedded in the family psyche for generations. One passes these things down to one's children and grandchildren. Frequently a man will marry a woman who carries a similar lunar configuration to his own, because many men act out these mother issues through their female partners and female children. It is always fascinating to see how repeating lunar patterns appear in the horoscopes of most, if not all, of the individuals belonging to the same family group. The instinctual needs of the family, embodying a particular archetypal theme, will seek fulfilment through all the members, taking more destructive forms according to the degree of unconsciousness and repression present in the family. Working with lunar issues really means working on family substance. As these dilemmas pass down, each succeeding generation has a fresh opportunity to find resolutions which the previous one could not. In this way, by working to resolve lunar conflicts, we redeem the past.

When we interpret the Moon in relation to the personal mother, we need to take nonastrological factors into account, such as collective expectations within the particular generation and social group to which she belonged. A mother who is the child of poor immigrants, for example, may grow up with profound anxieties which effectively paralyse her capacity to take risks in life, and these very legitimate problems must be taken into account if we are to get a truthful picture of our psychological inheritance. The Moon square Saturn may describe a mother who is emotionally withholding because of a deep flaw in her character; but it may also describe a mother who started out warmhearted but was so crushed by material hardship that she could not help herself. We also need to bear basic psychological mechanisms in mind, such as the fact that a mother who is by nature independent and spirited may find the role of mothering difficult for perfectly justifiable reasons; and children do, after all, want nothing less than everything.

If we look at this latter issue, we might make a broad generalisation that the Moon in the masculine signs, especially if aspecting dynamic planets such as Mars or Uranus, implies an inevitable dilemma. A mother who is represented by such a lunar configuration will inevitably suffer conflict simply by the act of mothering. Although this ought to be obvious, we often overlook such a simple truth because we are so aggrieved by our own sense of deprivation. How could such a woman, with the archetypal image of the untamed Mistress of Beasts alive within her, be wholly contented sitting at home and nursing you? Or we might consider the Moon in Scorpio. This placement, as I have mentioned, has considerable affinity with mythic figures such as Hekate and Circe. There is a powerful erotic component in these sorceress-women, and it may be difficult to reconcile such sexual intensity and passion, even if it is unconscious, with the role of mother—particularly if she has a daughter who begins to grow into a rival. So if you are a woman with the Moon in Scorpio, the component of sexual jealousy may very well be part of your childhood relationship with your mother. This is not "pathological"; it is just a fact of life. A passionate woman will not enjoy sharing her husband's emotional energy with a pubescent and erotically competitive daughter. And this kind of dilemma is usually deeply unconscious, because we are not taught anything about the Plutonian level of family life. No moral judgements are appropriate here. But in adulthood, if your Moon is in Scorpio, you may need to find the honesty to face the emotional undercurrents of your childhood so that you do not inadvertantly repeat the same mistakes.

Such characteristic scenarios are present with every Moon placement. They are simply dimensions of the particular archetypal pattern at work in one's early life. Probably we all need to go through phases where we are furious about what has been done to us in childhood, for loyalty to self sometimes must begin with righteous anger; and there is no such thing as a mother who gets it wholly right. This is particularly the case if idealisation of the mother has protected us from facing our early hurts. But at the other end of the tunnel of anger and blame, it is essential to recognise that lunar substance is shared between mother and child, so that we can really forgive and move on. This shared substance may not be the Moon's most benign, nurturing face. It may be wild and unpredictable, or deep and subtle. As we have seen, the Moon is not always comfortably maternal. Demeter is one of the most reassuring of lunar deities, yet even Demeter is

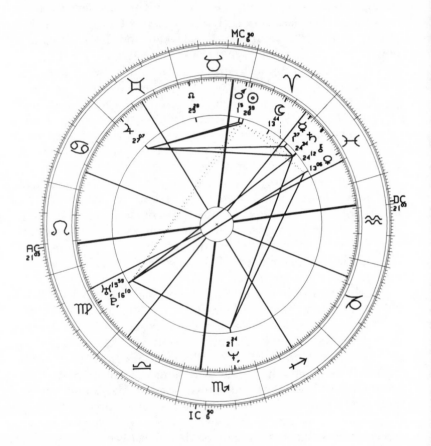

Chart 1. Julian. The birth data has been withheld for confidentiality. Chart calculated by Astrodienst, using the Placidus house system.

capable of scorching the earth and blighting the crops when her daughter loses her virginity. We may need to redefine that word "maternal" in order to understand the Moon. The lunar goddesses have sex with their sons and eat their children and do all sorts of things which one does not usually find in the Stephen Spielberg portrayal of family life. Yet they all faithfully reflect the different phases of the Moon.

Now I would like to explore the Moon's signs and houses by starting with Chart 1 (see page 32). The Moon in this chart reflects several of the archetypal dilemmas I have just been talking about. It has no major aspects, and is placed in a fire sign (Aries) in a fiery house (the 9th). It is thus a highly combustible Moon, but unrelated to any other planet in the chart, although it forms a trine with the Ascendant. Let me give you a few details about Julian's family background first, and then we can see what the Moon might have to say about his history and his present difficulties.

Julian is the son of a much-published and highly respected Cambridge professor of Classics. Now those of you who are familiar with the typical "Oxbridge" mentality might recognise that the Moon in Aries, along with the Sun in Aries conjunct Mars and a Leo Ascendant thrown in just to fan the flames, is not the most convenient thing to have if one's father is an aloof, intellectual and impeccably controlled sort of personality. Nor is Mercury square Jupiter and conjunct Saturn and Chiron altogether helpful if one is expected to follow in the paternal footsteps and become an Oxbridge scholar. I am not suggesting that Julian's father is the "villain of the piece." But before we explore the lunar issues in this chart, we can already surmise that Julian, with his self-willed, fiery, dramatic temperament and his intuitive, undisciplined mind, has been born into an environment which may not be altogether sympathetic to his essential nature. This does not have to be a negative thing. But it can easily mean trouble, as part of the archetypal journey of a man with the Sun in Aries concerns rivalry with the father.

With this broader background in mind, let's consider the Moon in Aries. Does this placement suggest any particular mythic images to you?

Audience: It makes me think of the Lady of the Beasts whom you mentioned, very fiery and wild.

Audience: What about the maenads? I always think there is something very uncontrolled about an Aries Moon.

Liz: I think both these images are very appropriate. The Moon brings out an instinctual, irrational level of Aries, very different from the Sun's conscious initiative and leadership. It is indeed the wild, combustible dimension of the sign, raw, touchy and full of life. There is a lot of the Amazon in this Moon, the warrior woman who loves the ecstasy of battle. I think your remark about the maenads is also very astute because, as I mentioned earlier, this word comes from the same Greek root as "mania." You will see as I go on how appropriate this is.

The Moon in Aries is very hot and passionate, like the Egyptian lioness-headed Sekhmet, goddess of battles, or the lionesses who accompany the ancient Anatolian Lady of the Beasts. Julian's mother had many of these qualities. Although he does not remember his early childhood at all well, he says that, before the accident which crippled her when he was 8, she was lively, "bossy," and had a dreadful temper. He recalls frequent rows between his parents, where his father became coldly cutting and contemptuously reasonable while his mother became so enraged that she actually foamed at the mouth. Yet he has a positive memory of her despite this unattractive picture, describing her as "exciting" and "never dull." He never felt emotionally close to her (this perhaps reflects the Moon's lack of aspects as well as its Amazonian nature), but she made a tremendous impression on him with the force of her personality. Then, when he was 8 years old, everything changed in a horrible way.

It seems that Julian's mother and father were having one of their flaming rows, and had left the bedroom to continue matters at the top of the stairs. Julian was reading a book in the sitting room below, and saw his mother lash out and slap his father in the face. She then lost her balance, stumbled, and proceeded to fall down the stairs, landing in an unconscious heap literally at Julian's feet. The injuries to her spine left her permanently confined to a wheelchair. The change in her personality struck Julian as even more horrible than her paralysis, since she became quiet, polite and formal, retreating to some isolated inner world which excluded both husband and son, and leaving both with an appalling sense of guilt. Julian cannot help blaming his father most of all, although he has tried to approach the trauma with the reasonable view that, horrific though it was, the episode was nevertheless an accident. But the repercussions on Julian have been as complex and tragic as the event itself.

This is a rather dark tale, redolent of Greek family curses; but Julian is afflicted with a rather dark problem which could have come straight from Aeschylus. He is a manic depressive, and like a great many manic depressives he is kept within reasonable bounds of behaviour by lithium. The symptoms began to show themselves just after Julian went through puberty, and have run their sad cycle many times since then; and they are typical of most manic depressives. Sometimes Julian feels grounded and sane, but then he begins to "go high." Despite the lithium (which can only temper, not eradicate, the emotional fluctuations) he alternates between severe, suicidal depressions and states of manic flight where he becomes like a maenad. In these states he is capable of climbing to the tops of buildings and shouting abuse at people; he believes he will live forever; he enters a kind of ecstatic trance where he knows everything and can penetrate all mysteries and possesses the answers to all the ultimate questions. He generally winds up being hospitalised, since sooner or later some offended person rings the police; and, once quieted in hospital by stronger medication, shows great reluctance to leave and resume a life in the world. His mother has never visited him in hospital, although he asks for her every time. But eventually he finds his feet and comes out, and then the cycle starts all over again.

The hot passion of the Moon in Aries is very evident in Julian's manic episodes, as well as the global philosophical perspective of its placement in the 9th house. This Moon, being unaspected, erupts in a pure, archetypal way, uncoloured by any other planet. It is a disturbing example of what can happen when an unaspected planet, which is usually disconnected from the ego, breaks through into consciousness. It has a way of taking over for a time, like a kind of possession. Julian himself disappears, and there is nothing but a pure, archaic Moon in Aries in the 9th house for the time that his manic episodes last. Then, when he crashes, the Moon drops into the unconscious again, and he is left bereft, lonely, guilty and ashamed.

The Moon in all the fiery signs reflects a profound need to feel special, to be acknowledged a child of the gods. Instinctively, one feels one ought to be exempt from the ordinary limits which apply to common mortals. This is an innate lunar need which cannot be reasoned away. If it is contained and balanced by more solid chart factors (particularly planets in air, which can give it structure without stifling it), a fiery Moon can give rise to a potent imagination along with the courage to express this rich inner world through creative forms. But in Julian's chart, only Jupiter falls in an airy sign, and Mercury, reflecting the capacity for formulating the inner world, is blocked by the Saturn-Chiron conjunction. This suggests that the faculties of reason and reflection, so natural to his father, do not come easily to Julian. Like many intuitive-feeling people, he tends to experience everything subjectively, finding it difficult to view life's limiting and hurtful experiences—especially his mother's accident—with any detachment. Life has injured him personally and deliberately, and so he will punish life—and his parents—accordingly.

Audience: Would this apply if the Moon were in another element but in a fiery house?

Liz: No, probably not. The signs in which the planets are placed symbolise the stuff we are made of. The houses are those spheres of life in which the planets express themselves. If Julian's Moon were in Taurus in the 9th, he would no doubt possess an instinctive need for some kind of all-encompassing philosophical perspective or worldview, along with a craving for travel and adventure. The 9th house is one of the houses of the mind, and Julian, with his Moon in Aries in the 9th, literally goes out of his mind and inwardly travels to some very exotic foreign ports. But if this Moon were in Taurus he would have different emotional needs, as well as a different mother; and he would not behave like a maenad, acting out her rage. I doubt that manic depression would be his presenting symptom. If the Moon were in Aries but in the 6th house, he might not climb buildings and shout Aristotelian philosophy at people. It might be his body which, maenadlike, expressed his rage through physical symptoms such as sudden fevers or migraine headaches.

The Moon in fire needs a sense of meaning, an imaginative connection with a deeper or higher pattern. Because we are dealing with lunar nourishment, this is not a question of formulating a philosophy or spiritual framework. It is an instinctual urge to infuse life with a mythic or archetypal dimension, so that one can feel part of something larger and more significant than the mundane world. In this sense the Moon in fire is a contradiction in terms, because the lunar realm is the realm of the body. But the Moon in Aries, Leo or Sagittarius instinctively tries to vitalise material reality with drama and imagination. What crushes a fiery Moon more than anything is a banal life, where there are no knights on white horses and no damsels in distress and no huge, giant, colourful figures crashing out of the fairy-tale world to compensate for the taxman and the grocery bill.

This tells us a little more about Julian's manic flights, particularly when we think of the ordered and restrained world in which he was brought up. Although English academia, like any other sphere, has its scandals and dramas, they are usually played out in a polite and well-behaved fashion. Domestic life among Oxbridge professors tends to be rather low-key, *Inspector Morse* notwithstanding. If a child with a fiery Moon is not taken seriously when he or she tries to bring the vividness of the imaginal world into daily life, then this can result in the child withdrawing into inflated fantasies which are split off from the everyday world. One is really a genius, a great artist or a spiritual avatar, but that lot out there are too stupid and philistine to recognise it.

Julian's manic episodes make him the absolute centre of his world. He has landed the leading role in the play, and everyone around him drops whatever they were doing to rush to his aid. This may comprise one of the reasons for his suicidal depressions, for when he loses his connection with being the gifted and brilliant child of the gods, he can see no point to life. He cannot believe he could be loved as a mere mortal. This is Aries operating on a compulsive and deeply unconscious level.

Audience: Then he is really unconsciously using blackmail against his parents.

Liz: Yes, it is unconscious blackmail, or more precisely, unconscious punishment. He is punishing his father for his "crime," as though the man actually pushed his wife down the stairs; but most of all he is punishing his mother for abandoning him in favour of her wheelchair and her silence. This latter is probably a key issue, although less conscious than his anger toward his father.

Audience: And when he breaks down and winds up in hospital, he is really asking for his mother to take care of him.

Liz: Yes, I believe so. Also, he becomes like her—an invalid, incapable of coping with life—and by becoming like her, he gets closer to her. The manipulative elements in Julian's behaviour are complicated but make a strong symbolic statement. His breakdowns serve a multiple purpose. He can punish his father for not validating him, and for being good at something he cannot hope to aspire to. He can punish his mother for her withdrawal. He can force the world to give him the mothering he is no longer getting (and possibly never did). And he can become a mythic figure, the absolute centre of the universe, without having done anything to earn it—which is one of the characteristics of the Moon, rather than the Sun, in fire. We could spend an entire seminar on the causes of manic depression and other disturbed psychic states, but I have used Julian's chart in this session primarily because it is such an exaggerated example of the Moon operating in an unconscious and compulsive way. Both his manic states and his very complex relationship to his mother are bound up with this unaspected Moon in Aries which, even if he expressed it more moderately, would probably still be abrasive to his father.

Audience: What would you recommend for Julian? Presumably he was not in a manic state when he came to see you.

Liz: No, although I was concerned that I might give him fodder for the next one if I talked too much about myths and archetypes. I suggested to him that he undergo very deep and frequent analysis, of the four- or five-times-a-week variety. The Kleinian analysts work best with this kind of damaged personality, which needs great containment on a long-term basis. Manic depression is not "incurable," contrary to conventional psychiatric opinion, but it is very difficult to work with, and requires a psychotherapist or analyst who can accept the periodic breakdowns which are inevitably involved without losing faith. Julian might also need an analyst who could validate the healthy dimension of his fiery nature, which tends toward the theatrical at the best of times. The alternative is a lifetime of lithium, which allows him some degree of moderation in his mood swings, but which cannot of itself stop the cycle.

Audience: You have not mentioned the semisextile to the Moon from Venus. Could this be seen as the way through in the chart?

Liz: I am not wildly enthusiastic about taking one aspect, especially a minor one, and using it to define the solution to a problem which involves so many complicated psychological factors. I do not feel the semisextile from Venus is powerful enough to provide a container for the Aries Moon anyway, never mind all the rest. Semisextiles are delicate aspects and require conscious effort, and although this Moon semisextile Venus might describe qualities of gentleness and artistic appreciation in his nature, Julian does not yet have enough of an ego to make the best use of it. I am more inclined to look at what might help him to build an ego strong enough to contain that wild Moon. The Sun is perhaps the most important factor here, and its placement in the 9th house suggests that the more Julian can understand his suffering in a broader context, both analytically (through examining his family background) and archetypally (through exploring the deeper pattern expressing itself through his symptoms), the better equipped he will be to cope with the pain that sends him off into manic flights.

I would also look carefully at Saturn, which conjuncts Chiron in Pisces in the 8th house, suggesting considerable fear around the sphere of intimacy and emotional openness to others. This fear I believe is connected with both parents, but particularly with Julian's father, who is described by the paradoxical combination of Sun-Mars in the 9th (the academic) and by Neptune in the 4th house. This Neptune, conjuncting the South Node, suggests a hidden sensitivity and confusion in his father which Julian, with his three planets in Pisces, may be acting out for him. Julian deeply loves and idealises his father, despite the rage he feels about his mother's paralysis. In fact I wonder to what extend Julian carries both his mother's rage (which she has never expressed since the accident) and his father's sadness and weakness (which he has never expressed either).

So although I take your point about the aspect from Venus, which in the 8th house might also suggest a very lively sexual outlet for the wilder side of the Aries Moon, I would first want to explore Julian's very convoluted feelings about his parents. The "way through" is more likely to involve the whole chart.

Audience: He must feel that he has not lived up to his father's expectations. Is it possible that he might please his father by some kind of academic success, perhaps of a different kind from Classics, but still something in this sphere?

Liz: He has already tried that route, and studied philosophy and comparative religion at university. But he could not keep up with the academic requirements. I agree that he needs mental food – the 9th house is not called the house of higher education for nothing – and this might indeed provide a bridge to his father. But it also might set him up as his father's rival, and the Sun in Aries conjuncting Mars suggests that his father is unconsciously highly competitive and does not want a son who challenges him on his own patch. I believe there are some very complex issues at work between Julian and his father which need to be brought into the light, since I associate Aries with the myth of Oedipus enacted through the classic family triangle.

Audience: Does an unaspected Moon mean no relationship with the mother?

Liz: It means a deeply unconscious one, and often there is not much real emotional communication. From what Julian has said about his mother, there was probably never much maternal feeling in her, even when he was a baby. Although her present behaviour might be blamed on her accident, something was wrong long before. The accident has meant to him that there can never be a chance to redeem it. Julian does not have a sufficiently strong inner image of a "good mother" to know how to contain and nourish himself. This results in the archetypal level of the Moon breaking through without any human mediator. Even the cyclical nature of manic depression echoes the cyclical nature of the lunar cycle. Julian's manic states suggest the full Moon that calls the maenads to the dance, while his black depressions are the dark of the Moon when the black dogs of Hekate run amok.

I would like to leave Julian for the moment, and look at the Moon in the other three elements. The Moon in an earthy sign seems to have affinity with the earth goddesses such as Gaia and Demeter, who preside over nature and the life of the body. Also, as we saw with the Moon in Capricorn, Hera can be seen as an earthy lunar deity, because of her rulership over roots and traditional family structures. It is the body needs which are of paramount importance for the Moon in earth, although many things can provide symbolic body security for us. For example, one's home is a kind of body, a womb within which we feel safe and protected. Selling one's home and moving to a new neighbourhood can be a terrifying and deeply traumatic experience for an earthy Moon (especially if it occurs in childhood), even if all the practical details have been impeccably organised and there are no financial problems and the move is accomplished without disasters. One has nevertheless been dislodged from one's body, and the abyss looms.

If one is unconscious of these earthy lunar needs, the anxiety and distress of uprooting can linger for a long time, even if the real source is overlooked or denied. There is also a deeply ritualistic quality to the Moon in the earthy signs. We all have our little daily rituals, whether this entails digging up weeds in the garden, or reading the morning paper over tea, or jogging on Hampstead Heath, or following a particular order of bathing and dressing. These rituals are terribly important for an earthy Moon, because they provide a kind of body centering which is needed for a feeling of well-being. The Moon in the earth signs often favours dietary and exercise rituals, and even if these are a little faddish and do not do much for the body's actual health, it is the repetitive security of the ritual itself which promotes the feeling of being in balance.

So there is a deep resistance to material change in the earthy Moon, and also a need for a ritualistic ordering of daily life on the physical level. These Moon placements are sometimes quite obsessive, especially if the person is stressed, but you can see why – if the Moon is being expressed unconsciously, it is likely to operate in a compulsive way, and those rituals provide protection against anxiety. The Moon in earth is often very concerned with material security and social acceptability, even if this is consciously denied, and once again you can see why. Beautiful or valuable objects, money and respectability all provide a kind of safe body, a bastion against the cold winds of chaos. When these fundamental lunar needs are denied because of an overvaluing of the intellectual or spiritual level of life, an earthy Moon has a way of generating body symptoms as well as compulsive-obsessive behaviour.

The Moon in earth also needs to feel useful. This is different from the earthy Sun's conscious goal of contributing something practical to life. With the Moon in Taurus, Virgo, or Capricorn, there is an instinctive need to be occupied, to be doing rather than wasting time. Everything in nature is constantly moving, albeit sometimes very slowly, and if you sit around watching the insects and snails in your garden or the wildlife in the woods, you will see that there is never a moment when purposeful activity is not taking place. Ants are busy carrying bits of food to their hill, bees are busy dipping into flowers, aphids are busy feeding off leaves, birds are busy digging up worms. Even in their winter dormancy, plants carry on a secret life of their own. All this movement serves the perpetuation of the universal life of the world, and the Moon in earth is naturally attuned to such rhythms. Even the Moon in Taurus, the most fixed and serene of the signs, is constantly in motion, albeit at its own leisurely pace.

The Moon in the earthy signs is also highly tactile and sensuous, and there is a strong need for physical affection and stimulus of the senses. Although Virgo and Capricorn have a justified reputation for being highly controlled, they are both extremely sensuous signs, albeit rather discriminating about where they find their pleasures. I am distinguishing sensuous from sexual, because sensuality is not necessarily related to sex. The Moon in Taurus can feel deliciously sensuous while eating chocolate ice cream, whereas the Moon in Aries might experience great sexual stimulus without being sensuous. If this basic need for touch and physical pleasure is denied because of an undemonstrative or inhibited family, the Moon in earth may react with feelings of deep shame about body needs and functions.

In some Kabbalistic teachings, the Moon is related to Malkuth, the lowest level of the Tree of Life. This is the insensible substance of which the body and all material reality are made. Malkuth is a kind of blind receptive container into which the seed of the spirit descends, but in itself it possesses no consciousness. Now I was speaking earlier about the Moon having its own intelligence, which is reflected in the ancient images of the lunar goddesses. I think we can see here a difficulty in many religious or esoteric teachings which devalue the level of the Moon because it is not "spiritual." Lunar intelligence does not evolve toward a goal as solar consciousness does, since it is geared toward safety, comfort and the survival of life. If something in nature doesn't work, such as the dinosaurs, then the line is discontinued. But if it does work, such as the gingko tree, the same model tends to remain in stock, with minimal improvements, millennium after millennium. There is no vision of a higher evolution based on ideals of potential perfection. From the solar perspective, the earthy Moon may seem dull, stupid, boring and unimaginative. It is precisely this feeling which many people with earthy Moons experience if their conscious values are aligned too powerfully with the "higher" realm.

We all suffer if we deny our lunar needs, for whatever reason. It is actually very easy for an earthy Moon to find satisfaction and contentment, provided the person does not assume natural means unevolved. Often when someone with the Moon in earth comes along for a chart, and they seem to be afflicted with apparently deeply complicated problems, I might suggest that they begin on the most basic level, by finding out what pleases the body and gives real satisfaction and contentment. Yet so often the response is, "Oh, yes, but . . .," because there is a complete undervaluing of these needs. Other, more meaningful pursuits must take priority. But if you have the Moon in earth, the foundation of your life depends for its strength on your appreciation of the reality of the body and all the mundane things which give you a feeling of pleasure and safety.

Perhaps we might look at the Moon in the airy signs now. How many of you have the Moon in Gemini, Libra, or Aquarius? What do you need most to feel secure and contented?

Audience: I need to communicate with people. I hate being alone with no one to talk to.

Audience: I need beauty around me. I cannot tolerate an ugly or coarse environment.

Liz: You both have expressed fundamental requirements for the Moon in air. The Sun in an airy sign may consciously strive for intellectual development, but the Moon in air simply needs verbal contact and stimulation on the mental level. There is no formulated goal of knowledge; instead, there may be a love of playing with ideas which make the mind feel alive. This is why the Moon in Gemini is such an incurable gossip. People are simply so fascinating, and talking about them is endlessly entertaining. The airy signs are social creatures, naturally gregarious, and even an introverted personality with an airy Moon will seek mental contact with others, albeit selectively.

There is nothing more painful for an airy Moon than an early environment in which there is no communication, or where the communication is dishonest and full of double messages. Also, there is a natural aesthetic feeling in the element of air. A childhood which is too dreary and disciplined, without any time for frivolity, is stultifying, and a world barren of beauty and light and style crushes the soul. The idealism of air, combined with the instinctual needs of the Moon, produces a profound hunger for a beautiful and intelligible world, and there is often an excessive hypersensitivity in these Moon signs which reacts with great distress to the usual confusion and ambiguity of human relationships. Although the Moon in air needs contact with others, it tends to shy away from complex emotional dynamics because of this excessive delicacy and aestheticism. Isolation provokes anxiety in an airy Moon, but so too do powerful feelings, which threaten to drown the airy Moon in dark undercurrents.

Audience: I have the Moon in Aquarius, and I find I am always looking for escape routes from relationships. I am afraid of getting stuck in too much emotion.

Liz: Yes, the need for breathing space in relationships is a necessary requirement for the Moon in all the airy signs. Although Libra loves romance, the romance must be clear, bright and uncontaminated with ambiguous vapours.

Audience: I have the Moon in Aquarius also, and I find that I talk about my emotions all the time. I talk about them so much that I don't have a chance to feel them. Once I have analysed them, I don't have to worry about them any more.

Liz: That is a characteristic airy line of defence against feelings. Just as the earthy Moon becomes compulsive and obsessive with its rituals when threatened by material upheaval, the airy Moon becomes analytical, dissociated, and evasive when threatened by too much intimacy.

Audience: Is the Moon in Aquarius evasive as well? I thought Aquarians placed such importance on truthfulness.

Liz: Aquarius is highly ethical, but we cannot be truthful with others unless we are honest with ourselves. Because the Moon in air may compulsively dissociate when faced with emotional conflict or vulnerability, one may deceive oneself about what one really feels. In this sense the Moon in Aquarius is just as evasive as the Moon in Gemini. It is not a deliberate act of dishonesty, but rather an instinctive defence against the threat of emotional pain. Air needs clarity, and nothing is so clouded and ambiguous as human feeling. Although the airy signs must communicate, communication can be very dangerous if it involves an emotional confrontation. It is much easier to change the subject, or reduce complicated issues to simple black-and-white formulae. Anyone with an airy Moon needs to create a private space within relationships, in which they can breathe and nourish themselves with those things that bring beauty and light and grace to life. Then the inevitable emotional confrontations are not so unendurable.

Audience: This may sound a little funny, but I have found that most men with the Moon in Libra don't like to kiss.

Liz: Yes, it does sound a little funny. I haven't found that to be the case, but never mind. I can see I had better avoid taking that comment any further!

The Moon in the airy signs recoils from fusion. There is a need to preserve the ideal intact, without too much contamination by another person's reality. The mind is a great boundary maker, just as feelings are boundary dissolvers. The mythic deities who preside over the realm of air are extremely independent creatures. For example, Aphrodite (Venus), who rules the sign of Libra, refuses to be possessed. She favours the hetaira and the lover, and shows a marked disinterest in the sanctity of marriage bonds. Hermes (Mercury), who rules Gemini, is the god of the roads and of the traveller, and favours the thief and the liar. He traverses the paths from heaven to earth and to the underworld and back again, a messenger with no fixed abode. And Ouranos (Uranus), the ruler of Aquarius, is the original god of heaven before there was a manifest cosmos. He embodies the Idea before the concrete reality, and when the reality is presented to him in the form of his Titan children, he is repelled and shuns them. All these planetary deities reflect a distaste for anything too fixed in form or bound by emotion. Thus the Moon in an airy sign tends to find its security in those crystalline spheres where the idea of life is not spoiled by the imperfections of reality.

If these lunar needs are blocked, the Moon may generate body symptoms just as readily as other Moon signs do. But I have found that one of the most characteristic spheres of suffering for a choked airy Moon is depression. This depression may be unconscious because of the dissociating propensities of the air signs, but if there is no air to breathe, the person may descend into a kind of bleak hopelessness and apathy, masked by brittle sociability. Sometimes the detached qualities of the Moon in air are not met with sympathy in childhood, and the person is perpetually being told that he or she is cold and unfeeling. An airy Moon is not cold, but its occasional lack of demonstrativeness, as well as a cyclical need for emotional withdrawal, may be the wrong mix for an emotionally demanding parent. I would emphasise once again that the need to communicate is not the same as the need for fusion. If the Moon's essential nature is rejected in childhood, then the person may grow up feeling deeply guilty and unlovable because he or she is "unloving."

Now we can finally look at the Moon in the watery signs before we finish this afternoon's session. How many of you have the Moon in water? What do you feel to be your essential requirements?

Audience: I need emotional closeness more than anything.

Audience: I have a great need of my family. I dread the time when my children grow up and want to move away.

Audience: I need to be able to express my feelings. I hate it when I am treated as though I am being hysterical.

Liz: You may sometimes get that response from a partner with the Moon in air. But all your comments are very apt. The Moon in water needs above all to receive emotional response from others. It is the most important thing in the world, even if the response is hatred or anger. At least that is better than one's feelings falling down a hole somewhere. For a watery Moon, exchange of feelings is a means of drawing people together. One is no longer alone and separate, because feelings are the solvent which allows the barriers to break down between oneself and life. Nothing activates anxiety in a watery Moon more quickly than another person's unresponsiveness, because it is like dropping into the void. One ceases to exist. The Moon in water feels safe only if one is merged with others. Your comment about hysteria is sadly apt, because if you do not value this side of yourself, you can easily be provoked into highly emotional behaviour by anyone who rejects your feelings.

Audience: I have the Moon in a watery sign, and I have been married for twenty years to a man with the Moon in Gemini. I am always trying to get closer to him, and he is always slipping away.

Liz: There is a good deal of the classic attraction of opposites in this. Each of you has an instinctive gift which the other one finds difficult to express. But I believe the most important issue for a person with the Moon in water is not to find the perfect partner who responds to one's every emotional fluctuation. One must be able to take one's own feelings seriously, and know that they matter. Even if one has a cool and detached partner, which can be very painful at times, it is ultimately the individual's capacity for self-value which feeds the Moon. Nourishing a watery Moon means knowing the worth and truth of one's own heart, even if this is not mirrored by others. As Goethe once said, "If I love you, it's none of your business." Perhaps you are trying too hard to get validation for your feelings because you do not quite value them yourself. You may want your husband to approve of your needs, but it is you who must do that within yourself. Then you might not mind so much when he plays Hermes and performs an emotional vanishing act.

The dilemma of a watery Moon is complicated, because if one needs response from others, how does one nourish oneself? A blocked Moon in the watery signs has a way of generating deeply manipulative behaviour in order to obtain the necessary care and attention. This has a sad tendency to backfire, as other people usually pull away when they feel manipulated, and one has thus created the very situation one fears most. Often there is a cool or rejecting parent in the early background, whom the child has internalised; this can result in considerable resentment in adulthood at the least sign of withdrawal from a loved one, because it brings up the old wound. Equally often there is a parent who is even needier than the child, and whose message is, "There is only room for one infant in the house, and it isn't you." So the person grows up ashamed of needing too much, yet remains full of anger at the deprivation. All that emotional dependency seems cloying and gummy, and no one will love us if we reveal the full extent of it. Yet it is a vicious circle, because the more resentful the watery Moon feels about being rejected or ignored, the more manipulative it is likely to become, and the more others will actually be driven away by the force of the covert emotional demands.

I think the key to this dilemma lies in our ability to enjoy and appreciate the richness and importance of our own feelings. Longing for intimacy, expressed so powerfully by the Moon in water, only drives others away when it is full of covert resentment, and it may remain full of resentment if we unconsciously expect others to provide that constant and unconditional acceptance, love and for-giveness we cannot give ourselves. If we can appreciate our own feelings, we may succeed in communicating them without the unspoken requirement that others should heal our parental wounds. This tends to bring people closer rather than driving them away. It is worth asking yourself, if you have the Moon in a watery sign, whether you can value what you feel without an external stamp of approval. The Moon is a watery planet, and in the watery signs it reflects the most archetypal level of its nature, the primal mother goddess as the source of life. She contains all things within her own womb, and does not need anyone or anything outside to give value to what lives inside her.

Audience: I don't have the Moon in water, but I have a question. I feel I validate my own needs and appreciate my Moon sign. But I have trouble finding other people who appreciate it.

Liz: You will never be able to please all of the people all of the time. Sometimes accepting this fundamental fact of life can make a great deal of difference, and one can relax. But if you can really find no one at all who values this side of your nature, perhaps it might be relevant to look at the kind of people you attract into your life, and why there is a pattern of rejection. There is probably a family complex at work, and if that is so, then you may have internalised a rejecting parent, and are unconsciously far more judgmental about yourself than you admit. Then you might express your unconscious self-criticism through projection, by getting others to do it for you. This is very common and very human, and most of us do it at some point. I have found that it is usually the case when someone says, "But I like this side of myself, it's just everybody else who doesn't." Who, after all, is this global "everybody else"?

FIRST LOVE

THE MOON AS A SIGNIFICATOR OF RELATIONSHIP

BY HOWARD SASPORTAS

> The mother becomes, for her young baby, an orienting fig-
> ure; she is her child's home base in the world. She is the first
> intimate partner—to be replaced one day by the orienting
> figure . . . who is the lover or mate. But it is in this first love
> relationship of existence that the immature human will have
> developed a crude template, or pattern, for being in a loving
> relationship. . . . The person in love is not only "resonating"
> to something that is reminiscent of the original beloved one,
> but is experiencing something of that relationship again.
>
> Maggie Scarf[1]

I want to begin by drawing your attention to the guidelines for
interpreting the Moon which can be found in Table 1 on page 52. I
only have a few hours to discuss the Moon with you, and because
time is short it would be impossible for me to cover all the different
permutations of the Moon by sign, house and aspect in the chart.
These guidelines are intended to help you work out the meaning of
specific placements—at least, it will spur your thinking and give
you ideas about how to interpret the Moon's position in any chart.

Liz has explored many of the different archetypal, psychological, and astrological implications of the Moon, but tonight I want to
examine the Moon in a very specific way—I want to consider its
role as a significator for relationship. Normally if we're looking at
someone's chart to consider what close partnerships might be like
for that person, most of us would naturally and immediately look

---

[1]Maggie Scarf, *Intimate Partners: Patterns in Love and Marriage* (London: Century,
1987; and New York: Random House, 1987), p. 78.

Table 1. Guidelines for Interpreting the Moon

Moon by Sign
1) Your Moon sign shows something about how you experience or see mother, and also how you are as a parent or mother; how you nurture, or like to be nurtured. It describes the anima image or image of the feminine.
2) Your Moon sign describes your feeling nature, how you instinctively respond or react to events and the environment. Provided the Moon is not too inhibited by other aspects (or by heavy contrary cultural conditioning), we will naturally respond to life according to its sign.
3) The Moon sign often shows a way of being that gives us comfort and security. It can also show where you retreat when you need a rest, pause or sanctuary. It can describe something about your domestic life.

Moon by House
1) The house shows where we are sensitive and responsive to the needs of others, but also where we are easily influenced by others. Where we mirror or reflect others – where we tend to blend in with what is around us.
2) The house shows where we are easily moulded and shaped by habit and past conditioning. Our experience of mother will in some way be tied up with the Moon's house. It is also where we might be bound by the notions, expectations, values and standards of our family or culture. Where we act in a regressive way or are pulled toward the past, where we might be childish or clingy.
3) One longs for the sphere of life associated with the house of the Moon because it makes us feel safe, comfortable or gives us a sense of belonging. The Moon's house is where we might retreat when we need a rest or sanctuary.
4) The sphere of life associated with the Moon's house is where we may experience ups and downs, many different moods and fluctuations of behaviour.

Table 1. Guidelines for Interpreting the Moon (cont.)

Moon by Aspect
1) Aspects to the Moon colour the anima image and what we experienced via the mother or caretaker. For instance, do we meet Jupiter or Saturn through the Moon (through females or mother)? Are we owning our anima image or projecting it?
2) Planets aspecting the Moon generally describe childhood conditioning, and further define our feeling nature. Are we open, closed, defended, quick or slow to react? The nature of a planet aspecting the Moon describes our instinctive responses to life as well as what we tend to meet in the emotional sphere. The Moon's aspects will also colour how we care for and nurture others, or how we liked to be cared for.
3) Aspects to the Moon describe something about our domestic life.
4) Planets aspecting the Moon can come out through the body and the way we move. In particular, aspects to the Moon will describe a woman's relationship to her own body.

to Venus or the 7th house as a source of information and insight into this area of life. That's our natural inclination. Venus is the planet of love, so we'd see how Venus was placed. The 7th house is the sphere of life to do with relationship, so we would look to see what is going on there—planets in that house, the sign on the cusp, its ruler, and so on. And no doubt this would help you get a sense of what someone meets in relationship, the kinds of issues, conflicts or experiences that would come up in partnership. But in years of work as an astrologer, I discovered that the Moon's placement tells you just as much as Venus about what you will meet in love, about what love will bring up in you—and this applies to *both* men and women. So, in my opinion, just assessing Venus or the 7th house isn't enough to give a full picture of love and close relationship. I remember when I first noticed this. I was doing a woman's chart and she had fine aspects to Venus and no big problems with the 7th house, yet she had a terrible (and I mean *terrible*) time in her love life – dreadful anxieties, fears, and a penchant for attracting violence. Her Venus was beautiful – you'd pay a lot for it if it were up for auction at Sotheby's – and her 7th house wasn't particularly troublesome. Her Moon, however, was a mess, with such challenging aspects as a square to Pluto and a close inconjunct to both Saturn and Neptune. Her unhappy Moon seemed to override the benign Venus and 7th house, giving real problems with relationship and intimacy.

So I want to explore the Moon with you in this light, to examine how it indicates what happens when we get close to someone, how it directly affects issues to do with merging and intimacy throughout our lives. The reason why the Moon is one of the prime significators for relationship isn't too hard to figure out. The Moon is a symbol for mother, and assessing its placement in a chart is a good indication of what that person's mother-child relationship was like. I've discussed this at length in the "Stages of Childhood" in *The Development of the Personality*.[2] For instance, if you have the Moon natally in aspect to Saturn, then you would have met Saturn in some way through the mother; if you have the Moon in aspect to Jupiter, you would have met Jupiter through the mother, and so on. I won't go into detailed interpretations right now. But the point I want to make is that mother is *not* just mother. Besides being mother – the one who is meant to love, nurture and care for you – mother is also the first important relationship in your life. She is not just your mother, she is the first big love of your life. Your mother is your first big romance – for both men and women. Every child falls desperately and madly in love with his or her mother. It may be hard to believe this when you look at your mother now or consider what happened earlier on, but it's true. In the time we have, I want to analyse the Moon's placement in terms of how your first big romance went – how you "made out" in the first grand passion of your life. And I'm not doing this just to wallow in the past; I'm doing this because what happened back then has an undeniable influence on our later close relationships.

---

[2]Liz Greene and Howard Sasportas, *The Development of the Personality*, Volume 1 in *Seminars in Psychological Astrology* (York Beach, ME: Samuel Weiser, 1982), pp. 3–82.

I'm sure you're all pretty familiar with my thinking on this matter, and you know I believe that the past has a way of haunting us. We don't consciously remember what passed between mother and ourselves in the first year or so of our lives, but we never forget it. This is where I find the chart so useful. It's like an X-ray. If you know how to read a chart properly, you can learn a great deal about what went on in early childhood. You can make fairly safe conjectures about what happened between you and mother by looking at the natal placement of the Moon, and also by examining the early progressions and transits involving the Moon. To put it another way, the chart shows the "inner child of the past" in all of us. Our past, particularly our childhood, with all its hopes, fears and expectations, with all its joys and terrors, is stored and recorded in memory and shown by the chart. Your "inner child of the past" is still there in you right now. No matter how mature you become, no matter how sophisticated and learned you are, you still have an inner child inside you. I've seen even the most educated, mature people fall to pieces and start acting like frightened and angry children when a boyfriend or girlfriend doesn't ring them up as promised. Current relationships have a way of bringing to the surface deeper emotions which originally stem from early child-hood bondings. Mother is our first important relationship, she is the first love of our life, and what happens in that relationship becomes a prototype for later close partnerships. What happens between you and mother sets up a pattern, template, or package of inner expectations which shape and influence what we meet and experience in later intimate unions. In her book *Intimate Partners*, Maggie Scarf comments on the link between mother and the eventual choice of a mate:

> It is from this primitive psychological state—of total emotional symbiosis with a responsive, intuitively comprehending, need-satisfying other—that we slowly awaken to the human world. And it is in the context of this awakening that we begin to form assumptions about what the experience of intimate loving is like. For even as we come to know and recognize those who care for us—particularly mother—we develop feelings of attachment that are so intense that it would not be at all exaggerated to term them "the first grand

passion of human life." . . . What is "right" when it comes to the choosing of a mate, is to some degree what has been and what is familiar; it is what "works" on that inner template, or pattern of assumptions about what an intimate partnership is like.[3]

To underline the importance of the mother-child bond, I'd like to quickly review a study carried out in the 1940's by a Dr. Renee Spitz. Women prisoners who were pregnant had to give up their babies at birth. These babies were then put in a hospital where there was one nurse to every eight babies. The nurses kept changing; there were day nurses and night nurses, so the babies were unable to form a one-to-one bond with either a nurse or their natural mother. Imagine how confusing it must have been for the babies—eight of them needing attention, and only one caretaker around at a time, and not always the same one. The conclusions of the study are quite dramatic. When these babies reached the age of 1 year, they showed profound signs of physical and psychological retardation compared to babies who were reared on a one-to-one basis with mother or mother substitute. The babies in the Spitz study cried much more often than other babies. They smiled less. You could say they were depressed. They were slower to begin talking, they were more apathetic and less responsive than the infants raised normally. They caught infections more easily; in fact, they had a higher mortality rate than babies cared for by one mother. The study demonstrates with a frightening clarity that a loving partner in early life is a precondition for healthy development.[4] You can die if you don't get this. So if we don't have a good, loving relationship there in the beginning, or if we have a lot of problems in bonding with mother—the first love of our life—we are left with what Judith Viorst in her book *Necessary Losses* refers to as "emotional scars on the brain," deep emotional wounds.[5] It is the mother-child bond which first teaches us about love, and first teaches us whether or not we are lovable.

Later, I'll be discussing a study of children deprived of their fathers in their early years and the kinds of problems that this can

---

[3]Maggie Scarf, *Intimate Partners*, pp. 73, 79.

[4]Maggie Scarf, *Intimate Partners*, p. 74.

[5]Judith Viorst, *Necessary Losses* (New York: Fawcett, 1986), p. 19.

give rise to. But now we're talking about the psychological significance of your relationship with mother. Speaking generally for a moment, if you have a number of difficult aspects to the Moon, then it usually means that your love affair with mother didn't go too well. If this is the case, you probably failed to develop a basic trust in life or in yourself, which can lead to a lot of fear and paranoia in partnership, to anxious feelings and deep uncertainty in close relationship. I believe that we all have the right to be loved, the right to a loving mother. And if you don't get that, you can be psychologically harmed and left not only with a distrust of life and a poor self-image, but you also may feel angry because you have not been given something which is a birthright. On the other hand, if the bonding with mother goes pretty well (which is normally shown by harmonious aspects to the Moon), then you feel safe, you feel cared for, you have your basic needs met, you feel understood. Obviously, this is going to be a blessing for you whenever you get close to someone later on in life. It's as if you already have a picture in your mind of closeness being okay, of love working for you.

Fortunately, all is not lost if our bonding with mother went awry. We can work through many of these issues, and part of this process involves getting to know the "inner child of the past" which is still alive in us right now. It is important to form a relationship to the child inside you, to befriend it, to recognise its needs and moods. In this way, we can begin to heal or make peace with the wounding or scarring that might have taken place. Many of us still need to mourn the loss of that blissful state of unity we once shared with mother. Many of us still need to grieve for the ideal mothering we never experienced; if we don't grieve and let go of the past, we are compelled to keep looking for that lost ideal mothering from mates and partners later in life—a search that is destined to fail because, no matter how much someone loves and adores us, no one can meet such impossible expectations. Soon we'll be examining all this in terms of astrological aspects to the Moon. But before I do so, I'd like to give you a short exercise which may help you reconnect to the child inside you.

Start by closing your eyes.
(If this exercise becomes difficult for you at any time, just open your eyes and write about what you are experiencing.) Take a minute to relax, a few deep breaths to help let go of tensions, and then let your mind and your heart recall the feelings you have about your mother.
When you think about her, do you feel warm and safe, or do you feel anxious and uncomfortable?
Now, let an actual memory come to your mind, some event or situation that happened between you and your mother. Just let it arise spontaneously.
Spend a minute reliving this memory.
Now, let go of that memory and bring to mind another event or situation concerning you and your mother.
Take another minute to reflect on this.
See if you can come up with an overall image, symbol or feeling which sums up or describes your feelings around mother.

When I've done this exercise with various groups, it's been interesting to see the range of emotions people feel and connect with. Some feel terror and dread at the thought of mother; others feel safe and warm. The Moon's placement by sign and aspect, along with the parental house you assign to the mother, will in some way reflect the kinds of feelings you have toward her.

I always manage to get around to talking about the womb in whatever lecture I give. Most of you are familiar with my thinking and ideas about the womb experience and how it can affect us later in life, so today I'm not going to talk about it at length, but draw you a picture instead (see figure 2, page 59). In the womb, and for the first six months or so after birth, our identity is totally fused with the mother. In figure 2, Mother is the big egg, and your identity is a little egg within that big egg. You can see at a glance that your whole being is immersed in her. By the time you reach six months after birth the developmental task is to somehow get the little egg (which is you) separated from that big egg (which is your mother); then you have a little egg and a big egg which can relate with one another because the little egg is no longer enmeshed in the big egg.

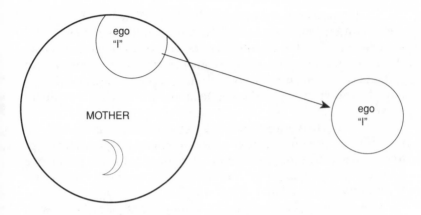

Figure 2. The need to differentiate your "I" or ego from that of mother.

Let me explain this further. For the first few months or so after birth, you really don't have a relationship with a specific or personal mother; instead you are fused with the Great Mother, someone who is the whole world to you. But by six months, you gradually begin to differentiate or distinguish an "I" that is not your mother. This is shown by the little egg which is now separated out from the big egg. Once your identity is no longer immersed in the Great Mother, you then have a specific, personal or "circumstantial" mother with whom to relate. You are beginning to recognise yourself as a separate person, and therefore you are forced to recognise your mother's separateness from you. So by six months we form what is called a *specific* mother attachment. It is only then that you can actually begin to make a one-to-one relationship with her—if you are the same as something else, you can't have a relationship with it because there is no duality. When you separate your "I" from your mother's "I," then you have to face the issue of how these two "I's" (yours and your mother's) are going to get along with one another. What do you think happens when it dawns on you that mother is not you, when you begin to distinguish her as a person separate and distinct from yourself? If you're dealing with someone who is not you, one of the first things you might feel is terror, fear or dread. Where there is other, there is fear. If mother is not me, what if she doesn't like me, what if she doesn't understand my needs, what if she decides to go away and abandon me? The key issue in the first few years of life is survival. We are born unfinished, we are banished from the womb without certain essentials, such as our own flat, our own car, and without any of our own credit cards. We need mother to be on our side to survive.

According to many schools of psychological thought, when we first differentiate our identity from that of our mother, we attempt to ease the ensuing fear and terror by trying to get her to fall in love with us, by wooing her and winning her love and therefore her loyalty and special attention. If she loves us, she will want to keep us alive and well. This is what I mean by having a romance with your mother; you try to impress her, you try to win her over like you would do if you were going on a date with someone you really liked and with whom you thought there could be a good future. Now remember, all this occurs around six months after birth. In terms of the transiting Sun in the chart, what happens to everybody at six months old? Yes, there is the first opposition of the transiting Sun to one's own Sun. I think this is an apt symbol of the fact that, for the first time, two separate selves are encountering one another. If we consider the Sun to be a symbol of the developing ego, the fact that it forms an opposition (an aspect long associated with relationship) indicates that your emerging ego is coming face to face with somebody else's ego or self. Of course, differentiating identity from mother doesn't happen overnight; it's a gradual process and usually takes about three years to complete. And it helps immensely if there is a father around or another key figure on the scene to draw us away from mother. I'll be going more deeply into how this works when we look at ways the father can help break the early mother-child symbiosis by being an attractive outsider who draws us away from a too-intense bond with the mother.

I've been emphasising how this *differentiation stage* gets into swing at six months old. We can learn something about what happened then by looking at the chart. For starters, I would examine the natal aspects to the Moon to glean a general overview of how your love affair with mother went. But I would also look at the transits and progressions involving the Moon from six months to three years old. The progressed Moon moves approximately one degree a month. Look to see what it was doing when you were six months old. Let's say your progressed Moon moved into an exact applying opposition to Pluto at this time, a time when you were beginning to view your mother as distinct from yourself. If this is the case, then you will have met Pluto just as you were entering the relationship arena, and therefore relationships will become associated in your mind with the kinds of qualities or issues to do with Pluto. If your progressed Moon at six months comes to conjunct or trine your Venus, then Venus will have bearing on what you will expect to meet in later relationships.

I would also look at transits to the Moon. Within six months after birth, most transits to the Moon from Saturn and the outer planets will be natal aspects as well. But if we consider the fact that differentiation can take up to three years to complete, then we should also examine any important transits to the Moon right up to age three in light of our later expectations in relationship. You may be born with Saturn at 1 degree Leo and the Moon at 29 degrees Leo. This is not a conjunction, but when you are 2½ or so Saturn will pass over your Moon. You're still very impressionable at this age, and therefore Saturn is going to influence your feelings about what it is like to be close to someone in a supposedly caring relationship.

Let's look more closely at a few natal aspects to the Moon to see what they might mean in terms of the link between mother and later partnerships. We won't have time to cover all the possible aspects to the Moon in depth. I also want to consider the Moon in another way—as a significator not just of one-to-one relationships, but as a measure of how you relate to society in general and how you behave in social situations.

We'll start now with Moon-Mercury aspects, examining these in terms of what your love affair with mother was like, how your first big romance went. I'll focus in on the hard angles and the inconjunct, because these are the trickier and more interesting ones. I don't want to do all the work, so please add your own comments and ideas. If you are born with the Moon in hard angle to Mercury, what kinds of problems could you have encountered with mother?

Audience: Problems in communication.

Howard: Yes, problems understanding one another, problems communicating with one another. It's pretty obvious why this is the case. The Moon is associated with your safety and security needs, your need to be held and fed and comforted. Mercury is associated with the transferring of information. Therefore when you have the Moon, the significator for mother, in trouble with Mercury, you may find that the two of you have difficulty understanding one another. To put it simply, she may not read you right—you get your wires crossed. This can happen if your mother has a very different temperament from you; for instance, if your mother is quite fiery and you're more earthy or watery. You may be trying to communicate that you need to be held or fed in a certain way, but she doesn't get the message, she doesn't pick up on what you are asking for or require. As an infant this could make you feel that you're stupid, that there must be something lacking in you. This becomes part of your personal mythology, an early impression you form about life and about yourself which might haunt you later on. In other words, Moon-Mercury problems can manifest as an insecurity about your intelligence or your ability to communicate and be understood. But we shouldn't just examine the past and early childhood in order to moan about what happened. We want to go into the past and into the unconscious in order to understand the present better, to see the connection between your later life or current relationship problems and what happened between you and mother as a child. So if you had trouble making yourself understood and you experienced communication difficulties with mother, what are the possible consequences in later relationships? What will you be sensitive or touchy about? I often hear people who have these aspects complaining "My partner doesn't understand me. We can't express our needs or feelings to each other." You see how this is the same problem which was there with mother in first few years of life.

Let's consider the hard angles of the Moon to Venus. What kinds of problems can these aspects signify in terms of your love affair with mother?

Audience: I have Moon square Venus and I can remember finding my mother ugly and coarse. I didn't like the way she moved or touched me.

Howard: Yes, I've heard other people report similar things. Even though the Moon and Venus are personal planets and you might not think that the hard angles between them would be as problematic as Moon in trouble with Saturn or an outer planet, difficult Moon-Venus aspects can create quite a lot of tension in relationship later on. Here we have your need for security and what you require to feel safe and included (the Moon and mother) at odds with what you find attractive or beautiful (Venus). Later in life, this conflict could repeat itself in a variety of ways. You may marry or get involved with someone who offers you security or who makes you feel safe, but this person somehow isn't the one who really turns you on erotically or excites you in a Venusian way. In other words, because these two planets are in conflict with one another, you may marry for safety at the expense of Venus. Or it could be the converse situation: the people you're attracted to (Venus) are not the ones who can offer you the kind of safety or security you need.

I've also seen Moon-Venus problems manifest in quite another way. When you have these two planets in square or hard angle, it signifies a tension or probable incompatibility between what these planets represent archetypically. We've looked briefly at the case of not finding the mother beautiful. But the reverse could be true – we might find her too exciting or too enticing. In other words, there is a mix-up between the maternal principle and the sexual or erotic principle. So mother may be feeding or holding you in the course of fulfilling your basic Moon/survival needs, but it actually feels sexual to you. Perhaps mother is not getting her Venusian needs met through her partner, and unconsciously turns to her child for that kind of excitement or pleasure. What we have here is the "seductive mother." This can create problems for the male child later in life because there is a taboo against sex with mother. So he starts getting close to a woman but as soon as she becomes too familiar or maternal with him, he feels funny about being sexual with her.

Moon-Venus aspects can give a slightly different problem in the chart of a female child. Mother may be seen as the one with a monopoly on beauty, style or taste, thereby leaving the child feeling inadequate by comparison. A kind of competitiveness can arise: "Mirror mirror on the wall, who's the fairest of them all?" This sense of not being as beautiful as the mother can stay with the female child right through life, manifesting in difficulties and rivalries with other women later on.

Audience: Is it possible with these aspects that the mother feels the child is unattractive and the child picks up on those feelings?

Howard: Yes, in some cases I think that the child may feel that he or she is not what the mother values or appreciates. Moon-Venus problems can also be seen as a tension or incompatibility between two different faces of the feminine principle, between the maternal and the erotic. Some women with these aspects experience a conflict as they get older between these two faces of the feminine. They might align themselves with being maternal and forfeit their Venusian side by letting their looks go or not really caring about their attractiveness, or they are *puella* or *hetaira* types who are happy being a flirt, a girlfriend or an inspiration to a partner, but are uncertain about commitment, marriage or maternity. The challenge is to make room in marriage or relationship for both the Moon and Venus—for instance, every once in a while leaving the kids with your mother for a week so that you and your spouse can go off alone on a romantic holiday for two. We've already mentioned how men with hard Moon-Venus angles may split their anima figures into the whore and the madonna. If they live with someone for a while, the partner is seen as mother and this gives rise to sexual problems because it's not on to have sex with mother. Some men attempt to "resolve" this tension by having an affair or something on the side to satisfy their Venusian needs, although I'm sure there are ways to have both the Moon and Venus in a marriage or long-standing relationship.

How about the Moon in difficult angle to Mars? What could these aspects indicate in terms of how your love affair with mother went?

Audience: There may have been battles.

Howard: Yes, I immediately think of a battle between two strong-willed individuals: you want it one way, she wants it another; you want it now, she wants it later; she wants you to behave in a certain way, and you're not in the mood to comply. You don't have the verbal capacity to quarrel or argue with your mother when you are six months old, but these aspects can manifest in fierce arguments and plate-throwing in later relationships. You'll very often have territorial or space problems in your early love affair with mother. The feeling is that mother is too intrusive, bossy or domineering. It's not hard to see why this could be the case with these two particular planets interconnected—the Moon is mother and it is linked with Mars, the god of war and assertion. I also have an image of an infant wanting to venture out and explore the immediate environment or the outside world, but mother comes along and intrudes. You start to "do" your Mars and assert your independence or sense of adventure, but if it is in hard angle to the Moon then mother is somehow dragging along after you or interfering, barging in with her view of what you should be doing or how you should be doing it. So if you have these kinds of experiences in your first major relationship, there might then be a tendency to attract or be sensitive to similar issues in later partnerships. Again and again I hear people with Moon-Mars angles complain about being invaded or not have enough space. In actual fact I believe that a hard Moon-Mars angle is an inner conflict, an inner dilemma between that part of you which wants to be adventurous and independent and another part of you which craves closeness, safety and security. The ego, however, hates ambivalence, so you may identify with and live out the Mars side and project the Moon—that is, see others as trying to cling to you or hold you back.

Audience: Is this also the case with the conjunction?

Howard: Yes, very often. But whenever you're assessing how a conjunction will work, you also have to examine any other aspects in the chart to the conjunction. If you have Moon conjunct Mars trine Venus it will be less of a problem than Moon conjunct Mars square Venus. Nonetheless, the conjunction of these two planets inevitably links your image of mother with the god of war. You'll usually view her as strong, powerful or angry. She may not show that anger, frustration or power: it may be simmering, it may be seething or hiding underneath, but it is there. Originally mother is the whole world to you, so what passes between you and your mother is a pretty good indication of how you will see or relate to the world in general later on. If we felt safe with mother, then the world feels safe; if mother didn't seem too steady or reliable a container, then later on the world feels more dangerous. If you have to fight with mother to establish your space or independence, then later on you may find yourself repeatedly in situations where you are fighting with close friends, partners or loved ones for more freedom and room to move.

Let's take Moon-Jupiter aspects. With the hard angles, the relationship with mother may go through noticeable—often quite dramatic—mood swings, from love and bliss to pain and despair, all wonderful one day and then all terrible the next. We love her and think she is the greatest thing on earth, and then for whatever reason the situation reverses, leaving us feeling betrayed and let down. Can you see why this is? The Moon is associated with emotions and feelings, while Jupiter is a planet associated with expansiveness and the tendency to over-do or go to extremes. People with Moon in aspect to Jupiter often have manic, rollercoasterlike relationships.

I'm reminded of a woman I know who has Moon conjunct Jupiter in Taurus square to Pluto in Leo. As a child, her feelings for her mother swung from worship and adoration to hate, fear and loathing—a pattern or prototype which she repeats in most of her adult involvements. The Pluto square serves to bring out the extremes of her Moon-Jupiter conjunction. After telling me about her wonderful and kind mother, she then added that there were times when her mother beat her badly or locked her up in a cupboard for a relatively minor misdemeanour. As a consequence of these early experiences, she came to associate relationships with dramatic ups and downs. She meets a man and rings me up to talk and rave about him: he is perfect, he is divine, he is Zeus incarnate. Her relationships usually get off the ground very quickly—two days after getting together, she and her new lover are planning their future life together, and this usually involves starting up a business or project which magically will bring money and fulfilment to them. I mean this woman functions like clockwork. Whenever she calls and tells me these things, I look at my watch and check the date. I know that in approximately two weeks I'll be hearing from her again, and she'll be moaning about what a bastard and disappointment he is. I've been observing this pattern in her for years and years. So just by assessing the Moon in her chart, you have a good idea of what her relationships are like. This is the point I'm making, that the Moon is as much of a significator for relationship as is Venus.

If you have a Moon-Jupiter aspect in your natal chart, it could also mean that your mother had a conflict between mothering and wanting to be out in the world doing something she considered more adventurous or exciting. She may literally be foreign or travel a great deal, or have a penchant for religion, philosophy or sport, anything expansive. So the image of your loved one is linked with qualities of Jupiter. In a man's chart, he may later seek a partner who somehow embodies Jupiter, someone who is exciting, inspirational, adventurous. This is fine so long as it's not at odds with another side of him that wants a more sedate or settled woman for a mate.

Let's briefly consider some possible manifestations of the hard aspects of the Moon to Saturn. What could these aspects indicate in terms of your urge to love and relate with mother?

Audience: You might meet some form of coldness.

Howard: Yes, you could encounter someone who is uptight in some way, who seems to be burdened with difficulties, or who simply has problems responding to your needs in a fashion which makes you feel at ease. In some cases, mother may be trying her hardest to be attentive to your comfort and satisfaction, but she might be so nervous about doing her job right that what you ultimately pick up on is her insecurity and doubts. We could also look at it in another way. Picture yourself at six months or so wanting to be fed or held but for whatever reasons, your mother fails or is unable to meet these needs. You run into a brick wall; maybe she's busy with other responsibilities or has read in a book that babies should be fed according to a timetable and not just when they express a desire to be fed. So you have real emotional or physiological requirements, but they're not being met. What might this do to you? How is this going to affect you inside?

Audience: You then feel frustrated and insecure.

Howard: Yes, that is very likely. It's also likely that you'll feel you're to blame, that there's something wrong with you: "She doesn't give me what I need, therefore I must be bad and unlovable." This is called "introjecting" the bad mother, or identifying with the bad breast. Early impressions cut deeply, so if you think you're bad, no good, or unworthy of love, then what kinds of feelings are you going to bring into relationships with you later in life? Even if someone truly loves you, on some deep level you are unable to believe it. People with Moon in hard angle to Saturn often lack self-confidence and carry the conviction that others will fail to meet their needs. They form touchy, nervous attachments; they find it hard to relax in a relationship, and their anxieties and insecurities may, in the end, drive the other person away. In this way, they manage to turn their worst fears and expectations into a self-fulfilling prophecy. Or (according to the doctrine of repetition compulsion), you may go for those people who, by nature, have difficulty showing love or meeting your particular needs. There may be suitors around who truly desire you and want to make you happy, but they're not the ones who interest you. Instead you're drawn to the difficult people who can't quite respond to you in the way you need, as if some part of your psyche is still trying to turn a "bad" mother into a good one.

Moon-Saturn aspects also can give rise to someone who doesn't feel okay about even having needs or wants. If as a child you had difficulties getting your needs fulfilled, it may be easier for you to stop needing, rather than going through the pain of not getting what you seek. If you needed mother to be there in a certain way, and over and over again you were let down, you begin to feel that loving and needing hurt too much. Emotional detachment becomes a strategy or defence against the pain of unfulfilled needs—it is better not to acknowledge or show your needs because it hurts too much when these are not met. So you cut off from what you really want, you deny your feelings. In doing so you become seemingly self-sufficient. A rock feels no pain: you appear tough and strong, but underneath is someone who is hurting, someone who is fearful and who doesn't feel worthy of love and fulfilment.[6]

Compensation also may come into play here. If you had a Moon-Saturn type relationship with your mother and you ended up feeling unlovable or unworthy, you may then try to make up for this by being superproductive and by doing things to prove your value to the world. But there is a compulsion or complex underlying this kind of compensatory behaviour. If you're not being productive or doing what you consider are worthwhile things, then you don't feel you deserve love. You have to keep proving yourself; you can never really fully relax. In order to feel worthy or safe, you *have* to be responsible, successful and achieving in a Saturn-type way. All this is a means of making up for your deeper underlying sense of inadequacy. I'm sure some of you can identify with what I'm talking about, or know others who behave in this way. It is especially important for Moon-Saturn people to grieve for the ideal mothering they never received, to work through the pain, guilt and anger engendered when the bonding with mother has failed, or was too weak, or tenuous.

Now, let's briefly examine difficult Moon-Uranus contacts in terms of our early romance with mother. Try to picture the consequences of these two planets at odds with one another. You're attempting to bond with mother and then you run into Uranus; in other words, you run into some kind of disruption, something erratic, uncertain or unconventional—any of those qualities we normally associate with Uranus. Mother may be felt as a shaky or unstable container; she may be there physically but for some reasons you don't feel sure about her. Something in you senses she's restless and might get up and leave at any moment. She can be holding or feeding you, and yet she doesn't feel solid and fully attentive—her mind may be somewhere else, thinking about other things she would like to be doing or contemplating abstract theories and philosophies rather than being totally present for you. If you have these kinds of aspects, you may feel that your safety and security could be disrupted at any moment, things could change in a minute.

---

[6]Judith Viorst, *Necessary Losses*, p. 23.

If you meet these kinds of situations with mother in your first big romance, it's likely that similar apprehensions or expectations will consciously or unconsciously remain with you into adult life. Later on you find yourself in a relationship, but you have a nagging sense that it could all change or end suddenly. Conversely, because you have not had the experience of a solid and safe container, you don't know how to be one yourself; therefore you may be the one who feels restless in partnership, who is easily bored or distracted. Or you grow into the kind of person who appears totally autonomous and self-sufficient, when, in actual fact, your self-sufficiency is a defence or armour concealing a frightened child living underneath, a child afraid to trust or rely on the love of others.

In a man's chart, it can indicate an almost compulsive attraction to women who are fairly independent or Uranian in nature, whether or not they show that side of themselves at first. In a woman's chart they indicate confusion about whether she really wants to mother at all or lead a conventional married life. Anyone with these aspects could have inner conflicts between wanting the type of partner who offers security and can make a settled home, and finding they are attracted to people who display a high degree of autonomy and independence.

Because these two planets represent very different principles or archetypes, their hard aspects often produce a "closeness/freedom" dilemma. The Moon craves closeness and inclusiveness, but Uranus likes its space and freedom. If you have Moon-Uranus aspects in your chart, you need to make room in your life for both sides of the polarity. If you just identify and side with your need for closeness, you're denying your need for greater autonomy and individuality. Should this be the case, your partner will likely be the one who acts out what you are suppressing in yourself. Your clingingness or your conventionality may drive away the partner in a search for someone more exciting, or in search of a freer and more expansive life. In other words, there is a split going on, what has been labelled by Maggie Scarf as an "emotional division of labour."[7] You carry the closeness needs, and the other person becomes the one who lives out your denied Uranian urges. Or the

---

[7]Maggie Scarf, *Intimate Partners*, p. 60.

reverse is true: your partner is the one who provides the stability, and you're the one who is uncertain and variable. Either way, the situation is usually not very satisfying, and it doesn't make for relationships that last.

I'll be discussing the freedom/closeness dilemma in greater depth in my lecture on Venus.[8] For now, suffice it to say, that it's better for you to accept that you have both the desire for closeness and the desire for autonomy within yourself and work out some way to make room in your life and your relationships for both of these needs. The task at hand is how to be close and intimate and yet also leave some space for yourself. It's likely that your mother had a similar dilemma or tension inside her, and now it's in your life and can be seen in your relationship patterns.

We will cover Moon-Neptune and Moon-Pluto aspects in the joint session on the Sun and Moon (in Part 3, pp. 197–201). Right now, I want to change gears slightly and broaden how we are looking at the Moon. We've been discussing it as one of the indicators of what we encounter or expect in intimate, one-to-one relationship based on our early love affair with mother. However, the Moon is activated anytime you seek to belong or be included. To put it another way, the Moon represents your inclusion needs. Just think about all the different kinds of situations you experience in life where you want to belong, where you want to be included: it can be a dinner party or other kinds of social gatherings, or even at the office where you work.

I'm expanding the significance of the Moon to include what happens in group situations such as at a party, and to signify what you need to feel safe and secure in whatever environment you find yourself. I'd like you to observe yourself and see if you can get a sense of what you need to feel comfortable there, how you act or behave in order to feel safe and okay in a social setting. What makes you feel secure and included? What makes you feel unloved or unwanted, dislodged or the odd person out?

These are not original ideas. I'm borrowing from Stephen Arroyo, who in his book *The Practice and Profession of Astrology*,

---

[8]The discussion on Venus will appear in the next volume in this series: Liz Greene and Howard Sasportas, *The Inner Planets: Building Blocks of Personal Reality*, Volume 4 of *Seminars in Psychological Astrology* (York Beach, ME: Samuel Weiser, 1992).

analyses the Moon as an indicator of how you interact with the environment in order to feel at home, in order to feel welcomed or included.[9] In fact, we can play a kind of game with this. Project your mind onto an upcoming party and try to imagine what the different Moon signs will need or what they might do in order to feel comfortable at such an occasion. Arroyo suggests that a good way to do this is to use the phrase "Let us . . ." or "Let's do . . ." I'll illustrate what I mean by using the Moon in Aries as an example. Unless your Moon in Aries is severely restricted or impinged upon by more downbeat planets, you're likely to feel at your best if you can activate and arouse the environment in some way, so a phrase associated with the Moon in Aries may be something like "Let's get this thing going; let's energise the environment." You might be impatient or easily bored, so you want to get the party moving. You may be the one who initiates speaking to someone you don't know, or you might be the first one to dance. For the majority of people with the Moon in Aries, doing anything is better than doing nothing: the way they feel comfortable and at home is by making things happen or getting things going.

Contrast this with people who have Moon in Taurus. They usually need to feel physically comfortable or settled in order to feel safe. They'll look for a space to sit or stand that feels right. They may make themselves secure by heading straight for the food table — they may not feel safe until they have had something to eat. I'm joking to some extent. When I first read Arroyo on this, I was a little surprised when he wrote that the Moon in Taurus feels most safe if it has control over the environment. I had never really thought of Taurus in terms of control issues. But it is true. I have this placement and I know that I feel most at home or happiest when things aren't too hectic, chaotic or haphazard, when things are in order and I have a say about how they're going to be run. For instance, if I found out suddenly that we had to change our lecture room tomorrow, I'd probably have trouble sleeping tonight. Will the new room be adequate, will it have what I need? The more familiar I am with an environment, the more comfortable I feel.

---

[9]Stephen Arroyo, *The Practice and Profession of Astrology* (Sebastapol, CA: CRCS Publications, 1984), pp. 159–62.

What about Moon in Gemini? What might their "let us" statement be?

Audience: Let's communicate and exchange information.

Howard: Exactly, they usually feel more comfortable and at home when they start talking with people and making connections with others. For instance, let's say a Moon in Gemini person meets someone at a party and discovers that they both know someone in common, or both have brothers who work in computers. Bingo! Now, they are off, now they fit in. They may want to impress you with their knowledge on a wide range of subjects. The Moon in Gemini also likes to observe, almost a voyeur who enjoys drawing conclusions or making deductions from what it sees. These are the sorts of things that instinctively make them feel secure or included. What about the Moon in Cancer? What would the most obvious need be?

Audience: To merge with the environment, or to be helpful and caring for those they are with.

Howard: Yes, if they're not too threatened by their surroundings, their instinct is to merge and blend. So if they're in a room full of saintlike people, they will mirror back their saintly side. But if they are in a room full of criminals, people with the Moon in Cancer may try to blend and be included by displaying that they too can be bad. And what you say about their need to mother is often true. They may offer to go to the bar to get you a drink, or they are the ones to get the coffee for everyone. So by feeding others or being sensitive to other people's needs, the Moon in Cancer person feels more comfortable as well. But I've noticed something else: if those with the Moon in this sign really don't like the environment or are in one of their withdrawn moods, then their instinctive reaction is to retreat, to sit in the corner talking to no one, or even to leave the party or scene altogether. They just want to get back home into their shell, into what is familiar.

What about the Moon in Leo; what does this fire sign Moon need to do in a social situation to feel safe or included?

Audience: They will probably need to make some sort of impact on the environment.

Howard: Yes, their statement might be, "Let's vitalise the environment, let's get noticed, let me do something which allows me to shine or stand out." It's when people see that they are a little bit special or unique in some way that they feel okay. A karmic astrologer once remarked that if you have the Moon in Leo it probably means that you were royalty or someone famous in a past life, and now you come into this incarnation expecting to be treated special, expecting to be discovered or noticed. Some Moon in Leo people have come to me for readings and they look so shy and unobtrusive, but when I talk to them about these instinctive needs for recognition and admiration, they have to admit that such feelings are there strongly within them. Also, I've noticed that there can be quite a bit of one-upmanship going on in them. So if they're with a group of thieves or robbers, the Moon in Leo person would like to be able to say that "I've robbed more than you," or, "I have the best idea of all for a bank job." If they can do one better, then they feel good about themselves, then they feel worthy of inclusion and love. As children, the more special we are to mother, the safer we feel. This is especially true for the Moon in this sign. And this need for specialness in order to feel good about themselves stays throughout life, long after they have left mother's side.

How about the Moon in Virgo? This placement can be quite contradictory, but what do you think of first?

Audience: Maybe they feel most at home and at ease if they are emptying ashtrays or clearing the table? Or if they can find someone with whom to discuss their health.

Howard: Yes, these fit with the textbook idea of the Moon in Virgo. I think they need to feel useful and productive in whatever environment they are in. So they may offer to do the washing up, or even before the party begins they ring up to see if you would like them to make the sandwiches or to bring anything along. Or, as you suggest, they'll feel as if they've arrived when they meet someone with whom they can compare cholesterol levels—that certainly would be in line with the typical Virgoan preoccupation with the body and physical well-being. More seriously, to feel safe, Moon in Virgo often needs to size up the environment, to analyse it, to "clock" it. So their statement might be, "Let's study the environment, let's figure out how it works and then I will feel more relaxed, at home, safe and comfortable." After all, it is a Mercury-ruled sign. If someone with the Moon in Virgo is supersensitive or very uptight, then what do you think they'll do to feel comfortable? Probably, they will instinctively start to criticise the environment, to dissect or tear others apart a little in order to feel all right about themselves. They might comment on how the room should be decorated differently, or remark on the low quality of some of the other people around. But this is usually only when they are extremely nervous or ill at ease.

What is the most obvious way that a Moon in Libra would approach a social situation?

Audience: Their statement might be, "Let's be pleasing."

Howard: Yes, you often get the Moon in Libra with a strong desire to harmonise with the environment in order to feel safe and secure. Or they might want to beautify the surroundings in some way. But again, I think it is a misunderstanding to think that the Moon in Libra is just motivated to be nice or sweet. This sign is also equipped with an instinct to redress imbalances. So if they're in an environment where everyone is being sickly sweet to one another, some people with the Moon in Libra will instinctively want to act out the opposite, to be aggressive or a little rude, a little crude or pushy in order to balance out the phoniness or lopsidedness they see around them. So their statement could be, "Let's oppose the environment," especially if they decide it's not worth the effort to be liked. There is something of the flavour of the Moon in Virgo in this regard; they too can be judgemental and critical, measuring the party or the people there against their own ideals or expectations. There is a theory that Virgo and Libra were once one sign in the distant past, and I've certainly observed some similarities between these two Moon sign placements. The shadow side of having high expectations is the tendency to be critical and judgmental when others don't live up to your ideals. This is very different from the stereotype of the sweet and charming Libra Moon type.

What about the Moon in Scorpio? How are they going to approach an environment or behave at a party to feel most safe or comfortable?

Audience: Maybe they'll have a "Let's wait and see" attitude.

Howard: Yes, that's an interesting way of putting it. Many people with the Moon in Scorpio will want to keep a close watch on what is going on around them, and that makes them feel less wary and more at home. So they might, at least at first, be on guard, not revealing too much. They are sharp-eyed like eagles. So their statement might be, "Let's understand the hidden workings going on in this environment; let's check out the undercurrents and subtle interactions between people." They are not inclined to be satisfied just knowing what is happening on the surface, but they have a need to see the little games going on, who is chasing after whose date, and who is giving off what vibes and why. Then they start feeling more comfortable, more at home. And if the party is boring, they may resort to devising ways of stirring things up: "Who can I shock or upset in order to make all this more interesting?" I hate to say it, but people with the Moon in Scorpio often have something of the drama queen in them. If life or the environment is getting too dull or boring, there is nothing like a little crisis to liven things up.

What about the Moon in Sagittarius, what do you think their statement might be?

Audience: "Let's make the environment more lively."

Howard: Yes, "let's make things more interesting, let's stimulate or arouse the environment, let's be expansive or more adventurous." It might even be "Let's move the party to somewhere bigger!" Unless the Sagittarian Moon is in serious trouble with Saturn or the outer planets, people with this placement are usually fairly gregarious. They feel good if they're learning from others, they feel at home if they're teaching or sharing their ideas and their enthusiasms, if they're meeting new and interesting people. But if they are insecure or uptight for some reason, then you may see an arrogant or slightly haughty side coming out: "These are not my people, this is not my scene, I'm above this, goodbye."

What do you think about the Moon in Capricorn in terms of how they make themselves comfortable in social gatherings or social situations? This is another complicated one, but what are the first ideas that come to your mind?

Audience: "Let's use the environment to get ahead in life."

Audience: Maybe they hope important people will be there and mixing with brass would make them feel good.

Howard: Yes, a fair number of people with the Moon in Capricorn have difficulty just relaxing, just letting go or playing. They like to be productive and they could be ambitious, so there is a chance they'll use social situations for ulterior motives such as achieving a desired goal or getting ahead in life. Their statement could also be, "Let's control and regulate the environment." They may feel safest when things are structured or well organised, if there are timetables and clear rules of behaviour, clear-cut guidelines defining what is allowed and what isn't. Another statement might be, "Let's assume responsibility for the environment." So if something needs to be done like changing the music or wiping up a spill, the Moon in Capricorn may take this on as his or her duty or responsibility. But what if they can't manage to feel at ease? They may then deal with the environment by keeping up their staunchest defences, acting in a rigid way, drawing clear boundaries between themselves and the other people around.

The Moon in Aquarius has a few different sides to it. If Uranus is strong in the chart, their statement could be, "Let's electrify the environment, let's bring new energy and life here, or let's disrupt things a little to make it more interesting or lively." Like the Moon in Gemini, this placement is usually curious about life and interested in observing how others function and operate. There is a need to learn and discover things in order to feel satisfied and at home, so a person with the Moon in Aquarius is likely to circulate and talk to a whole range of people to find out where they are coming from, what they believe in, how they conduct their lives.

Certain individuals with the Moon in this sign are happiest when they have an opportunity to spout their views or share their political or social beliefs with others. "Now that you're all here at this party, I want to tell you about animal rights."

The Moon in Pisces is an interesting and varied placement in terms of how they negotiate social situations. One obvious statement may be, "Let's love, care for and help the environment." They feel they've arrived when they nab some poor soul who needs succour or sympathy. The reverse is also true. They may not feel safe or at home until they've poured their hearts out to another person and found someone who understands, who is sympathetic to them, then they can relax and enjoy themselves. They usually like to blend or merge with the environment. You see how different this is from the Moon in Aries. The Moon in Aries isn't all that bothered about blending or merging, but the Moon in Pisces feels good if this is possible. So you may see the Moon in Pisces behaving one way with one group or one type of person, and completely differently with another type of person. Or they spend a lot of time just having fantasies and daydreaming, imagining that this or that is going on.

Audience: I know a lot of people with the Moon in Pisces and their statement is "Let's drink!"

Howard: Yes, I'll buy that. They feel good when they can let go, when their boundaries are loosened. There are certain similarities here with the Moon in Cancer: if they can't manage to feel comfortable where they are, they'll usually find some excuse to slip away, to do a disappearing act and escape the scene altogether.

These are just some ideas about how the Moon indicates what you need to happen in order to feel included, to feel that you're safe and that you belong. Please excuse me for being so general and brief, and a little light with all this. You all know that it's necessary to take the 11th house and the whole chart into consideration to discern a more accurate picture, and especially to consider what other planets are aspecting the Moon.

PART TWO

THE SUN

THE HERO WITH A THOUSAND FACES

THE SUN AND THE DEVELOPMENT OF CONSCIOUSNESS

BY LIZ GREENE

I would like to start this morning's session by talking about one of the oldest and most profound mythic representations of the Sun: the ancient symbol of kingship. Until the beginning of the present century, kingship was perceived as the earthly embodiment of the godhead, the mortal vessel through which the will of the divine made itself known in the world. Some of you may find this peculiar, especially since Switzerland is the oldest democracy in Europe and has never had a king. But there is an archaic layer in all of us which even today still responds to the magical symbol of kingship. In ancient times the king was also a priest, and the role of governing his people was combined with the role of the *pontifex*, the bridge-builder who mediated between heaven and earth. As we explore the mythology of the Sun this morning, it may help to keep the symbol of kingship in mind, because it binds together the various mythic solar figures.

Yesterday Howard and I talked about the Moon as an innate, instinctive dimension of the personality. Although we may need to work at expressing the Moon, our lunar nature does not consciously strive to develop goals in the world. Our self-nourishing capacity is intrinsic to us; we have only to listen to it. The Moon is also regressive in nature, always pulling us back toward the past and the mother-child bond, because our basic emotional and bodily needs do not change at core. But the Sun is progressive. It is an active, dynamic principle which unfolds during the course of a lifetime. We never really finish developing the Sun, for this aspect of the personality is always in a process of becoming, of moving toward some future vision or goal. Some of you may be familiar with what Joseph Campbell calls the "monomyth," the story of the hero which recurs in every culture's mythology. The hero myth is a solar myth, for the hero is always on the way to becoming something. He is not automatically born a hero. He must earn his right to become hero and king and a fitting vessel for the god who parents him.

I should emphasise at this point that the hero, who is always masculine, is not the exclusive property of men, any more than the lunar mother is the property solely of women. We all possess a lunar and a solar dimension to our natures. The unfolding of the hero myth through the development of the Sun is just as relevant to women as the self-nourishing wisdom of the Moon is to men. The adjectives "masculine" and "feminine," when used to describe a symbolic image, do not refer to one sex or the other. They refer to a quality of energy, receptive or dynamic, for which male or female deities in myth are the most appropriate images. In a similar fashion, as I hope you will see later in the week, the mythic conjunction or marriage between Sun and Moon describes a potential of inner relationship between these different aspects of the personality in either sex.

Now perhaps you can have a look at our diagram for the Sun (see figure 3 on page 83). Much of the material which I will be using to describe the myth of the solar hero comes from Joseph Campbell, whose book, *The Hero with a Thousand Faces*, is one of the best psychological explorations of myth.[1] Before I link it up with astrological symbolism I would like to outline the basic stages of the hero's journey. First of all, the hero has a strange or portentous birth; he is usually fathered by a god on a mortal mother. In some cases, such as the Greek hero Achilles, this is reversed; his father was the mortal Peleus but his mother was the sea goddess Thetis. There is also the Roman hero Aeneas, fathered by the mortal Anchises on the goddess Venus. But whichever parent is the god, one of the characteristics of the hero is that he is a hybrid between human and divine, and is thus destined to be a pontifex.

As a child the hero has no idea of his true parentage. He thinks he is just like everybody else, but he has a nagging feeling of being different and an intuition of a special destiny. One of the main

---

[1]Joseph Campbell, *The Hero with a Thousand Faces*, Bollingen Series No. 17 (Princeton, NJ: Princeton University Press, 1968).

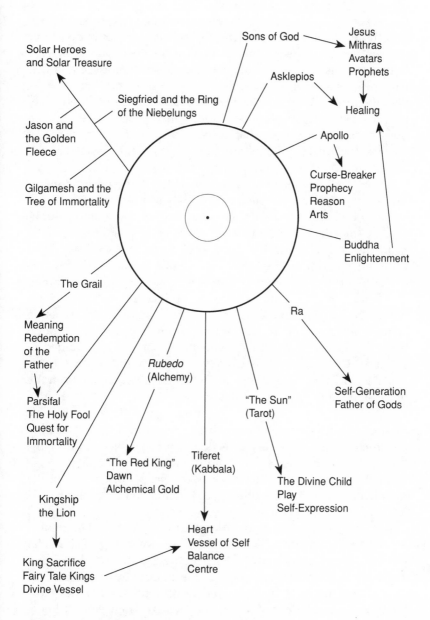

Figure 3. The mythology of the Sun.

themes of the hero's quest is the discovery of his true origin, which is both mortal and immortal. In this mythic image of hybrid birth we can perceive a deep sense of duality, a conviction that we are not merely made of earth and doomed to eat, reproduce and die. Each of us is special, unique, and has a personal destiny, an individual contribution to make to life. The Moon is our body life, parented by mortals and fated by our genetic inheritance. It is the Sun in us which senses that there is a quest to be pursued, a journey toward an unknown future, a profound mystery at the core of "me."

Many children have a fantasy that they have been adopted. Those two ordinary people bumbling about the house could not possibly be our real parents. We were actually fathered or mothered by someone special and wonderful, a prince or a princess or a head of state, but this has been kept secret. This fantasy is so common amongst children that we can assume it is archetypal. It is one of the places where myth finds its way into ordinary human life, before "reality" stomps all over the imaginal world of childhood. The same motif also occurs regularly in fairy tales, where a stepmother or stepfather has replaced a missing parent. Although this missing parent may not be divine, he or she is shrouded in mystery. The stepparent is usually obnoxious and a comedown, and the child has a special destiny which involves escape from the oppressive environment and the discovery of his or her true birth.

Our awareness of the Sun may first express itself in this early fantasy of a mysterious unknown parent, or of a "high" destiny awaiting us. The solar part of us does not feel subject to the same lunar cycles and laws of fate that our emotions and bodies are. It stubbornly refuses to be ordinary. Many people discover it in the middle of life, and I have often heard clients in their forties say, "I have this feeling there is some deeper purpose for my being alive. I am no longer satisfied by the old goals of money and emotional security and worldly achievement." This awakening of the solar principle may coincide with the beginning of a period of inner exploration, and this in turn may be precipitated by a crisis of some kind which leaves depression and discontent in its wake. How many of you have experienced this feeling? Then you all know what I am talking about.

Audience: At first it's very difficult to articulate it in terms of concrete goals.

Liz: Yes, it is, because the Sun is not really concerned with the concrete world as its final destination. Material reality is the domain of the Moon, and often what we think of as goals in the first half of life are really the lunar security needs translating themselves into mundane terms. Solar goals are inner, and are concerned with self-realisation and experiencing one's life as special and meaningful. These goals are very difficult to define, and they differ from one person to another in the kind of outer expression they need. Socrates called this mysterious inner driving force his *daemon*, the destiny that impels an individual toward becoming his or her own ideal. The Sun says, "But I am not just any old mouse or rabbit or cabbage. My life means something, I have potentials that I have not yet fulfilled." You can see why we ignore this solar drive at our peril, for if we do not take the heroic leap and make a unique creative contribution in some way, however small, we are doomed to the nagging torment of an unlived self. Then we have every reason to fear death, for we have not truly lived.

Another important element in the solar hero's childhood is that he is usually envied or persecuted without knowing why. Sometimes the enemy is his mother's husband, who is really his stepfather. Sometimes it is a usurping or wicked king who has had an omen or augury and fears that the hero, having reached manhood, will overthrow him. We can see this theme in the stories of Greek heroes such as Perseus as well as in the story of Jesus, who as an infant was persecuted by King Herod. The theme of envy, and the potential threat the hero holds for the ruling powers, is one which I will refer to many times as we explore the solar journey. The Sun is special, and the expression of specialness often invokes destructive envy in others. If the Sun remains unconscious, it may equally invoke destructive envy of others in oneself. Whenever we explore a myth, we can be sure we will find it everywhere in ordinary human life.

This archetypal problem of envy and persecution of nascent solar potentials, which may be seen enacted in a great many families, is one of the reasons why many people find it hard to express the Sun. They fear that, if they are truly themselves, then others will react with anger and attack them, verbally or emotionally. Often one's actual mother or father unconsciously did exactly that, because the parent's unlived solar life has turned sour and envious; and one has a direct experience of the mythic hero's persecuted childhood enacted in one's own formative years. The young hero-to-be may have his mortal mother's protection for a time, but sooner or later he must learn to cope on his own with the envious stepparent or ruler. He has to develop realism, since envy is a fact of life and an indelible part of human nature. He cannot always run home bleating when his specialness is attacked or called into question. And he must acquire toughness, self-sufficiency, insight, intelligence, and loyal friends in order to survive as an individual. Otherwise he might as well quench his solar light and crawl back into the womb again. This is in fact what many people do, for they find mother surrogates such as unfulfilling jobs or stifling relationships to protect them, and suppress their own individual potentials to avoid the competitive world outside.

At some point in his growing-up process, the hero receives what Campbell refers to as "the call to adventure." This can come in a number of forms. The divine parent may appear in a dream or vision, saying, "All right, son, pull your finger out, it's time to grow up and go after the treasure hard to attain." In other words, the call may come from within us – a sudden intuition of meaning and destiny – which frequently occurs under major heavy planet cycles such as the Saturn return at 30, or in midlife coincident with the Uranus half-cycle or the second Saturn half-cycle. The hero's call in myth may also come through apparent external upheaval or disaster – the crops are failing, or a plague or invasion has struck, or the old king is dying and there is no known heir. Those of you who are familiar with the Arthurian legends will recognise that this last situation, when the Saxons are invading and King Uther Pendragon is dying, is the backdrop for the moment young Arthur is revealed as the rightful heir by drawing the magic sword Excalibur out of the stone. The mythic call to adventure can thus express itself in our lives as a major crisis which, unlike our usual everyday troubles, challenges us to plunge into the unknown and discover new resources that we did not know were there. I believe this is how the majority of people experience the solar call to adventure which, as well as being signalled by heavy planet cycles, is often reflected by a major transit or progression involving the Sun.

Not many of us get struck like Saul on the road to Damascus, where the god appears in a vision and announces one's unique destiny to save the world. When it does happen so floridly, especially in youth, there are often some questionable elements involved, such as deep-rooted feelings of inferiority which generate a compensatory messianic identification. There is a difference between the real adult emergence of the Sun in a relatively solid personality, and the global messianic fantasy which reflects a poorly developed ego structure. The Sun's uniqueness is not incompatible with realism and humility, and its sense of specialness does not need to look down on lesser mortals, unless it has become badly mixed up with unhealed childhood wounds.

The timing of the hero's call to adventure has a strange preset quality in myths and folklore, rather like an alarm clock going off at a programmed time. It is inevitable, like the rising of the Sun. As Hamlet says:

> If it be now, 'tis not to come; if it be not to come, it will be now; if it be not now, yet it will come: the readiness is all.

The time is often specified at the hero's birth, right at the beginning of the story. This suggests the built-in timing of the astrological chart. Theseus, for example, discovers that his real father is the King of Athens when he lifts up the great stone under which the king's sword has been hidden. He is instructed by his mother to do this only when he has reached his seventeenth birthday, for that was his father's wish. There is a sense of unavoidable destiny about this timing, which is reflected in the feeling I have heard many people express, that the crisis which has awakened them was "meant" and happened "at the right time." In myth the divine or royal parent may provide a test which must be passed before the hero's real identity and quest can be revealed to him. Thus he demonstrates that he is now fit to become himself.

The timing of the call becomes very interesting to the astrological student when we consider transits and progressions involving the Sun. We all get many transits of heavy planets to the natal and progressed Sun, and many progressed planetary aspects to the natal Sun as well as progressed solar aspects to natal planets, during the course of a lifetime. Unlike the hero, we are given more than one chance to respond to the call, and it may come in separate segments, disguised as disparate life situations linked by a single meaningful thread. The hero's journey does not occur for us once and for all. It seems to operate on many levels, and repeats itself throughout life. Perhaps during this morning's session you might think about the ways in which the heroic call to adventure has arrived in your own life, and whether you recognised it at the time. But try to remember that the call may look like something entirely different, although the results are usually apparent later. Sometimes it occurs through an important encounter. Relationships can provide us with our awakening, especially if they begin or end under significant chart movements involving the Sun. The intervention of another person into our lives, whether this is a lover, a child, a teacher, or even an enemy or rival, can transform our consciousness and send the solar hero on his quest.

Once the hero has been called, he usually acquires a helper, or receives assistance from divine or human or animal sources. Interestingly, he generally does not have to work for this initial assistance. It is provided by the divine parent, or by the mortal parent, or by other benign deities who are on his side for their own reasons. For example, when Theseus sets out to slay the Minotaur, Ariadne, who is in love with him, gives him the ball of thread which will enable him to find his way out of the Labyrinth. Jason, when he flees Colchis with the Golden Fleece, is aided by the priestess Medea, who deflects her father's pursuing ships by chopping up her brother and sprinkling the bloody pieces on the water. Perseus, when he goes forth to destroy the Medusa, is given a shield by Athena in which to see the monster's reflection. This help, sometimes morally questionable (as with Jason) but always exactly the right sort to ensure success, reflects the hero's divine right—he will be tested, but he is given every possible leeway, other than shirking, to help him achieve his goal.

The issue of shirking, or even of blowing it the first time around (as Parsifal did), may also be part of the hero's story. I am reminded of a very amusing television sketch I saw long ago, in which Bill Cosby played the part of Noah. God keeps calling him to warn him about the Flood, but Noah, far from being the righteous and humble figure of the Old Testament, keeps turning his back, making various excuses and offering the religious equivalent of "Not tonight, dear, I have a headache." God eventually becomes so irritated and threatening that Noah gives in, but most gracelessly. It is extremely unheroic behaviour, but it faithfully reflects the way most of us feel when we are called upon by life to find heroic resources. In myth, the hero never whinges.[2] In real life, it seems we all need to whinge a little in the face of the call. This is probably the voice of the Moon, which feels very aggrieved and sorry for itself because we are dragged away from our comforts by the demands of our own souls. It is a bit like the old Jewish joke— Thank you, Lord, for making me one of the Chosen, but couldn't you choose somebody else for a change?

It is of course possible to refuse the call absolutely, in which case it generally comes back again in a different form, with harder tests. The divine parent—who is a mythic image of something within ourselves—will not leave us alone simply because we don't feel up to it. I have met many people who have tried to escape the destiny which the Sun reflects during a time of important chart movements, and they have paid dearly on one level or another for their refusal to become themselves. Often the result is deep depression and a sense of failure and emptiness. Or the test may pass on to the next generation, and one's children and grandchildren may suffer by being the recipient of unfinished solar parental business, grown larger and more demanding with each generation's avoidance. More drastic forms of refusal may also be part of the constellation of breakdowns and serious physical illnesses. It is possible to refuse the call so violently that one retreats completely and self-destructively into the lunar world, which is perhaps connected with chronic "lunacy." The world is full of lost people who have refused their solar call to adventure, not once but many times. Many of them seem "normal" in collective terms, except that there is nobody home, and I am reminded of T. S. Eliot's poem:

> We are the hollow men
> We are the stuffed men
> Leaning together

---

[2]This British word may be unknown to American readers. To whinge is to whine and complain peevishly and seemingly without end—a tactic often employed by tired, small children.

Headpiece filled with straw . . .
Those who have crossed
With direct eyes, to death's other Kingdom
Remember us—if at all—not as lost
Violent souls, but only
As the hollow men
The stuffed men.[3]

Now I would like to go back to the issue of the hero's assistance from outside sources, and consider it in astrological terms. This help comes from within us, although sometimes it is embodied by another person who miraculously provides support or a key of some kind at precisely the right moment. In myth it is often the mortal mother, or lunar goddesses such as Hera or Artemis, who offer the boon; and this might reflect the instinctual wisdom of the Moon, which can be depended upon in times of crisis because it shows us how to look after ourselves. Sometimes it is benign natal aspects which constitute our internal help—innate gifts or abilities which can be relied upon in a pinch. Where we have harmonious aspects, we often have what is called luck, because we are in harmony within ourselves and therefore intuitively approach life in the right way. For example, a Venus-Jupiter conjunction in the natal chart, ready at hand when the Sun is being triggered by a difficult transit or progression, might respond to this challenge with an innately optimistic and hopeful outlook which communicates itself to others, or a spontaneous generosity which makes people want to be generous in return. Mercury trine Saturn might respond with great shrewdness, realism, and a canny knowledge of the rules of the marketplace, so the person avoids the blunders which entrap more gullible souls. We all have "helpers" in our charts—planets in harmonious aspect, planets dignified or exalted by sign or house—which can form the psychic components of the hero's support team.

Help generally follows on the heels of the hero's acceptance of his call. It is as though something powerfully supportive within us is activated when we face and accept our own individual path in life. It is also quite revealing that other gods become involved who

---

[3]T.S. Eliot, "The Hollow Men," from *The Complete Poems and Plays of T.S. Eliot* (London: Faber & Faber, 1969 [p. 83]; and San Francisco: HarperCollins, 1952).

are not directly related to the hero. They have their own reasons for wanting him to succeed. For example, when Perseus goes after the Medusa, a whole crowd of deities joins in the fun. Perseus is the son of Zeus, but Athene offers a shield, Hades contributes a helmet which confers invisibility, and Hermes produces a pair of winged sandals out of his magician's hat. All these gods have an investment in the Medusa being destroyed, and I think this suggests, in mythic language, that the hero is really redeeming a problem which is bigger than his own personal quest.

The solar hero is thus doing something for the collective, although he believes he is only doing it for himself. The Medusa in the Perseus myth symbolises more than a personal dilemma. She is a problem within the collective psyche, a universal human inheritance of resentment and poison which generates paralysing depression within families and social groups and even nations. The gods, it seems, cannot deal properly with their own business, and they need a hero to do the deed for them. Thus the collective unconscious depends upon each individual's authenticity to fulfil its greater design. We can glimpse the links between the solar hero, the priest who mediates the wisdom and intent of the gods, the artist who serves as society's prophetic voice, and the king who embodies the divine will through worldly authority. All these are mythic images for the deeper function of the Sun which, becoming the conduit for an individual's authentic self-expression, inevitably contributes something to the larger psyche from which the individual has come. But the hero must perform his task because he is driven to it from within. If he does it merely to please others, however humanitarian he might wish to sound, he will wind up in awful trouble, because he is not being true to himself. He must pursue his quest because he is pressed to do it by his own inner necessity, not because it will make other people love him. Yet in the act of becoming an individual, he contributes something to others by that act. You can see that the Sun is deeply paradoxical. By becoming ourselves, we have far more to offer than if we are rushing about trying to save the world in order to compensate for an empty place within.

The hero eventually reaches what Campbell calls the Threshold Crossing. There is usually something rather nasty awaiting him here which attempts to block the goal of the quest. The dilemma of the Threshold Crossing reflects a basic life conflict within us. This may be described by many factors in the birth chart. Even the Sun sign portrays an innate conflict, since there are always weaknesses as well as strengths in every zodiacal sign. Difficult aspects to the Sun may suggest the obstacles which lie inside, albeit projected outside, that seem to stop us from growing. Saturn can also describe, by sign and house and aspect, the nature of the Threshold Crossing, since it portrays our defensiveness and fear and reluctance to reveal ourselves. When we look at an example chart later, we shall see how other planets might be linked up with the various characters in the solar hero's story.

Myth describes some typical forms for the enemy at the Threshold Crossing. Often the opponent is a dark brother, an embodiment of the shadowy, destructive or amoral side of the hero himself. Sometimes the enemy is female, a wicked stepmother or witch, and here we meet the lunar goddess in a most unmotherly guise. This reflects a situation where the instinctual needs, rooted in the family and the past, fight against the development of the independent individual. Sometimes the threat comes from a monster or a giant; and these are also images of the instincts, huge and blind and primeval. A good example of this is the hero Siegfried, who must first kill the giant Fafner, who has taken the form of a dragon, before he can pass through the ring of fire to find Brünnhilde. This giant embodies all the inertia and apathy and regressive conservatism of the instincts, which resist any kind of change or transformation; and he exists to a greater or lesser degree in us all.

The dragon may also be seen as a lunar image. It is a cold-blooded, archaic creature, a portrait of the uroboric primal mother in the shape of a huge winged snake. This is what mother often feels like to a young child, for she is still the all-powerful life-giver and death-dealer. The dragon-snake at the threshold can personify what the Moon feels like to a hero who has not yet grown up. The Moon is mythically portrayed not only by goddesses; it is also the Hindu cosmic serpent Ananda, the Great Round of the womb, self-fertilising and world-generating. Our early perceptions of mother span a vast spectrum of experience, ranging from the benign Greek Demeter to the child-eating Babylonian Tiamat.

So the solar hero must confront the mother-snake, as Osiris the Egyptian Sun god did every night when he descended into the underworld. If you are a child reaching the first Saturn square Saturn at 7 years, or a pubescent 14-year-old coming under the first Saturn opposition Saturn, there is great conflict between the longing to return to the womb and the urge to separate and become an individual. The whole process of adolescence reflects this conflict, and often the breakdowns and illnesses which afflict university students reflect that terrific collision between lunar and solar needs. When we are struggling to free ourselves from the grip of our need for mother, we may experience her as the dragon. Thus the Threshold Crossing is also a reflection of puberty and adolescence with its typical family conflicts. We are formed enough as solar entities to know that the backward pull is a kind of death; yet we are too unformed to feel we can face such regressive needs without a violent fight.

Erich Neumann, in *The Origins and History of Consciousness*,[4] calls this stage of development that of the "Struggler." Although it is an archetypal stage of youth and an inevitable stage of the solar hero's journey, it may also be a place to which we are compelled to return later in life if the Sun has remained undeveloped. For the Struggler, everything feels like a battle, and the feminine—whether the actual mother, the bonds of the family, the emotions, women, mother surrogates in the workplace, or one's own mortal flesh—is not viewed with kindness. We might understand certain adolescent battlegrounds such as anorexia in this light, for the violent rejection of food is the violent repudiation of mother. She is a dragon, and must be defeated. There is not yet the possibility of genuine relationship, because one is still too close. There is deep ambivalence in this early stage of the Sun's emergence, and many people become stuck there at the threshold, battling the mother-dragon all their lives. I think we are all familiar with the feeling of being caught between the need to be loved and wanted and the need to stand loyally for our own values. The dragon fight has many emotional levels, and can occur whenever we are confronted with this inner conflict. From the solar point of view, the Moon at

4Erich Neumann, *The Origins and History of Consciousness* (Princeton, NJ: Princeton University Press, 1954).

these moments is only life-destroying, and must be vanquished. And no doubt there are times when it is appropriate to feel this way and act accordingly – even though the conquered dragon reappears later, secretly disguised as the hero's bride.

One of the most ancient myths describing this dragon fight is the Babylonian myth of creation, imaged as a battle between the Sun god Marduk and his mother, Tiamat. Tiamat, the saltwater ocean, is a personification of the primal world-creating mother in the form of a sea monster. She is both the lifegiver and the maw of death which devours all that it creates. This myth is an ancient portrayal of our earliest experiences of the womb and the life-threatening process of birth and separation. At the beginning of time, before any manifest cosmos has come into being, Tiamat and her consort, Apsu, the sweetwater ocean, contain within them all the lesser gods who are their children. Tiamat becomes bored and angry with her noisy offspring, and plots to annihilate them. But the children discover the plan, and Marduk the Sun god, the strongest and boldest of them, slays his father Apsu and challenges Tiamat to mortal combat. He shoots his flaming arrows into her throat and destroys her, and out of her body creates the vault of heaven and the earth beneath. Thus the manifest world is made.

This ancient tale is a stark portrait of the process of the solar individual emerging from the darkness of the womb and the collective unconscious. As with dreams, we may read all the characters in myth as unfolding their story inside us. Tiamat and Marduk are still alive and well within the child and the adult still grappling with the problem of separation from the mother. Marduk, the solar principle, must battle against the regressive pull of his own lunar hunger, and while this struggle continues, the needs of the instinctual nature are experienced as bitter (saltwater), monstrous and life-threatening. His victory results in the making of the world, which might be another way of describing the formation of individual reality. Myths are images of feelings as well as patterns of development, and some of you may recognise the stage of development which the Marduk-Taimat story describes. It is our ongoing battle against inertia, apathy, stagnation and addiction, and on a small scale we experience it in everyday skirmishes like sticking to a diet, or pursuing an exercise programme, or following through a difficult course of study. We may also see it in the struggle to leave an unsatisfactory but compulsive relationship or marriage, or a safe but stultifying job, or a reliable but devouring family. Marduk is the voice of "I am," and although this unity with the oceanic mother is destroyed, this is replaced by the creation of individual reality and individual values.

In some myths, the Threshold Crossing is not a dragon fight, but involves the actual death of the hero, prior to transformation or resurrection. This is the case with Dionysos and Jesus, both of whom are destroyed but who can only assume their true form as divine redeemers through such ritual dismemberment. In these stories the hero is subjected to great suffering, which burns away his mortal aspect. This process is really the same as the dragon fight, but it is imaged from a different and more sophisticated perspective. In the archaic tale of Marduk and Tiamat, it is the mother-dragon who undergoes the suffering and dismemberment, while Marduk experiences only victory. In the Dionysian and Christian stories, the god experiences the suffering himself, for the mother-dragon is his own body which must be transformed or freed from the grip of instinctual bondage. We can see in this a kind of evolutionary process at work where, in the later myths, the deeper meaning of the dragon fight is revealed.

The dragon fight is a noble enactment, heroic on the grand scale. Its image still grips us and reappears perennially in the cinema in such films as *Alien*, not to mention the Hammer House of Horror epics where the hero battles the werewolves, vampires, ghouls and goblins of Hekate's underworld. Yet the internal experience is really a kind of dismemberment or crucifixion, because as we separate we suffer. There is always a problem of suffering—loneliness, isolation, guilt and the enmity of others—when the Sun begins to emerge. If we deny this process of suffering, we will always need to find a dragon outside upon whom to project our own pain.

The mythic image of crucifixion is one of the most powerful symbols of our isolation and alienation on the Saturnian cross of matter. In this state we are unparented and forsaken. There is no home to return to, no comforting bosom to enfold us, no group or collective which can offer a palliative. This is the stark existential state of "I am," which can tell us a lot about why the Sun only really emerges at midlife, when the person is sufficiently strong and formed enough to meet the challenge. The problem of aloneness, which always accompanies any expression of the individual self, is the deepest meaning of the Threshold Crossing in the hero myth. It constellates our greatest anxieties about loss and separation, for there is always the risk that, if we emerge, no one may love us. So the battle with the dark twin, the dragon fight, and the dismemberment or crucifixion are all images of taking on the burden of one's separate self, which is the first important stage of the solar journey. The hero is then equipped to pursue the real object of his quest, because he has proven that he can stand alone.

Now we need to explore this "real" quest, the prize or treasure which awaits the hero after his ordeals. The treasure is often literally a treasure—gold or jewels, or the water of life, or the rulership of a kingdom, or the gift of healing or prophecy. It is a highly individual goal, but it is always something of great value to the hero. The Sun, embodying the mythic hero, strives toward an ultimate reward, an indestructible nugget of identity which justifies and validates one's existence. The hero and his prize are really the same thing. The treasure is the essential core of the hero, his divine side which was always hidden in his mortal body. This may sound terribly abstract. But the sense of being a real, solid, indestructible "me" is a very precious and magical thing, and it is also hard won. Every life situation where we are called upon to separate ourselves and stand for our own values and goals forges a bit of this "me," and we suffer for it each time, because the eternal mother-dragon must be fought again and again in different guises.

Sometimes the hero's treasure is a bride, and the *hierosgamos*, the sacred marriage, is the end of the quest. The divine hero is fully united with his other half, his humanity, in the form of a woman. He then creates a dynasty, from whom are descended famous kings and queens, all of whom have a little bit of the blood of the immortals in them because of the hero's divine parentage. In pagan times, many rulers claimed they had some of this divine blood. Julius Caesar, for example, claimed descent from the goddess Venus through her son, the hero Aeneas, founder of Rome. If you

have read *The Holy Blood and the Holy Grail*,[5] you will know that
there is a secret society in France who believe their proposed claim-
ant to the French throne is descended from Jesus, who married
Mary Magdalen. Because the theme of descent from the god
through the semidivine hero is archetypal, it remains a potent
symbol for us even today.

One aspect of the sacred marriage and the founding of the
dynasty seems to be the anchoring of the divine seed in mortal life
through the continuity of successive generations. There are
descendants who carry the hero's blood down through time, which
means he lives forever through his bloodline. What might this
symbol mean for us psychologically? Perhaps it reflects the solar
drive to create something which outlasts one's own life. The archetypal masculine longing for a son expresses the most basic, biological level of this drive. But there are inner levels as well. If we live
the Sun as fully as we can, we may experience the feeling that we
have secured our bit of eternity by offering something of lasting
value to the collective. We have given something of our own lives —
to life. The 5th house of children is ruled by the Sun, which offers
its essence to the future in order to experience the eternal realm.
The Moon has its own instinctive need to bear children, but this
reflects nature's continuity of life on earth. The Sun's longing for
progeny reflects the quest for immortality.

For many people, however, children are not the only channel
through which the solar drive may need to express itself. Although
this may be the most "natural" level, some individuals choose not
to have children, or are unable to. Finding another dimension for
the solar urge then becomes extremely important. The 5th house in
the chart reflects the artist's longing to create something
indestructible – an inner or imaginative child which will outlive its
creator and contribute his or her essential being and vision to
future generations. I have known people who fulfil this longing by
planting trees. They know perfectly well that, by the time the tree
reaches maturity, they will no longer be here. But this act gives
them the feeling that they are transcending time. So the sacred
marriage which generates a dynasty is a powerful symbol of the

[5]Michael Baigent, Richard Leigh and Henry Lincoln, *The Holy Blood and the Holy
Grail* (London: Jonathan Cape, 1982; and New York: Dell, 1983).

Sun's need to contribute a little piece of its divine essence to the future.

Another image of the hero's goal is reunion with or redemption of the father. One of the stories which portrays this theme most vividly is that of Parsifal, the holy fool who sets off in quest of the Grail. The finding of the Grail is only one aspect of his journey; redemption of the suffering father, the sick Grail king, is the other. This brings us to the issue of the Sun as a symbol of the inheritance from the personal father. If we are to fully live the Sun, we must, in the words of the *I Ching*, "work on what has been spoiled by the father" by infusing it with new life. The sick or wounded father in myth is an image of spiritual decay and the loss of hope and faith. It is interesting in this context to consider Jung, who had the Sun in Leo and who was impelled to redeem his clergyman father's lost faith by restoring life to the Christian symbols in a new way. Jung's *Answer to Job* aroused considerable confusion and even hostility when it was published, but it is a brilliant analysis of this problem of redemption of the father, who in Job's case is God himself.[6] Jung's thesis, put very simplistically, is that the necessity for Christ's incarnation arises from the fact that God the Father makes a bit of a mess of things with Job. The paternal deity's relationship to humankind is faulty and lacking in compassion, and God recognises that it needs to be redeemed through the suffering of Jesus, his only son. Just as the Moon represents an essential substance which we share with our mothers on the instinctual level, the Sun reflects an essential vision which we share with our fathers on the creative level, and which can only reach its proper fruition over many generations of solar striving.

The hero's prize is sometimes an elixir, which he must steal. This elixir may confer immortality or healing gifts or prophecy, or it may save the kingdom. The motif of the stolen elixir appears with great regularity in fairy tales as well as in myths such as that of the Babylonian Gilgamesh, who stole a branch of the Tree of Immortality, or Prometheus, who stole Zeus' sacred fire, or Jason, who stole the Golden Fleece. The magical substance is usually in the hands of a monster or dragon or sorcerer or witch, and the hero must nick it and bring it back into ordinary life. The illicit nature of the hero's

---

[6]Carl Jung, *Answer to Job* (Princeton, NJ: Princeton University Press, 1972).

task is a most interesting theme and we should look at it more carefully, for it can tell us yet more about the innate conflicts and dilemmas of expressing the Sun.

I have spoken about loneliness and the enmity of the collective as the emotional equivalents of the dangers the hero faces in his struggles. The issue of guilt (and the accompanying fear of reprisal) surrounding the theft of the elixir is also a fundamental aspect of the solar journey. There is something illicit about becoming oneself, because it involves stealing something from the mass psyche, something which was the common property of the collective unconscious. This dilemma can easily clothe itself in political garb, although the essence of all political ideologies is ultimately to be found in the individuals who formulate them. The more separate we feel, the more we experience an archetypal sense of guilt. The word *guilt* comes from an Anglo-Saxon root which means "debt." And a profound sense of reneging on a debt—to mother, to the family and to the collective—is constellated by any act of individual creation which separates us from them.

I have worked with many people who are afraid to express the potentials they know are in them because on some level they fear the separation from the family psyche which such self-expression would entail. To be free enough to move beyond the family circle, especially if the parents themselves were blocked, repressed and stifled in their own lives, is tantamount to the dragon fight. It is better to stay where one is, however frustrated, and know that the magical umbilical cord remains unbroken. After all, the inner collective voice tells us, who do I think I am? What right do I have to become something my parents were never able to be, after all they sacrificed on my behalf? There is thus considerable guilt around expressing the Sun, because it means stealing an elixir which is the common property of all—albeit unused. The elixir can do nothing on a mass level until a hero comes along who knows what to do with it. But for an individual to possess it means that, at least initially, something is taken away from the mass. Of course it remains the hero's task at the end of the story to give something back to the collective. But this does not mitigate the initial sense of sin. In Wagner's *Ring* cycle, the dragon-giant who guards the gold and the ring of the Niebelungs does nothing with them. He lies asleep on top of his hoard, and would do so unto eternity. The solar gold is a human potential, common to us all, but if it is buried in the unconscious, it remains forever potential. It takes an individual to actualise the elixir. Yet in doing so, it is a theft, and the hero suffers for it. So the hero must return as a culture bringer, and make good his debt. I always find etymology interesting, because so often it gives us the key meaning of a word which we ordinarily take for granted. The word *redeem* comes from the same root as *ransom*, to buy back. Thus the hero must become a redeemer for his people, paying off the debt he incurred when he stole the elixir. He cannot use it for himself alone. He owes something to the mass psyche, and must create something original in return. Guilt is the shadow face of altruism, and we will always find it sitting side by side with the impulse to redeem which is so unconsciously powerful a motive in the helping professions.

We meet the same theme in the Biblical tale of Adam and Eve, for they, too, are embodiments of the solar hero. The apple which gives knowledge of good and evil is the fruit of consciousness, which inevitably separates us from fusion with mother and the collective. Adam and Eve have stolen something which previously belonged only to God, an elixir sitting unplucked and uneaten on the Tree, and for their sin they are expelled from Paradise. Nor are they allowed back in again until the solar hero-redeemer appears in the form of Christ to pay off their debt. Once the Sun has begun to shine we cannot enter the gates of Paradise again, unless we can also find within us the stuff of the redeemer who can buy back our debt. Unfortunately we usually try to find this redeemer outside.

So the theft of the elixir is a profound rite of passage, and once it has been made, things cannot go back to where they were before the Fall. We can only move forward, and make something of the elixir which is really our own precious uniqueness. Even if we do a little backsliding and regressing now and then under heavy Neptune transits, we cannot undo what has been done, for with the light of the Sun the fantasy of fusion must cease. There is also the fear of reprisal, and the hero must usually run for his life once he has stolen the elixir, with all the legions of the angered guardian in hot pursuit. This threat of reprisal is not just paranoia, either, for the collective does indeed strike back, and we can see it most clearly in the operation of family dynamics when an individual breaks free of an enmeshed family unit. We can also see it in political, religious and professional groups when one of the members voices too original an opinion, or achieves more creatively or financially than the other members. Thus the ancient myth enacts itself outside us, until we recognise that all the characters lie within.

The hero must eventually make his return, which is no more simple than the process of his setting out. He must pass the Threshold Crossing once again, with the elixir or the bride or both, and reenter ordinary life. Because the hero myth does not occur once in our lives, bur repeats itself over and over on many levels, this difficult process of return follows every act of creation and triumphant self-actualisation. Sometimes the return is reflected by a time of depression, because mundane reality contrasts painfully with the great inner tasks we have been engaged upon. Sometimes the hero must be rescued by his helpers at the very last stage of the quest. He may face yet another dragon or witch (which is of course the same one) barring the path of his return. And sometimes he doesn't really want to go back. The fiery temperament, which applies to Sun-ruled Leo as well as to Aries and Sagittarius, may find this return to ordinary life particularly difficult because it seems so boring, and the hero may already be planning his next quest before the old one is completed.

We cannot simply look at a horoscope and say, "Ah, here is the story of Theseus and the Minotaur, that is your hero myth." All the stages of the hero's journey are relevant to everyone at some point in their lives, although there may be more of a focus on a particular theme. For example, I have found that Gemini tends to repeatedly meet the dark twin in one form or another, while Scorpio favours confrontations with dragons. But these motifs may reflect other factors in the chart, such as Moon conjunct Pluto or a Gemini Ascendant, and they will interweave with the themes of the Sun's placement. We should also remember that sooner or later all the other planets will transit in aspect to the Sun, and the Sun will progress to aspect many planets during a lifetime. We all get a glimpse of what it might feel like to be somebody else, sooner or later. And as I have said, we enact the hero's journey many times in many different forms, some of them so small that they come to completion during the course of an ordinary week, or even a day. As soon as we have made any step in consciousness and self-unfoldment, another call to adventure comes, and off we go again. We never really finish the process of the Sun.

The sign in which the Sun is placed at birth is in theory the most basic of astrological factors, and is usually interpreted on the level of character. But it can also tell us a great deal about one of the main themes of the hero's journey. Each sign relates to a particular set of mythic figures, and each sign also has a planetary ruler or presiding deity with its own set of stories. The planetary ruler of the Sun sign can give us insight into the god who engenders the hero, for this planet, even more than the ruler of the Ascendant, describes the special potentials within us which we must work to find and develop. The chart ruler can give us information about what life will require of us and, in combination with the Ascendant itself, may describe the kinds of situations the hero will meet on his journey. But the Sun ruler is our presiding deity; and the hero and his prize are ultimately the same thing.

We can view the Sun sign from the perspective of what role we are called upon to play in life, and what unique contribution we can make by finding an individual channel for this archetypal energy. For example, if you are born under Gemini or Virgo, your Sun ruler is Mercury. On the level of character reading, you can say, "I am a Gemini, therefore I am communicative, intelligent, versatile and get bored easily." But what happens if we think about Hermes? What is his domain? What spheres of life does he govern?

Hermes has many myths, from his theft of Apollo's cattle and his invention of the lyre to his role as psychopomp, magus and messenger of the gods. You will hear a lot more about Hermes when Howard gives you a broader mythic background for the planet Mercury.[7] But very briefly, Hermes is the god of the roads. He rules the ways in between, the linking routes between different domains or levels of the psyche. He presides over the wanderer and the merchant, for he belongs nowhere and travels every-where, speaking every language and dealing in every currency. He

---

[7]The discussion on Mercury will appear in the next volume in this series: Liz Greene and Howard Sasportas, *The Inner Planets: Building Blocks of Personal Reality*, Volume 4 of *Seminars in Psychological Astrology* (York Beach, ME: Samuel Weiser, 1992).

is a negotiator and a messenger, without ambition of his own, serving the purposes of the other gods as well as his own mischievous whims. All his spheres of activity involve exchange or communication of one kind or another. It is possible to view this figure as the image of a particular *daemon*, a calling or destiny which needs individualised vehicles in ordinary life.

There are other myths which concern the sign of Gemini, and these too will be relevant in terms of the calling or destiny of the Gemini individual. The best-known Geminian myth is that of the Twins, Castor and Pollux (or Polydeuces), one of whom is divine (the son of Zeus) and the other mortal. One of the characteristic themes of the hero's Threshold Crossing, as we have seen, is the confrontation with the dark twin. This particular motif often enacts itself very literally in the Gemini person's childhood, through a competitive and difficult relationship with a sibling who may even be an actual twin. Or the theme may express itself through a particular pattern in friendships. The issue of sibling rivalry, whether literal or metaphoric, tends to occur over and over again in the lives of many Geminians. Yet all the while the Gemini may be heard to say, "Oh, but I'm not competitive, I haven't done anything to cause this problem, it's my brother/sister/friend who started all the trouble." Yet the battle with the dark twin is the story of confrontation with the dark side of oneself, and those upon whom Gemini hooks this mythic image are really carriers for hidden aspects of oneself.

The mythic themes which reflect the Sun sign and its ruler are extremely rich. They describe some of the main archetypal patterns behind the person's unfoldment as an individual. Now what would you say about the two Venus-ruled signs, Taurus and Libra? Can you try to approach these from a mythic rather than a character perspective?

Audience: The mythic ruler is Aphrodite. She is the goddess of love.

Liz: She is the goddess of a particular kind of love. All the feminine deities concern themselves with relationships of one kind or another. Aphrodite has a very precise domain over which she presides.

Audience: Beauty.

Liz: That is part of her function; she embodies and presides over the creation of beauty, harmony and pleasure. Her love is erotic love, rooted in sensual pleasure and aesthetic delight. It is not concerned with marriage bonds or family ties. Plato once described love as passion aroused by beauty, which describes Aphrodite's love very nicely. Venusian love is not self-sacrificing like that of Neptune, nor is it concerned with fusion, empathy or security. Venus' principle is that of self-pleasuring, and you can take this on all possible levels. Through Libra, Venus pleasures the mind with its longing for a perfect, harmonious world; through Taurus, Venus pleasures the body with its longing for sensual satisfaction and beauty in concrete form. If you are a Libran or a Taurean, this capricious goddess is your presiding deity, and she will strive to be given creative expression in the world through vehicles which are appropriate for her nature.

The conventional listings of personality characteristics which are used to describe the Sun sign may fit some people up to a point; but often they do not fit at all, to the confusion of the layman who then assumes astrology does not work. I have heard many people rightly point out that they do not "behave" like the usual descriptions of their Sun sign. It is not sufficient for us to say, "Well, other chart factors are stronger." The Sun is, after all, the Sun, the centre of the chart and the solar system. It must be hiding somewhere. But if we can understand that the Sun describes a process rather than a set of behaviour patterns, and can comprehend the core of each sign's inner drive (which is what myths portray), we can be far more helpful to a client struggling to express his or her individuality. We may not "behave" like our Sun signs, but we *are* them, in the deepest sense. The Sun ruler is our divine parent, and if this inner striving is thwarted or repressed, it is, in effect, tantamount to a refusal of the mythic call.

If there is no expression of the Sun ruler, and no capacity to recognise the divine parenting, then the hero never grows. He refuses the call to adventure and remains a psychological child, unformed and uninitiated. In effect, nobody is home. Now perhaps you might think about the Saturn-ruled signs, Capricorn and Aquarius. What kind of presiding deity is this?

Audience: Isn't Uranus the true ruler of Aquarius?

Liz: Both Saturn and Uranus rule Aquarius, and neither is more true than the other. One facet of Aquarius's complexity is that its two rulers have a certain mythic animosity toward each other. Uranus banishes Saturn (Kronos) to the underworld, and Saturn castrates his father and steals his throne in revenge. This is a psychological dynamic, a collision between ideal (Uranus) and reality (Saturn) which tends to repeat itself in various forms throughout the Aquarian's life. But if we focus on Saturn for the moment, who is this god? What is his function?

Audience: Working efficiently.

Liz: That is one way of putting it. But efficient work is really a character trait, rather than the essence of the god. Saturn creates forms and structures. In myth he is a Titan, an earth god who presides over the productivity of the land. He embodies the laws governing the growing of crops—not the fecund receptivity of the soil, but the immutable structures which define the changing seasons and dictate the timing of seeding and harvesting. He teaches human beings how to obey the laws of nature in order to survive and flourish.

Audience: What about his destructiveness? What is the motif of castration, and swallowing his children?

Liz: These are the inevitable concomitants of his function. If you take an unlimited idea (Uranus) and bind it in a formal structure, you are destroying its endless future possibilities. You have curtailed its fertility, and it is now limited by the choices you have made. A person may have the dream of a beautiful Edenlike garden with luxurious plants flowering all year long. In reality nothing flowers endlessly, and the gardener must contend not only with the immutable laws of the seasons and the climate but with slugs, aphids, black spot, mildew and the neighbour's cat. Have any of you ever written an essay or a story or a book? You begin with an idea, and it proliferates in your mind. You can do all kinds of things with it when it exists solely on the mental level. You can even fantasise receiving the Nobel Prize for Literature. But when you put your idea down in words on paper, and then finish your essay within the required number of pages, you have castrated it. That is the end of it. You might write another essay on a similar idea, but it will be different. Can you understand how incarnating something limits and castrates the original idea, as well as making it real and permanent? The swallowing of the children is a similar image. In myth Saturn does this because he has been warned that one of his sons will overthrow him. There is always the possibility that the unknown future will disrupt any present structure we build. Saturn swallows these dangerous future potentials (his children) because they are unknown and threatening to his law. The destructive feeling-tone of these images of castration and swallowing describes how the incarnating process looks from the Uranian or Jupiterian point of view. But Saturn was also the god of the Golden Age of humanity, when the earth was fertile and productive and everyone lived happily in accord with divine law. And if you are Saturn-ruled, it is important to understand things from *his* point of view.

Audience: I understood that it was the Ascendant which described this kind of journey you're talking about.

Liz: Like you I also understand the Ascendant as a development pattern. But it doesn't seem to describe the essential core of character as the Sun does. The Ascendant is rather like a guide who accompanies us on our life's journey, and who requires us to learn certain lessons or attributes *to help us become what is symbolised by the Sun*. If I were to look for a mythic image to describe it, I would consider a hero such as Theseus, and understand his quest (the slaying of the Minotaur to redeem the kingdom) as the unfoldment of his essence (the Sun); but he must first develop certain skills and abilities in order to fulfil his task. If you read Mary Renault's wonderful novel about the Theseus myth, *The King Must Die*, you will see that he undergoes a kind of training before he achieves his goal.[8] He must undergo the humiliation of slavery in order to learn control of his anger; he must learn the art of bull dancing in order

---

[8]Mary Renault, *The King Must Die* (New York: Random House, 1988).

to discipline his body; and he must develop diplomacy and strategy to become a fit leader of his people. In the novel he is very much an Aries type of hero; but his Ascendant is probably Capricorn. I believe the Ascendant reflects the particular training to which life subjects us.

One of the things I have noticed about the Ascendant is that on some profound level we seem to intuit that we will be required to develop its qualities and confront its archetypal situations. So we acquire a kind of beginners' version of it in the first half of life, an outer mask which often fits all the typical textbook descriptions. You know the sort of thing – Gemini rising is chatty, and Virgo rising is neat, and Aquarius rising is reasonable, and so on. But in fact the Ascendant presents us with an enormous dilemma, for it is very hard to internalise its meaning and take its values on board. Usually there is a lot of resistance to it, because it feels somehow alien, and is often projected out onto the immediate environment, so that we meet its positive and negative faces in the people close to us. But the Sun is not alien, unless it is severely repressed; and even in such cases, once the individual has discovered it within, there is usually a profound relief and sense of homecoming.

When we express the Sun, we feel authentic and possess a quality of personal authority. Howard and I had a look at the etymological dictionary to find the roots of those words *authenticity* and *authority*, and of course the root is the same – the Greek word for "self." All kinds of words spring from this root – automobile and automatic and autoerotic and autonomous and so on. The Sun gives us a feeling of personal potency and validity. Without this feeling, we are left feeling rather empty and awful, and desperate for reassurance from others. I think there are times when we all lose our connection to the Sun, and wander around in a fog seeking other people's affirmation to make us feel real again. The Sun says, "Whatever cockup I have made of my life, I am myself, and I don't wish to be anybody else." But when we encounter the Ascendant, we often say, "Oh, there must be some mistake about my birth time. I couldn't *possibly* have a Pisces Ascendant, it must be Aquarius."

Audience: How does the Sun show itself if it is not yet developed? Through its lower qualities?

Liz: I am not very comfortable with distinctions such as "lower" and "higher." These evaluations are highly subjective, and depend upon your personal frame of reference. What happens is that the Sun expresses itself *unconsciously*. Sometimes some of its qualities are projected, which can happen with any unconscious factor in the birth chart. Someone remarked before the session that there are still many cultures where women have little opportunity to express the Sun. What happens to it? It is projected onto their husbands and fathers, onto their male children, and onto authority figures in the outer world. It may also be projected onto other women, for women can also carry solar qualities. The sense of authority and meaning then lies outside, and the woman feels empty and bereft without the objects of her projection.

Audience: But you cannot project everything belonging to a sign. You must surely retain some of its qualities.

Liz: I think I said that *some* of its qualities are projected. I quite agree, it is not a clear black-and-white issue. We may live bits and give away other bits, and this changes as life progresses. Also, projection does not mean we don't behave in that way ourselves. It means we do not realise it, but prefer to think everybody else is doing it instead. One of the peculiar characteristics about the mechanism of projection is that the person can usually be spotted by others as having those particular attributes. Projection does not stop us acting things out, but it creates a kind of self-blindness. The qualities may indeed be what you are calling "lower"—the less attractive face of the sign. But they may also be "higher," for we also project some of our best potentials onto those whom we feel have everything we lack.

The difference between conscious and unconscious expression is this quality of self-blindness, rather than a "good" or "bad" side of the Sun sign showing itself. Also, the more unaware we are of something within ourselves, the more likely it is to drive us compulsively, and take away our options for choice. Then we may set up situations where we feel it is all out of control, and we are the passive victims, when in fact it was really the unconscious Sun working relentlessly toward its goals from its headquarters in the basement. For example, some Sun in Aries people may be relatively unconnected with it because of childhood complexes, environmental pressures or other factors in the birth chart which mitigate against it (such as the Sun in the 12th opposite Saturn and a lot of planets in earth), they will have the normal Aries quota of aggression, competitiveness, fiery energy, imagination and hunger for challenge, but may not see themselves this way. There may be quite a lot of unconscious aggression and determination to have their own way, but it will all be very low-key and the anger may surface in manipulative ways; and these people will tell you they are really very compromising and indecisive and that others push them around. This might be superficially true, but the Aries qualities have fallen into the shadow, and will make themselves known sooner or later. There will usually be people about who provide a hook for the projection of these attributes, both positive and negative—a lover, perhaps, who is seen as incredibly potent and dashing and exciting, and a father or employer who is seen as domineering, selfish and insensitive.

Anger in such a case may come back to the person via others, who are irritated by the unconscious assertiveness and impatience which are being expressed. I have heard quite a few Aries women complain that they could not understand why their friends turned against them; the Aries competitive spirit manifested unconsciously in trying to chat up all the friends' boyfriends but the woman was utterly unaware of it. So you can see that it is not as simple as just dumping the Sun sign and having none of it oneself. Projection is a fascinating and extremely subtle mechanism. We all have dimensions of the Sun which are unexpressed, for it reflects a process of becoming, and we never finish this process.

An undeveloped Sun may also be very envious. I have mentioned this problem already. Envy is one of the most basic of human emotions, and it can be turned into very creative fodder if we are honest enough to face it; for we envy in others what we value most highly, and usually this includes some of the untapped potentials of the Sun, which are projected onto suitable hooks. It can be very valuable to work with envy in this way, for we discover a great deal about ourselves. Venus may admire, but the Sun envies, and there is a high charge around the people upon whom we project this ideal of what we wish we could be.

Now I would like to mention some of the functions of the Sun god in myth, because this might help to clarify the Sun's role in the chart. In some cultures the Sun is represented by a female deity, but in such cases the goddess's attributes are "masculine" in the sense of being dynamic. One example is the Egyptian solar goddess Sekhmet, daughter of the Sun god Ra, who was called the "Eye of Ra." She was portrayed with a lion's head crowned by the disc of the Sun, and was a deity of battle and bloodshed. But Ra himself, one of the most ancient of solar gods, is more characteristic of the Sun's symbolism; he is the world creator and dispenser of justice, the All-Father who generates all the other gods from his own seed.

Apollo, the Greek Sun god, is a much later and more humanised figure. He is the gentleman of Olympus, and we can learn a lot about the deeper meaning of the Sun from him. Perhaps most importantly, Apollo is the breaker of family curses. If you are in an awful mess like Orestes, and have inherited a seething mass of family complexes which are driving you mad, Apollo is the only deity who has the power to break the grip of the Erinyes (the Furies), the avengers of matriarchal law. Another myth about Apollo which carries a similar meaning is his conquest of the giant female snake Python. Having destroyed the snake, he sets up his shrine of Delphi over her former lair, and honours (or integrates) her by calling his oracular priestess the Pythia or Pythoness. The function of curse breaking is a most interesting one. What do you think this might mean?

Audience: The Sun helps us to work through unfinished family business.

Liz: Yes, that is how I would understand it also. The more we are able to feel separate and individual, the less we are at the mercy of the unconscious conflicts and compulsions of the family psyche. This does not mean that living the Sun makes one reject the family. On the contrary, the more one is oneself, the more one has to give others in a genuine, openhearted way. But it is the psychic skeletons in the cupboards which taint families—the power ploys to keep people close, the subtle undermining of talents and potentials, the envy and resentment and fear accruing over generations – and it is these which the light of the Sun has the power to dispel.

In Greek myth, family curses are usually initiated by someone offending a god (through hubris or arrogance), who then casts a blight on successive generations. Because the deity is not offered the proper respect, the descendants must suffer until the curse is fulfilled or broken. Offence against a god is a way of describing offence against an archetypal principle, a fundamental life urge. Something is denied honour and value, and it strikes back through the psyche of the family, causing conflict and suffering which is psychologically passed down from parent to child. This happens in families all the time. It is the dark side of communal life, always hiding in the shadow of the warmth and support which a loving family can offer. Some families have a great deal of warmth and support and mutual respect to offer their members, and the dark side, which is perfectly human, causes those ordinary petty relationship problems we all encounter in life. Other families are truly blighted, carrying a vast reservoir of repression, manipulation and destructiveness, and all the members suffer. It is not always easy to spot this, since a tightly enmeshed family may present a united "loving" front to the outside world, while the problems are hidden or blamed on one individual's bad or sick behaviour. And sometimes all but one of the members seem perfectly satisfied to remain unconscious cells in the organism. It is the one who possesses a stronger need for individual expression who will often initially wind up as the "identified patient."

For example, certain emotions may not be permitted expression within the family circle. Perhaps affection is never openly displayed, or sexuality is never talked about, or no one ever gets angry, or everyone is expected to remain happily living in the same country town. There is a tribal feeling to such families, and members are warned by every possible covert means not to break the unspoken rules. If an individual attempts to challenge them, he or she may be made to feel bad, selfish, and unloved – or may even be labelled sick or evil. There is something about solar consciousness, the sense of "me," which has the power to break the spell these unspoken family rules have over us. We are all vulnerable to loneliness, guilt and manipulation, since everyone has a Neptune and no one has a perfect childhood; and the threat of being outcast is painful to all human beings, although to some more than others. But if we can believe that we are what we are meant to be, and that challenging the unconscious system does not make us bad or worthless, then we can make efforts to retain positive relationships with family members while still preserving our own independent values and path in life.

There is a lunar dimension to psychotherapy – containment, empathy and the building of a human relationship. There is also a solar dimension, which is related to Apollo's function of curse-breaking. The object of Apollonian analysis is not simply to dig up all the horrible traumas so that one can blame one's parents for all one's ills. It is consciousness of family patterns and the ways in which we still go on enacting them, which dispels the family curse. A curse is compulsive; we are trapped in behaviour which is destructive and self-defeating, yet we are blind to the source of the compulsion because there is not yet a sufficient sense of separateness from the collective, from the family psyche. The Furies which hunt the offending victim in Greek myth may be interpreted in many ways. I have found that for most people, they take the form of guilt, anxiety and resentment. Guilt tells us we do not deserve to be happy; anxiety makes us fearful of change and future potentials; and resentment makes us destructive toward others or ourselves. These are archetypal human feelings, and it is not possible to rid ourselves of them altogether. But the curse-breaking function of the Sun means that the more we value ourselves, the less we rush about trying to fulfil others' expectations, the less frightened we are of life overwhelming us, and the less resentful we feel about unlived potentials.

Apollo is also a prophet. He is called Apollo Longsight, and his Delphic Oracle was consulted for many centuries as a sacred source of guidance and prescience. The idea that one might consult the god in order to find the right course of action or have a question answered, is a very ancient one; we can see the modern version in astrology as well as the *I Ching*. But Apollo's oracular nature is not what we would call "psychic." Psychism is a kind of *participation mystique*, a capacity to lose one's own boundaries and fuse with the psyche of another. Solar prophecy is foresight, and there is no loss of self. It is intuitive rather than psychic, and bases its wisdom on a perception of the outcome of choices made in the present. The oracular side of Apollo was also called Double-Tongued, because one could never be quite sure about the meaning of the answer. Everything depended upon the level of interpretation. It was not predictive in the literal sense, but allowed choice to the querent in the same way that the images in a dream are multilevelled and may be interpreted or even acted upon in numerous ways.

Oedipus, for example, consults the Delphic Oracle because he has begun to wonder whether the King and Queen of Corinth are really his parents. The Oracle tells him that he will be his father's slayer and his mother's husband. This is like a dream image; what might it really mean? Freud thought that we are all symbolically our parents' murderers and paramours; it is the essential truth of the child's world, and enacts itself throughout life whenever we overthrow some old authority structure, inner or outer, and strive toward union with a beloved ideal. Oedipus, however, takes this oracular statement literally, and runs away from Corinth to avoid his dreadful fate. But Apollo is double-tongued, and in running away Oedipus creates this fate. There is a great flaw in his nature— uncontrollable rage—and when he meets his father unknowingly on the road, he loses his temper and kills him. You know the rest. The outcome of the Oracle is strangely interwoven with the choice of the person to whom the Oracle is given. There is a pattern at work which cannot be changed; but it is up to the querent to understand the inner level of the pattern and act accordingly. By the way, Apollo is also the only god who succeeds in cheating the three Fates of a preordained death. He gets them drunk.

So Apollo Longsight reflects a solar capacity to intuit a pattern at work in life and to foresee the consequences of our choices. We often make decisions blindly, out of emotional need or intellectual analysis or the desire to please. But we may fail to understand the broader picture—who we really are in relation to our environment, and what the deeper patterns of our own individual journey might be. Then we are astonished when the fruits of our past choices come ripe. Consulting the Oracle in myth is really a kind of turning inward, a meditative act which puts us in contact with a more prescient side of ourselves. Many people accomplish this with prayer or meditation, and it is a sacred act in the deepest sense, just as it was in ancient times when one approached the god. The more we know who we are, the more likely we are to act according to our own truth, or according to what is right for us—and even if the consequences are difficult or painful, we can retain our integrity and strength. This is why Apollo is a gentleman. Or, as Polonius says in *Hamlet*:

> This above all: to thine own self be true,
> And it must follow, as the night the day,
> Thou canst not then be false to any man.

Apollo's prophetic function is inside all of us. This dimension of the Sun reflects our vision and foresight, and our capacity to sense inner potentials which have not yet come ripe. The Sun is also associated with the image of the Divine Child, which is portrayed in some versions of the card of the Sun in the Tarot deck. The Divine Child embodies everything we have yet to become but which has not yet crystallised with time (Saturn). Experience, and the attitudes we acquire in response to experience, crystallise all those potentials and shape the adult. The Divine Child is our solar blueprint, which is present in us as a seed but takes a lifetime to unfold. The Sun gives us the feeling that we have a future, that it has meaning, that our lives follow an intelligent design. We are then able to retain trust in ourselves and can gamble a little with the unknown. Even if our gambling brings the roof down on our heads, we know we will survive to try again another time. From all this you should be able to work out what it is like to be disconnected from the solar principle. It is very dreary, because there is no vision of a future. There is only the past with all its mistakes and lost possibilities. That is the family curse. In the Tarot deck, I associate this feeling of hopelessness with the card of the Devil— the bondage which we cannot see but which casts a chain around our necks and stops us moving out into life.

Finally, Apollo is the god of music. He is also the father of the nine Muses, each of whom represents a different aspect of the arts. This rulership over the creative realm is different from Aphrodite's function as goddess of beauty and ornamentation, for Aphrodite takes what already exists in raw form and refines it. Apollo, on the other hand, creates something out of nothing; he symbolises the creative urge itself. Why music in particular?

Audience: It comes from the heart.

Liz: Yes, but so do other forms of creative expression. Perhaps it has more to do with the immediate nature of music. I am thinking again of Mary Renault's novel, in which Theseus comments that if you go to Apollo with your grief and make it into a song, he will take the grief away. Music can embody any human emotion at the moment that the emotion is felt. This is not transcendence or transformation; it is distillation of an essence. Music does not convey feelings through images or words, both of which require interpretation and reflective distance. It is the most spontaneous of all the creative arts, and was probably the first—I should imagine people were rhythmically moving their bodies and beating sticks on rocks long before they worked out how to paint bisons on cave walls. Rhythm is basic to the body, rooted in the beating of the heart. In this sense music is the most primal art, preceding thought and perception, emerging from the very origins of life. And you need no implements to make music—all you need to do is tap your foot and open your mouth. Music somehow magically carries unbearable feelings and allows us to bear them. It is very difficult to be articulate about this function of the Sun, but I hope you can make some sense of what I am saying. I am not suggesting that everyone should become a musician or a music lover. But in expressing ourselves spontaneously, we are making music. This dimension of the solar principle fuses life and art.

SUN, FATHER, AND THE EMERGENCE OF THE EGO

THE FATHER'S ROLE IN INDIVIDUAL DEVELOPMENT

BY HOWARD SASPORTAS

Individuation involves the subtle but crucial phenomenological shifts by which a person comes to see him/herself as separate and distinct within the relationship in which s/he has been embedded. In it is the increasing definition of an "I" within a "We."

Mark Karpel[1]

> This plant would like to grow
> And yet be embryo
> Increase, and yet escape
> The doom of taking shape . . .
> Richard Wilbur[2]

I can't emphasise enough the importance of the Sun. In my opinion it is the very heart of the chart. This shouldn't be surprising when you think that it comprises 99.8% of the solar system. It is the Sun which directly or indirectly furnishes all the energy that supports our earthly existence; all the foods and all the fuels we need are derived from plants which require sunlight for photosynthesis. So it makes sense that the Sun should stand out in the chart.[3]

---

[1]Mark Karpel, "Individuation from fusion to dialogue," in *Family Processes*, 15:65–82, 1976.

[2]Richard Wilbur, "Seed Leaves," from *The Norton Anthology of Poetry*, 3rd edition, Alexander W. Allison et al. eds. (New York: W.W. Norton, 1986), pp. 1201–1202.

[3]Toni Glover Sedgwick, "The Sun," in *Planets*, edited by Joan McEvers (St. Paul, MN: Llewellyn Publications, 1989), p. 15.

I'm certain that in order to feel complete and fulfilled we need to be giving expression to our Sun sign; we must strive to develop ourselves in the sphere of life associated with the house our Sun is placed, and we should try to find constructive ways to personify, integrate and utilise any planet which is in aspect to our Sun. When people come to me for readings, I always want to make sure that they're in touch with the qualities of their Sun sign—I want to know that the qualities of the Sun are being consciously expressed in a purposeful, positive way. Provided that the data is correct, I believe in the chart more than I do in the person sitting beside me. I also hold the opinion that most Sun sign columns start from an incorrect premise. The writers often assume that you are *automatically* like your Sun sign. So all Ariens are described as dynamic, egocentric and impulsive, and all Geminis are characterised as inveterate flirts and butterflies. Not true. Sun sign columns would be much more worthwhile if they began with the underlying premise that the Sun sign represents qualities which you need to build in and develop in a constructive way in order to *become* who you uniquely are, in order to be true to yourself and feel good about yourself. Instead of saying, "You are an Aries, therefore you are assertive," they could write, "You Sun is in Aries and this is an indication that one of your main purposes in life is to develop your courage, dynamism and the ability to assert yourself in a manner which is viable and workable." You see the difference. Now the readers have a goal or quest, they have something to strive for. If we then take the whole chart into consideration, we can analyse how other factors in the nature will work for or against the healthy development of the Sun sign qualities.

Figure 4 on page 120 gives a list of pretty obvious keywords for the Sun principle. Take a few moments this week to reflect on these words. Also take some time just to meditate on the glyph or symbol for the Sun. It is a circle which represents infinity and unboundedness, but there is a dot in the middle. The glyph shows the circle of wholeness encompassing the dot of individuality, and is therefore descriptive of what Jungians refer to as the "ego-Self axis." The dot symbolises your individuality, your individual and unique self which is a vehicle or vessel through which your "spirit" or your transpersonal Self (sometimes referred to as the higher Self) can express itself. The principle of the Sun defines a process by which we differentiate and develop an "I" or personal ego; however, in terms of fullest possible growth and evolution, there will come a time when the personal ego is asked to acknowledge and honour something greater than itself, to realise its role as a channel through which the transpersonal or universal Self can express itself. In his book, *What We May Be*, Piero Ferrucci describes the transpersonal Self in this way:

> The transpersonal Self, while retaining a sense of individuality, lives at the level of universality, in a realm where personal plans and concerns are overshadowed by the wider vision of the whole. The realization of the transpersonal Self is the mark of spiritual fulfillment.[4]

In *Myth and Today's Consciousness*, Jungian analyst Ean Begg explains how the archetype represented by the Sun can be associated with the ego/Self axis:

> I shall summarise how I see in psychological terms the archetype of the Sun. These terms are the ego-Self axis, and the transformations in the relationship between Self and ego in the course of the individuation process. The Self is psychic totality, the original, unconscious, all-inclusive, genetic potentia, from which, at first in isolated flashes in early childhood, the ego, subject of consciousness, emerges. The ego on its hero-path of achievement, slaying the dragon of dependence on mother and family, taking responsibility for being an individual in a world of individuals, one-sidedly plays its strong suits and journeys ever further from its first home, ascribing everything to its own strength and cleverness. At some point, however, the fascinating pull of the primal wholeness reasserts itself and, from the subsequent agony of awakening, death and rebirth, a new alignment is constellated. The relativised ego acknowledges the existence of the other psychic contents and becomes aware of its responsibility as the exponent of the Self, its source and its goal, as well as the path between, and the urge to tread it.[5]

4Piero Ferrucci, *What We May Be* (London: Turnstone Press, 1982; and Los Angeles: Jeremy P. Tarcher, 1982), p. 45.
5Ean Begg, *Myth and Today's Consciousness* (London: Coventure, 1984), p. 16.

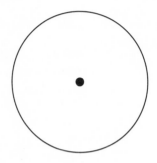

Basic character
urge for autonomy

Drive for power and recognition

The will

Animus issues

Creativity, Self-expression

Life force, Vitality

Strength

Courage

Faith and spirit

Leadership

Givingness

Generosity

Figure 4. Keywords for the Sun.

While the Sun represents the process of defining our individuality and separate-self sense, it also is our link to that part of us which partakes of the wholeness of life. By expressing our uniqueness and true individuality we are pulled into participating in some greater scheme or plan through which life's wholeness becomes evident. Like the different musical instruments in an orchestra, every individual has his or her own part to play in the overall composition of life. But we first need to develop a strong sense of "I," a healthy, honest and functional ego, before we can be a rightful vessel for something greater than ourselves.

"There is no ache more deadly than the striving to be oneself."[6] We examined the Moon and mother; we learned that as newborn

---

[6]Yevgeniy Vinokuriv, cited by Judith Viorst, *Necessary Losses* (New York: Fawcett, 1986), p. 7.

infants we are enmeshed and merged with the Great Mother. Now we come to the Sun, and we are ready to separate from her, to differentiate who we are or are meant to be from the mother or caretaker, to stand on our own feet and be a person in our own right. Last night I talked about the Moon in terms of the early love affair we have with mother, the first big romance of our lives. By the time we're nine months old, however, we are ready to have a love affair not just with mother but with the world. We begin to crawl, we learn to walk, and we discover there is a whole world out there to be explored or mastered. I equate the Sun with the urge to disentangle ourselves from our symbiosis with mother in order to pursue the desire we all have to become a separate and distinct self, a private "I."

Now we'll examine the Sun as a symbol of the ego and also as a symbol of Father, themes Liz has explored earlier. Before we delve into all this, let's briefly look at the guidelines for interpreting the Sun which I've drawn up (see Table 2 on pages 122 and 123). I really do hope that you'll make use of these guidelines when working with charts. Honestly, if you feel "stuck" with a chart, if it isn't coming alive for you, I would suggest that you focus first on the Sun and its placement by sign, house and aspect and use it as a way to start, as a way of getting a handle on the chart (if you'll excuse the jargon). Just analysing the Sun in terms of what a person needs to tap, work on and integrate can get the reading off the ground. From there you can then bring in other facets of the chart to see how these interact with the Sun's position. Although I'm emphasising the importance of the Sun, there are nine other planets which will describe other aspects of our nature. Some people may be too identified with the Sun and not have integrated their Moon sign or any other planet properly. Others may be obviously like their Moon, but their Sun sign is still in the background and needs to be expressed. In any case, if you find yourself having difficulty getting into or working with a chart, try starting with the Sun.

Let's play around for a while with these guidelines to illustrate how they can be used. I know some of you may find this pretty elementary, but there are definite reasons why I believe it's important to get back to basics. With the recent expansion of psychological astrology, many astrologers have become more psychologically

Table 2. Guidelines for Interpreting the Sun

SUN BY SIGN
1. The sign your Sun is in shows the route you need to take to develop a healthy ego and sense of individuality. By developing the positive and constructive qualities of your Sun sign, you feel more complete and fulfilled. We need a place in our lives where we can express and radiate the qualities of our Sun sign (perhaps through a vocation or calling).
2. The Sun sign is a symbol of what needs to be (consciously) struggled for and attained, not just that which comes instinctively.
3. The Sun sign will also colour the animus-father image.

SUN BY HOUSE
1. The Sun's house (and the house with Leo on the cusp or contained within it) designates an area of life where you need to achieve and distinguish yourself in some way. It is where you need to stand out or feel special. Through engaging in the activities associated with that house, you will forge a clearer sense of selfhood, ego and identity. (It is in this area of life that we separate from the archetypal mother and further define our separate self.)
2. Life can be a struggle in the house of the Sun. We have to do battles with dragons which hold us back or obstruct our unfoldment and development in the sphere of experience associated with the Sun's house. Often we feel that we could do better than we have already done in this domain.
3. Father or animus issues can show up in the Sun's house.
4. The Sun's house could give clues to a natural vocation or calling.

Table 2. Guidelines for Interpreting the Sun (cont.)

ASPECTS TO THE SUN
1. Any planet in aspect to the Sun represents an energy or archetype that is linked (positively or negatively) to the development of your individuality, selfhood and self-expression. You need to find constructive ways to express and include that energy in your life (perhaps through a vocation or calling which involves that planet). For instance, someone with the Sun in aspect to Neptune is bound to encounter Neptune in some form in the individuation process; this person might also give expression to Neptune through a "Neptunian" career such as healing, music or the arts.
2. You may meet aspects to the Sun via other people in your life (especially in the case of the opposition). For example, someone with the Sun opposition Saturn may see others as limiting or blocking. Ultimately we have to own and integrate those qualities we habitually project onto others.
3. Issues to do with the father and animus will be coloured by the nature of any planet which aspects the Sun.

knowledgeable and sophisticated; besides just knowing their astrology, they're taking courses in counselling or have trained in various schools of psychological thought. As a result (and I must confess that I was guilty of this myself), some of these astrologers may be inclined to delve straight into an analysis of deep psychological issues with their clients, such as infantile complexes and other baggage from early life which the client is still carrying around inside, all of which will be reflected in the chart. In doing so, however, some psychological astrologers run the risk of neglecting or overlooking certain basics, such as the meaning and significance of something as apparently simple and straightforward as the placement of the Sun by sign. So let's start by using the sign of Gemini as an example of how to work with these guidelines. Guideline number one states that your Sun sign shows the route you need to take to develop a healthy ego and sense of individuality. What qualities or traits immediately come to your mind if you think of the sign of Gemini?

Audience: The ability to communicate and exchange information.

Howard: Yes, we're concerned here with self-expression, whether verbal or through any other medium. Gemini is an air sign, therefore we're in the realm of the mind and intellect, the capacity for objectivity and analysis, to be able to look at oneself, other people and life in general from a variety of angles rather than just responding emotionally or instinctually to situations. There is also the need to make connections, to see how one thing influences or relates to another, to explore a wide range of the facets of existence. It is essential for our fulfilment that we have a place in our lives where we are able to radiate and give expression to the qualities of our Sun sign. I'm especially happy when people are in a vocation or a career which naturally allows them a lot of scope to use and develop the characteristics of the sign in which their Sun is placed. A few years ago I was approached by a publisher and asked to write a book describing which careers suited which Sun signs. It was intended to be a commercial, mass-market type book. In a moment of insanity I agreed to cowrite it with a friend and colleague, and it came out in Great Britain under the title of *The Sun Sign Career Guide*.[7] This was my most extensive foray into pure Sun sign astrology, and I felt slightly apprehensive about doing it, a little embarrassed to put my name to such a book. How can you assess career just by the sign of the Sun? What about the 10th house or the 6th or other parts of the chart which would obviously influence one's calling or profession? After a bit of thought I was less apprehensive because I realised it would be a good thing for people to find work which somehow expressed their Sun sign. Think about it: it's essential for self-development that we realise and live out our Sun sign, and it's also a fact that many of us have to spend a great deal of our time working. So why not try to find a job whose very nature requires us to make use of the qualities or

---

[7]Robert Walker and Howard Sasportas, *The Sun Sign Career Guide* (New York: Avon Publishers, 1991; and London: Arrow Books, 1989).

traits associated with our sign? That's how I justified it, at least. I am pleased when Geminis tell me they work as journalists or in the media, or even that they are cabbies or train drivers, provided they themselves are happy with what they're doing. You can see why – these professions fit with Mercury-ruled Gemini, with the need to communicate and exchange information, with the need to move around and transport knowledge, people or goods from one place to another. To be in a career which correlates with your innate archetypal make-up is a blessing.

Let's move on to point two under the guidelines for interpreting the Sun by sign: "The Sun sign is a symbol of what needs to be (consciously) struggled for and attained, not just that which comes instinctively." To varying degrees most of us will have to work quite hard to develop and manifest more fully the nature of our Sun sign. Although it may be suppressed or denied, your Moon sign is what comes instinctively to you, but the fullest expression of your Sun sign usually requires conscious effort, determination and choice. And I don't think we ever feel finished where the Sun is concerned. If you're an Aries, you will probably always feel that you could be better at asserting yourself. If you're a Gemini, you will probably think you could still be more intelligent or more adept at communication. Point three states that the Sun sign colours one's animus-father image. The latter part of this talk will examine this idea in greater depth.

Now take the Sun by house. Point one says that the facet of existence associated which the Sun's house is an arena in which we should actively involve ourselves, a domain where we need to distinguish ourselves in some way, to stand out and feel special. If you have the Sun in the 5th, you will find yourself through being creative, and I mean that in the broadest sense. Your path of self-actualisation requires that you give birth to something, whether these are children or the concrete realisation of an inspiration or bright idea that comes to you. Involving yourself in your Sun's natal house helps you come into your own. I remember doing a reading for a woman who had the Sun and Mars in Aries in the 5th. She consulted me over a number of years. When we first met, she really was quite meek and mild, which surprised me considering her Sun/Mars placement. A few years later, however, she had given birth to her first child and you wouldn't believe the difference it made. She came into my study beaming with strength and confidence; she had found her power and authority through this obvious 5th-house activity.

Point two asserts that life can be a struggle in the house of the Sun. This is similar to what I was saying about developing and refining the qualities of the Sun sign. If you're born with the Sun in the 7th house, you may in time become quite adept and sophisticated in the sphere of relationships, and yet you'll probably feel that there still is more to learn and unfold in this area. If you have the Sun in the 11th, you can attain the status of being a powerful force within groups, and yet you may feel that you could somehow do better or achieve more in this domain. No matter how great our accomplishment, our Sun always wants to shine more brightly. Point three relates father and animus issues with the Sun's house (something we'll be taking up in greater detail later). Finally, point four is that the Sun's house can also give clues to a natural vocation and calling. So if you're born with the Sun in the 9th, what field of life could you shine in?

Audience: You could be a natural teacher or even a born travel agent.

Howard: Yes, those professions are consonant with the meaning of the 9th house. There are many different levels and dimensions to each house, and for the reasons I've discussed earlier, it makes good sense to find work which relates to one of them. Of course, you may want to change or switch levels at certain times in your life, probably in synchrony with transits or progressions which affect the Sun. If your Sun is in the 12th, you can strengthen your identity and sense of self through working in an institution, being a nurse, a museum curator or a prison warden—it can be as obvious as that. Of course, the Sun in the 12th is in some ways an odd or conflicting placement. The 12th house has so much to do with merging with something greater than yourself or sacrificing your own needs and desires for the sake of other people or to the larger context of which you are a part; and yet the Sun's domain is where we are meant to develop our authority, specialness and individuality, where we are meant to shine and stand out. So some people with this placement have the curious task of finding themselves by sacrificing themselves. But it's important to remember that you can't give up your self until you have established a self to give up. So you have to forge an identity and define a sense of self, and then be prepared, given certain situations, to let go of it. If you have this placement, I would say that this might be one of your main lessons, tasks or purposes for this life.

Finally we come to the guidelines for interpreting other planets in aspect to the Sun. Point one reminds us that any planet aspecting the Sun represents an energy or archetype that is crucially linked to the development of your individuality. Planets aspecting the Sun are fellow travellers in terms of the route you need to take to find out who you are as a distinct entity. When I see a planet in aspect to the Sun, I picture the Sun going arm in arm with that planet along the path of individuation and self-realisation. So if you have a Sun-Jupiter aspect, Jupiter needs to be included in your self-definition. If you have a Sun-Saturn aspect, you will need to honour and include Saturn in the formation of your ego-identity. If you were born with the Sun aspecting Neptune, you have to find a way to incorporate at least one or more of the qualities associated with Neptune into your identity and self-expression—music, art, healing or even sea travel may be integral to the formation of your self.

In addition to showing qualities that are linked with your self-hood, aspects to the Sun can also suggest what might be an appropriate work or vocation. Sun conjunct Neptune could find the self through art or any other calling which evokes Neptune. Many people drawn to the acting profession have Sun-Neptune contacts. I think immediately of Clint Eastwood and Rock Hudson, who were both born with Sun square Neptune—their unfoldment and self-realisation involved Neptune quite literally in the form of film. Even though the contact was a hard angle they were highly successful, although one can see other ways the Sun-Neptune square was operating in terms of the discrepancy between Rock Hudson's film persona and his private life. Nonetheless, it pleases me to see people constructively integrating the nature of any planet aspecting the Sun into their work, life or identity. As you well know, you won't have too much difficulty finding drug addicts or alcoholics born with Sun-Neptune contacts. Obviously this is not the most ideal Neptunian route to self-realisation, and yet some people may need to go down that road as part of their individuation journey, although they risk self-destruction in the process. I've often been impressed by people with Sun-Neptune aspects who have fallen into the morass of addiction and yet climbed back out again; they seem to gain a certain kind of strength, wisdom or knowledge which may not be there in someone who hasn't gone through the difficult and challenging process of addiction and recovery.

Aspects to the Sun also suggest something about the pace, rhythm or nature of your self-unfoldment. With Sun-Neptune, it's possible that you may spend a lot of time wandering around in a fog, confused about what your true identity is. People born with the Sun in easy aspect to Jupiter are usually eager and enthusiastic about expressing themselves, although any Sun-Jupiter aspect may correlate with self-inflation. Sun-Saturn people often need a much longer time to get where they have to go, and they may have to work very hard in the process. Point two in the aspect guidelines is about projection, the process by which you deny or disown a planet aspecting your Sun and consequently experience it as coming at you via the agency of other people. The example given is that of Sun opposition Saturn, where you may see others as limiting or blocking you when really this is a facet of your own psyche which you are projecting onto others. Something in you is holding yourself back, but you deny its existence and then experience it as coming at you from the outside. Ultimately the process of becoming whole will require that you take back such projections. Point three covers the relationship between planets aspecting the Sun and our father or animus image.

I know the question in many of your minds right now: what happens when you have more than one planet aspecting the Sun? In certain cases you may come across rather curious combinations; for instance, Jupiter conjunct the Sun but Saturn square to the conjunction. So Jupiter is on one arm pulling your Sun one way, and Saturn is on the other arm pulling it in another direction or influencing you in a very different manner. The task is to accommodate the principles represented by both Jupiter and Saturn into your self-definition. The expansiveness of Jupiter will be countered by the doubt, insecurities and restrictions of Saturn; this will produce a fair bit of psychological tension, and yet there are ways to balance them, to make them work with one another rather than against each other. I apologise for all these examples being so sketchy, but my main purpose in reviewing these guidelines has been to elaborate briefly on how you can use them yourselves.

Someone asked me about Sun-Moon aspects and I promised I'd cover them, so let's discuss these now before we embark on examining the Sun in terms of father and ego-emergence. While I firmly believe expressing and "living" your Sun is the most important factor in self-fulfilment, this should not be done at the expense of your Moon sign and placement. We have to be our Sun while also acknowledging the Moon in us. When we separate from the body of mother and begin to form our own ego identity, this does not mean totally abandoning what our Moon represents. We shouldn't deny our inheritance from mother or our caretaker. We shouldn't deny our past. What I'm talking about is the distinction between *differentiation* and *dissociation*. We have to expand our identity and yet include what has been there before, not just cut off from it. Historically and mythologically speaking, when humanity emerged from its fusion with Nature and the Great Mother, people became more solar—that is, more conscious of themselves as separate from everything else in existence. This process allowed for the development of mind, reason and intellect, which has led to the remarkable technological advances of our civilisation and a fair degree of mastery over nature. But it appears that we might have gone too far, that we have become too rational and technical at the expense of heart and instinct. To put it another way, there has been a mythic dissociation from the Great Mother rather than a mythic differentiation.[8] Dissociating from the past means denying it ever existed or that it is part of us. Differentiating from something means we still recognise and include it, even though we have moved beyond it. The same rationale applies to the relationship between the Sun and the Moon in the chart. The Moon shows how you instinctively act and respond to any situation or environment you are in—although as I've said, many people may be out of touch with it. The Sun, however, has more to do with self-determination and the will, the capacity to choose to act in a certain way rather

---

[8]See Ken Wilber, *Up From Eden: A Transpersonal View of Human Evolution* (London: Routledge & Kegan Paul, 1983 [p. 187]; and Boston: Shambhala Publications, 1981).

than just respond or react in the instinctive manner of the Moon. You can see how life starts to get complicated if you happen to be born with the Sun and Moon in a challenging angle to one another.

Let's take an obvious example – the Sun in Aquarius square to the Moon in Scorpio. What in general would your instinctive reactions be like if you had the Moon in Scorpio?

Audience: You would probably respond emotionally and with strong feeling to most situations.

Howard: Yes, your instinctive response is likely to come from an emotional place. But if your Scorpio Moon squares your Aquarian Sun, you have some growing to do, some work to do on yourself. What do you think you are meant to build in and develop if your Sun is in Aquarius?

Audience: Aquarius is an air sign, which means that you need to be more objective, to stand back and view things from a broader perspective rather than just responding emotionally.

Howard: Precisely, a struggle or war is going on in the psyche. You are here to realise and develop Aquarian qualities in order to achieve a more fully formed sense of self, and yet your innate responses are Scorpionic. So I might advise someone with this combination in this way: "It is important for you to acknowledge, accept and allow your strong feelings and emotions rather than denying or condemning them, but in the name of growth and individuation you need to move beyond this place. Your Aquarian Sun asks that you work on developing the ability to view situations in a more detached or objective way as well." Having said this, I must admit I've run into cases where certain people with the Sun in Aquarius square the Moon in Scorpio appear to respond in a very cool, objective and detached way to life, and this leads me to conclude that they are in touch with the Aquarian Sun but are denying the Scorpio Moon side. So in this case my advice will be quite different: "I'm pleased to see the qualities of your Aquarian Sun in operation, but I fear that you don't realise just how emotional, vindictive and Scorpionic you also are. Have you acknowl-

edged this Scorpionic side to your nature, or are you simply denying it exists in order to come over as being reasonable, objective
and fair?" It is never healthy to denigrate any part of ourselves,
especially the Moon which is so vital to health, relationships, and
emotional well-being.

For the sake of argument, let's consider the reverse placement,
someone born with the Sun in Scorpio and the Moon in Aquarius.
This is a different story. With the natal Moon in Aquarius, what
kind of innate responses and reactions might a person display?

Audience: They will probably react in an Aquarian fashion, more
objectively and rationally than someone with the Moon in a water
sign.

Howard: Yes, the emotions are sifted through the rational mind or
intellect—this is the natural Moon in Aquarius way of reacting.
Have you noticed that it's often very hard to know what people
with the Moon in Aquarius are really feeling? They put up a front
which is laid back or cool, a bit like the persona Clint Eastwood
presents in a number of his movies. Many men would give their
right arms to be so self-possessed and unshakeable. But what if
this person was born with the Sun in Scorpio? I understand this to
mean that growth and consciousness-raising entails greater
acknowledgement and exposure of one's Scorpionic nature, which
is more intensely feeling and emotional, even though there are
many Suns in Scorpio who desperately try to hide or suppress
such traits. I must add that this doesn't mean they should allow
themselves to go berserk, because the Sun in Scorpio also asks that
one learns to manage—that is, to control, to direct but not to
repress—intense emotion. Nonetheless, growth and self-formation
for this person would require moving beyond the sole honouring
of rationality and objectivity, and allowing out into the open the
more feeling side of the self as indicated by the Sun in a water
sign.

So you can see that with a square, opposition, inconjunct,
sesquiquadrate or even a semisextile between the Sun and Moon,
you have very different archetypes or styles of being at odds with
one another in your psyche. This often produces a more tense and
jittery personality than someone with the Sun and Moon in com-

patible signs. We could say it is a conflict between the emotions or instincts and the will, the instinctive nature and response patterns versus those qualities you need consciously to develop in order to fulfil the individuation process indicated by your Sun sign.

Audience: Can you say something about the Sun in Aries in opposition to the Moon in Libra?

Howard: Yes, this should be fairly clear. In general, the Moon in Libra possesses a natural inclination to compromise, harmonise and balance, although I wouldn't take this to mean that all people with this placement are sweet and charming peacemakers. But if the Sun is in Aries opposing the Moon in Libra, these people actually need to learn that it is all right to stand up for themselves and what they want and believe in, even if it means causing disruption and offending others. Try it the other way around, the Sun in Libra opposing the Moon in Aries. Most people with the Moon in Aries are pretty adept at asserting their needs and feelings, but if the Sun is in Libra then perhaps they are here to develop a greater ability to compromise and balance their wants, beliefs or desires with those of others around them. Semisextiles and inconjuncts between the Sun and Moon are particularly interesting and challenging because they ask you to accommodate or include archetypal styles of being which are by nature very different; when these angles occur between such key planets as the Sun and Moon, they highlight a collision between two signs which are incompatible not only by element but also by quadruplicity, something you don't get with a square or opposition. An Aries Sun has entirely different requirements from a Taurus Moon; a Taurus Sun may not feel all that comfortable with the impulses of a Sagittarian Moon.

Pure trines and sextiles of the Sun to the Moon (I'm using the word *pure* to mean that the aspect isn't out of sign) are beneficial in the sense that your will and emotions are in compatible energies, so there is not such a great discrepancy felt or adjustment needed between instinctive lunar responses and conscious, solar self-determination and choices. Someone with the Sun in Cancer and the Moon in Pisces will have innate responses and reactions which are more naturally in accord with what the solar quest is asking of the person. Life may run a bit more smoothly if this is the case, because there is less conflict within you; consequently you might not meet so much external opposition or challenge, which is created by the outer world reflecting your own inner conflict or turmoil back to you. Get the picture? Of course, you could argue that there is no gain without pain; in other words, without the stress and tension inherent in a difficult Sun-Moon contact, you might not necessarily achieve the kind of positive transformation which a juicy inner struggle often yields.

I see a few hands up. Don't even ask, I have a pretty good idea what one of your questions is going to be: "What if the Sun and the Moon are in the same sign?" Right, I see nods. This question always comes up. I'm going to have it engraved on my tombstone along with that other classic, "What does it mean if a house is empty?" which is a ridiculous question because as you well know a house is never empty—there is always a sign there and the planet ruling that sign to be considered. But that's another lecture entirely, and don't you dare even ask that question today. Any conjunction (and any aspect or placement for that matter) is always a little tricky to talk about authoritatively for the simple reason that how it manifests depends on its relation to the rest of the chart. A Sun-Moon conjunction square Pluto and opposed by Saturn is a very different kettle of fish when compared with the same conjunction trine Jupiter. We can approach it this way for now. Every sign generates many different levels or dimensions of expression, like a note in a chord. An archetype can be compared to a lift (or elevator) in a department store; one level takes you to women's fashions, another level lets you off at men's shoes, and if you're hungry and have the time and money you can travel right up to the restaurant on the top floor.

Let's say you are born with both the Sun and Moon in Taurus; we'll make it a conjunction but just the fact these two lights are in the same sign is relevant to this discussion. The sign Taurus has numerous facets. True, all these facets will be connected by some common archetypal thread, but there are still fairly distinct levels. The Moon in Taurus probably means that certain dimensions of the sign come instinctively to you, but the fact that the Sun is also in Taurus suggests there are other dimensions of this sign which require attention in terms of the solar process of ego-building and self-formation. You may instinctively know how to create structure and security in your life (the Moon in Taurus), but the Sun being there as well could mean that the more sensual, creative and artistic side of Venusian-ruled Taurus is calling out for further unfoldment. Or let's say you have both the Sun and Moon in Virgo. The Moon there could mean that being critical and analytical come instinctively to you—these are qualities which are innate or inbred. But if you have the Sun in Virgo as well, there are other dimensions of the sign which you need to focus on to really evolve in this life. Virgo is the sign of the craftsperson or specialist, so it may be that you are meant to work very hard at something and become highly skilled in your chosen field in order to build a healthy ego, a strong sense of "I," or in order to feel fulfilled and complete as an individual. All right, that's enough on Sun-Moon aspects for now. At least we've cleared up some of the unfinished business from last night.

The general discussion so far was really intended to serve as an introduction to a more in-depth examination of the Sun as a symbol of ego formation and the role that father plays in this process. So let's dive in. I'd like to start with a few lines from Homer's *Odyssey*, Book XVI:

I am that father whom your boyhood lacked
and suffered pain for lack of. I am he.

This is not princely, to be swept away
by wonder at your father's presence.
No other Odysseus will ever come
for he and I are one, the same.[9]

I find this quote very moving. Odysseus was away on his adventures and trials most of the time his son Prince Telemachus was growing up. When he returned, Telemachus didn't recognise his long-lost father. This is when Odysseus said, "I am that father whom your boyhood lacked and suffered pain for lack of. I am he," and so on. The point I'm trying to make is that many of us didn't really know our fathers very well, and that for a great number of children—both boys and girls—father was, and could still be, a

---

[9]Homer, *The Odyssey*, trans. by Robert Fitzgerald (New York: Anchor, 1963), pp. 295–296.

somewhat mysterious, unknown, and possibly even a forbidding presence. How deeply do *you* know your father? A year or so ago I was preparing a new lecture on the topic of fathers and sons. I spent so many years going on about the womb and mothers that I thought it was time to get my teeth into the father-child relationship, choosing to focus on male children and their fathers; in the process, however, I also learned more about the father-daughter relationship as well. But let me start by talking about fathers and sons for a while before bringing in fathers and daughters.

According to various studies, chances are if you are an adult male between the ages of 20 and 55 brought up in North America or Britain (and I suspect these statistics apply to a number of other European countries as well), you probably didn't have a father who was significantly involved in your upbringing, who was openly affectionate and nurturing as well as strong and directive in a healthy, positive way.[10] When I was gathering information for the Fathers and Sons lecture, I talked with many men about their fathers, and explored more thoroughly my own relationship with my father. As I was saying, what stood out was how mysterious a figure the father was, and how deceptively complex the father-son relationship is in general. Whether describing heroes, saints, sinners, villains or anything in between, most men (and many women as well) knew very little about their fathers' inner lives—what their fathers really thought and felt as people, as human beings.[11] For many of us, he still remains a puzzle.

Things are beginning to change now. Freud and his followers generated a vast mountain of literature on mother's undeniable importance to a child's development, but until relatively recently you couldn't find much written about the father-child relationship and the vital role fathers play in the developmental and maturation process of their sons and daughters. You could almost say that father was the forgotten parent. Currently, however (at least in the United States and Britain), fathers are becoming more visible, more present. Broadly speaking, we are experiencing the gradual emergence of a new kind of man—the 70's man, the 80's man, the 90's

---

[10]See Andrew Merton, "Father Hunger," in *New Age Journal*, Sept./Oct., 1986, p. 24.

[11]Samuel Osherson, *Finding Our Fathers* (New York: Fawcett, 1986), p. 20.

man: a man who is not so embarrassed to be seen as thoughtful and sensitive, who is less afraid to show his feelings, who wants to play a more active role in bonding with, bringing up and nurturing his children. How different from the male/paternal stereotype of the 1950's, when men who fathered were relegated mostly to the position of the macho breadwinner. They were cast as the protectors and providers for the family, but they were not meant to be openly emotional, to cry or to be the one who nurtured and bonded with the children in the same way as the female parent.

There are certain clear sociological reasons for the changing role of men and fathers. Curiously, these revolve around the Women's Movement, which has expanded rapidly over the last few decades. As women change and grow, they are better able to stand up and speak for themselves, to reject stereotypes or projections that men and society have put onto them for centuries. Men have long been projecting unlived or undeveloped sides of themselves onto women – the woman is the nurturing one, the woman is the feeling one. Now an increasing number of women are contesting being labelled solely by these roles. A woman may be very nurturing or caring but she is now beginning to demand more space and time to explore and realise other facets of her nature. Men are therefore almost forced into finding within themselves what they have let women carry and live out for them over the years. In any system, if one component of the system alters, the other components of the system have to change if the system is to survive at all. Although I live in Britain and it is a little behind America in this respect (you know what they say, "When America sneezes, Britain eventually catches a cold"), I frequently visited the States in the mid 70's and 80's. It was while watching American television that I first registered the degree of sociological change taking place within the family; advertisements for baby powder, for instance, now showed the father changing the baby. A greater number of fathers are choosing to be present at the birth of their children; you can see fathers out on the street with their kids and the mother is nowhere in sight.

Just as you don't have to search too far afield to detect new images of male parenting, you don't have to look too hard to find astrological reasons for these new role models. Presently there is a traffic jam in the heavens happening in the sign of Capricorn, one of the signs traditionally associated with father. Neptune has been in Capricorn since 1984 and will remain there through the end of 1998. You could almost say that Neptune is dissolving a whole range of things associated with Capricorn, softening some of the rigidity of this sign, asking that the Capricorn principle (which covers fathering) become more pliable and empathetic. Uranus joined up in 1988, and will remain there until mid-January 1996, signifying new ideals and new images challenging existing Capricorn structures. In 1988, Saturn came along as well and did its number on Capricorn until February 1991. It's as if Saturn is saying the time has come to concretise these new images of fathering instigated by the movements of Neptune and Uranus.

A further astrological correlation with the changing role of father can be found through the sign of Leo, another sign that has long been associated with the hero-father archetype. Leo and Capricorn both represent aspects of male parenting; if these signs are prominent in someone's chart, I definitely would make a point of examining father issues with the person, just as I would dwell on stuff with mother if a client came along with seven planets in Cancer. At present, the generation of children born with Pluto in Leo are smack in or coming up to midlife, a time of self-examination and reappraisal. Just to be born with Pluto in Leo suggests complexes around the father. Pluto is now moving through Scorpio and you know what that means—sooner or later those people born with Pluto in Leo will experience transiting Pluto square natal Pluto. The transit of Pluto square its own place is very good at aggravating and bringing what is buried in you to the surface, casting light on unresolved complexes which have been doing their job of insidiously influencing the choices you make in life and the kinds of complications you attract in relationship. I know from my contemporaries that many men and women are presently discovering issues and feelings they have about their fathers which up to now they haven't acknowledged consciously. Many more books are being published which pertain to fathering, and there seems to be an influx of movies about fathers and their children. We'll shortly be examining the Sun as a significator for father and as an indication of what might have passed between you and him; right now, however, I'd like to continue looking at the father from a more purely psychological or sociological point of view.

In the early 1980's, Harvard University psychoanalyst James Herzog coined the term *father hunger* to describe the psychological state of children who had been deprived of their fathers through separation, divorce or death.[12] More recent research has re-evaluated and expanded this definition to include the offspring of fathers who were physically present but psychologically distant or inadequate. I would define father hunger as a subconscious yearning for a lost ideal father, for the father you didn't have, for the father who wasn't there in the way you desperately needed him to be. Herzog found that children thus affected (sons in particular, but much of this applies to daughters as well) had problems in four basic areas later in life. Firstly, with caretaking—it is very hard to give something you didn't get. If you experienced paternal deprivation, you'll probably find the role of parenting or fathering more difficult to play should your turn come up. The second area where Herzog detected problems relating back to a lack of fathering is in the capacity to be close to or intimate with others in one's adult life, whether with another man or another woman. Father is the first role model of the masculine principle, of what men are like. If he is distant and remote, a male child will assume that this is what it means to be a man; a female child might deduce that this is what men are all about. Carrying around such images influences who and what we meet throughout life, not to mention how we react to and interpret other people's behaviour. I believe it was the humanistic psychologist Jean Houston who once said that life has a way of obliging our expectations.

Thirdly, Herzog noted that the lack of proper fathering could lead to problems with aggression and assertion. Interestingly enough, psychological sketches of the early lives of convicts and prisoners often reveal the absence of a father or an aggrieved relationship with him. If you are overly aggressive or hostile as a child, you will benefit from a father who teaches you limits. Mothers can do this as well, but triangular relationships activate important questions about boundaries and assertion (such as the Oedipal complex), and we have the chance to learn valuable lessons in life

---

[12]See Andrew Merton, "Father Hunger," p. 24.

through facing these conflicts. If you are not assertive enough, a good father can model ways to be more forthcoming or courageous. Herzog's fourth point relates back to what I was just discussing: paternally deprived children often have difficulty with achievement and mastery in the world. By the way, there may be someone around who is not the biological father but who serves as a father substitute in respect to all the issues touched on so far.

I think it's wonderful that an ever-growing number of men are now seeking to take a more active role in fathering. But as I was saying before, it isn't always easy to give something you didn't get. It will be more of a challenge to father adequately if you don't have positive images of fathering recorded in your memory. Furthermore, when a father attempts to nurture and care for his newborn and helpless infant, distressing feelings left over from his own infancy can be reawakened—hitherto deeply buried pain, frustration and anger. The resurgence of such emotions is likely to interfere with a father's sincere desire to be a good parent. So in order for the "new man" to fulfil his desire to participate in the nurturing process, he may have quite a bit of psychological housecleaning to do first; in particular, working through unfinished business between his own father and himself. The same rationale applies to mothers and their sons, and of course to mothers and daughters.

There is a definite connection between ego formation and the kind of interaction you had with your father. This can be illustrated quite simply by a diagram (see figure 5 on page 140) which is an extension of the diagram I used in the talk on mothers and lovers last night. In the beginning your identity is fused with that of the mother as shown by Egg A, where your incipient ego or "I" is encased within her. The developmental task from about six months onward is to free the ego (or what also might be called your sense of being a separate self) from Egg A so that it stands distinct from mother. Needless to say, there is usually a great deal of ambivalence or separation anxiety about this, because one part of you would prefer to remain fused with her in that uroboric state. The urge to individuate, however, is powerful and natural; and the point I wish to make is that the process of individuation is fostered when there is a father around (Egg B) toward whom you can move, another parent present with whom to interact. We can say that one of father's principle roles is to serve as an attractive outsider who

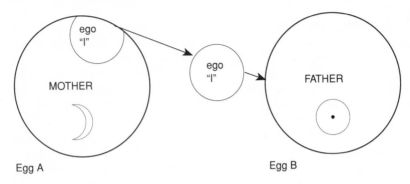

Figure 5. Father as an attractive outsider toward whom we can move in the process of differentiating from mother.

helps you to break the merger-bond or symbiosis you have with mother.[13] What is important is the *otherness* of father. At least this is the traditional way of looking at it. Obviously, one family is going to be different than another to varying degrees, and there are a number of alternatives to the conventional nuclear family setup. Nonetheless, we have to talk generally for now. So if mother represents closeness, fusion and security (what is known), then father stands for something other than mother—he enables us to develop a sense of self that is not solely tied to the body of mother, and in this respect he represents spirit, self-consciousness, adventure and growth. To repeat, a father can play a significant role in helping you to attain an identity separate and distinct from that of your mother. This applies to both male and female children.

The basic astrology of all this is pretty clear: Egg A represents the Moon and Mother, while Egg B is the Sun, symbolising father, but also the process of defining an individual self. We are drawn to him at that point in time when we are ready to break our uroboric bond with mother, when we first embark on establishing an "I" which is distinct from her. Therefore, what we meet when we move toward father has great bearing on our sense of individual identity. It's no wonder that astrology has traditionally linked the

---

[13]Arthur Colman and Libby Colman, *The Father: Mythology and Changing Roles* (Wilmette, IL: Chiron Publications, 1988), p. 78.

Sun both with father and one's striving for selfhood. I'd like to personalise this through a short exercise:

> Relax, take some deep breaths and clear your mind.
> Now spend a few minutes reflecting on or imagining what it felt like to move toward your father.
> Think about it.
> Was your father there?
> Was he an attractive enough force to encourage you to separate from mother?
> Does he feel better or worse to you than mother?
> What comes to your mind or what does it feel like when you picture interacting with him or being close to him?

Natal aspects to the Sun give one indication of what you meet through father, and because of the connection between father and self-formation, natal aspects to the Sun also indicate qualities closely associated with your sense of what it means to be an "I" separate and distinct from mother. We can play around with a few simple examples to amplify this concept. What if you are born with the Sun trine Jupiter? Obviously you may have other aspects to the Sun in your chart besides this one, but I want to keep it basic and straightforward for now. Picture yourself at that stage in infancy when the developmental task is to disentangle your identity from that of mother. In a sense you are moving away from the Moon and heading for the Sun. So if your Sun is trine Jupiter, what might going toward father feel like for you?

Audience: It should feel expansive.

Howard: Yes, it's likely to feel quite welcoming because you have positive Jupiterian images in aspect to the Sun: "Gee, separating from mother isn't so bad. It's quite interesting out here. Father is fun and how about all the new things I'm discovering and feeling with him." So if you encounter Jupiter through the father at the time your ego is beginning to take shape, your sense of who you are, your "I," will be coloured by qualities of adventurousness, spiritedness, and expansiveness. Such an experience will contribute to a stronger desire to express your individuality, to a joy, enthusiasm and zest for life. True, you'll probably hurry back to mother if the going gets tough, or check in with her regularly to make sure she is still there. But the die is cast; you've tasted some of the delights that exist beyond the range of mother's knee and there is no turning back. Now, for the sake of argument, let's say you are someone who is born with the Sun square Saturn. Picture yourself moving away from mother and in the direction of father, and you meet a Saturn square. What does this say to you about what it feels like to venture away from mother, to be more out on your own in the world?

Audience: There are difficulties, problems, blockages.

Howard: Yes, a bit like running into a brick wall perhaps. There you are on the verge of forming a separate-self sense and you meet Saturn via the father—a father who might be distant, cold or remote, who might be away working all the time, or who comes over as rigid, authoritarian, judgemental, controlling and punishing. So you think, "This is not much fun, this is not very welcoming or comforting, I'd better get back to mother." As a result, ego development could be retarded; you are not sure about standing on your own, your ego gets off to a faulty start, and this early insecurity and quite literal self-doubt (doubts about being a self) will haunt and challenge you in subsequent attempts to give form to and express your individuality. One hopes that with Saturn you'll make it there in the end, but it takes time and requires more effort because it doesn't feel as safe or as enjoyable when compared to a Sun-Jupiter contact.

Audience: What if you are born with really hard aspects to the Moon and much nicer ones to the Sun?

Howard: Good question. It may be that from the beginning mother never felt safe or never served as a solid container and provider of your needs. As a result, almost from the word go, father was preferred; he was the one to whom you were drawn—being close to him or held by him felt better than being close to mother. So, in this case, father is mother. I'm really not sure what this sets up in terms of separation and individuation, except to say that sooner or later in the name of psychological health and wholeness, you'll need to deal with the damage caused by a failed mother bond. But I feel even more pain for those children who couldn't find safety and nurturing from either parent—something that might show up in charts with mainly hard aspects to both the Sun and the Moon, or if the Sun and Moon form a close T-Square with Mars, Saturn, Chiron, or any of the outer planets (which also can indicate serious problems within the parental relationship itself). Imagine it, moving away from a "bad" mother toward father and then experiencing hurt and rejection with him as well. This doesn't bode well for your capacity to relate easily with others later in life, and certainly won't contribute to your forming an "I" blessed with a healthy sense of self-esteem. Some form of psychological, therapeutic or spiritual work on the self will be necessary to arrive at a place where you feel okay about being in the body and here on this planet. I've met successful and reasonably happy adults born with these kinds of solar and lunar aspects who have managed to come to terms with and learn from their early wounding; and I know people who haven't—some of whom are locked away in one kind of institution or another or should be, and others who are out in the world still having a truly difficult time in life. My heart goes out to each and every one of them, expect perhaps the one who decides to come at me with a knife because of something his parents "did" to him in childhood. Even so, if I survived the attack and set up his chart, I could come to some understanding of why it happened. Astrology can teach us a great deal about acceptance and tolerance. How can you judge someone born with such challenging aspects? Reincarnationists track these situations back to karma and past lives, and there are those who believe that the deeper Self chooses the chart according to the lessons and kind of growth you need this time around.

Let's continue exploring a few more natal aspects to the Sun in the light of father and ego formation. What if you are born with Sun well aspected to Mars?

Audience: Father appears strong, confident, assertive or stimulating, and this shapes your sense of what it is like to be an individual in your own right.

Howard: Precisely, just as you are establishing an ego identity, you meet a positive Mars figure in father, something which should help to equip you with a sense of potency and power. But what if you have a natal Sun-Mars square, especially one in cardinal or fixed signs?

Audience: You might find him too rough or aggressive, or immediately run into a conflict of wills.

Howard: Yes, he might seem gruff, angry, violent, unsafe or sexually unruly in some way. How will that affect a male child?

Audience: He'll grow up with problems around aggression.

Howard: Yes, let's look at that. Remember that father is likely to be our first role model of the masculine. A boy who repeatedly experiences his father as violent or aggressive could easily end up equating these qualities with what it means to be a man. A female child who encounters such a father probably will conclude that men are brutes, and you can imagine where that might lead later in life. Interestingly enough, I've seen people of both sexes with difficult Sun-Mars contacts who seem meek, mild and docile, or who try hard to control their anger and not appear too pushy or demanding. It's as if they've experienced an abusive or tyrannical father and decided, "I am never going to be that way." The trouble is that when you straightjacket Mars because you've only seen negative expressions of it, you also forfeit the potential to develop the positive things Mars has to offer—such as the power to affirm your identity through asserting your will and going after what you want in the world. It's like throwing the baby out with the bathwater.

Father is a role model for the animus, and we can embrace models or reject them. We can idealise him as a hero or cast him as a villain. In either case he is a force to be reckoned with because he is a manifestation of something within you whether you like it or not. I believe that the placements by sign, house and aspect of the personal planets in your chart show innate archetypal predispositions, the kinds of images or expectations you are born with (for whatever reasons) which influence what you experience in respect to the various facets of existence associated with the Sun, Moon,

Mercury, Venus and Mars. So if you "come in" with a negative animus image as symbolised by a square of Sun to Mars, this reflects something inside you which you may then project onto the father whether or not he is an appropriate hook. Your actual father may not be all that martial, but you are predisposed to notice or register when he is acting in that fashion; or something in the chemistry or timing between the two of you activates a negative Mars in him. Then again, he truly may be that way and exactly fit your inner image. You can read more about these and other basic premises of psychological astrology in my book *The Twelve Houses*[14] and in the chapter "The Stages of Childhood" in *The Development of the Personality*.[15]

Let's continue with a few more solar aspects. How about the Sun in hard angle to Pluto in terms of father's influence on ego formation?

Audience: Could he feel dangerous and threatening?

Howard: Yes, it might very well manifest that way. A difficult Sun-Pluto contact can give rise to a whole host of different issues around father. First of all, Pluto is the god of the underworld, which, as you all know, is equated with the unconscious in psychological parlance. Therefore you are not going to take him at face value: whatever he outwardly says or does, however he appears, you're likely to be more sensitive to what he is sitting on or hiding. What happens from there depends on the nature of the feelings or drives simmering away in his unconscious. Perhaps he appears fairly happy or content, but underneath he is depressed. You'll register the depression, not the facade. What if he seems to act lovingly and kindly towards you, but underneath he is feeling angry or explosive about some problems at work or in the marital relationship? You'll register his destructive or more threatening feelings, not necessarily in a conscious or mental way, but through

---

[14]Howard Sasportas, *The Twelve Houses: An Introduction to the Houses in Astrological Interpretation* (London: The Aquarian Press, 1985; and San Bernardino, CA: Borgo Press, 1988).

[15]Liz Greene and Howard Sasportas, *The Development of the Personality*, Volume 1 in *Seminars in Psychological Astrology* (York Beach, ME: Samuel Weiser, 1982), pp. 3–82.

undercurrents which hit you in the face or agitate your gut when you're in his vicinity. Like certain animals, you possess a sharp scent enabling you to smell what is in the air, to pick up on what is not immediately visible or apparent. Sexual undertones could riddle the relationship with father for a female child, and both parties could feel guilty, dark or bad because of such feelings. Are you getting the picture? Remember, all this could be happening just as you are beginning to define yourself as an "I"; so if you meet Pluto in the process, you're likely to conclude that being a separate self means having to be on guard, and it also makes life more complex. A Plutonic father may be seen as omnipotent and almighty. If you are to be safe and not sorry, you'll need to be deeply watchful, wary and probing, careful about what you give away or allow to happen. You'll want to establish as much control over your self and the environment as possible in order to guarantee things run your way—it's too risky otherwise. Power issues ensue, subtle games are played, and so on. I've even noticed these patterns in people who have Sun trine or sextile Pluto, although they seem more naturally equipped to adapt, work through and learn from the issues at hand than someone born with the conjunction, square, opposition or inconjunct.

A Sun-Pluto contact also suggests that you are very sensitive to those times when your father is in the process of change or transformation, or when he is contending with troublesome issues within himself. Again, this leads you to link selfhood with such things as crisis, self-examination and self-knowledge, and the periodic need to shed your existing skin for a new one—a propensity to create situations which require more psychological deaths and rebirths than other solar aspects might ask of a person. To be quite literal, Pluto is the god of death, and some people born with Sun-Pluto aspects experience the death or disappearance of the father while still at a tender age. Events that happen to us in early life do leave their mark, however clever you are at covering it up.

Audience: I've met a number of people with Sun conjunct Venus and they hated their fathers. I can't understand this.

Howard: I've noticed this as well, but I'm pretty sure the plot is more complex. To have the symbol for father linked to the planet associated with love and beauty has to mean that at some stage you adored or idealised him. Then, for whatever reason, he let you down or erected firmer boundaries between the two of you, perhaps because he felt it was getting a little too "hot," or mother was jealous and creating ripples. Sun-Venus also suggests that you were born with high expectations with regard to the Father archetype, that he should have embodied everything charming and wonderful, and offer you flawless love and affection. When the actual corporeal father invariably slipped up and failed to meet these unrealistic expectations, you may have been left angry and disappointed with him. I've seen a similar dynamic at work with Sun-Neptune contacts. In terms of ego formation, a Sun-Venus contact which is working well would mean that you did meet love and appreciation through the father and this will enhance your own sense of self-worth and esteem. Ultimately, however, I believe we all have to learn to love and value ourselves for ourselves, and not have our worth dependent on other people's validation.

Let's consider Sun-Uranus. Here you are moving away from the body of mother toward father and greater self-definition, but you have a difficult Sun-Uranus conjunction, square, opposition or inconjunct.

Audience: Maybe he is not around.

Howard: Uranus is a complex planet which can express itself in contrasting ways. But it's true that Uranus aspects often manifest as disruption, separation and unconventionality, so the family setup may not be a traditional one or may go through significant upheavals which disrupt and disarm you just when you thought life was settled. If your family differs from the norm, your sense of self is coloured by the idea that you are not quite like the kids you know from other families—you might come from a broken home or your father and mother aren't legally married. Father may reflect Uranus in that he gets restless and leaves for a while and then comes back to roost until the urge for change grabs him again, or he works at a distance and is only home on weekends. You can't be certain of him; he is an unknown quantity, changeable and erratic. A male child's sense of self and what it means to be a man could mirror what he sees in his father and he might find himself leading a similar life-style later in life. A female child with Sun in aspect to Uranus who strongly identifies with the father or prefers him to mother may grow up reflecting his attributes; or she might assume that men generally are not reliable, even though they can be rather fun or stimulating when they are around.

In Greek mythology, Ouranus was a sky god, and we can associate the expansiveness of the starry heavens with the mind and intellect, with beliefs, theories, philosophies, systems, anything abstract and conceptual. For this reason, strongly Uranian people (depending on rest of the chart) are sometimes disconnected or dissociated from their bodies and the realm of feeling. Very often, they think or make a decision about how they "ought" to feel and try to be that way rather than allowing the emotions free reign or a natural expression. They're great to talk to, they have principles and strong political or social beliefs, they spark off ideas in you and you spark off new ideas in them; but if you're needing reassurance, comforting or holding and you ask them if they truly love you, their reply might be, "Well, what is love really?" after which they launch into an abstract diatribe on the topic. Not much solace at a time when what you are actually craving is physical or emotional warmth or stroking. If you are a child with a Sun-Uranus contact and your chart is predominantly fire and air, a Uranian father is probably just your cup of tea. You'll readily identify your nature with his, and provided that your father is not the overly dogmatic type of Uranian who is certain that his truth is everyone's truth, you'll develop an "I" that relishes space, freedom and room to move. If you have a close Sun-Uranus aspect but the rest of your chart is comprised mostly of water and earth, a Uranian father may not be able to meet your physical or emotional needs. In the process of separating from mother, you move toward him; you may find him exciting, stimulating and even enjoy his unpredictability and sense of humour, but when you need the kind of closeness or warmth I've just been talking about, you will probably experience him as a little distant, a little cold, unresponsive or unreliable. He can be kind to you, generous with you in many ways, and yet you get the feeling he would be that way with the neighbour's children as well. He's fair, he'll treat everyone equally. That's great, but what you really want is to feel special to him. If you have the kind of mother who can offer the emotional closeness and reassurance you need, you'll go back to her. But then you get bored with the known, you start to feel smothered or confined by her, so it's back to father again for a breath of fresh air, for a different kind of stimulation. You see how this sets up a pattern of to-ing and fro-ing. Later in life, you start a project, job or relationship in the hope it will offer you satisfaction or even lasting fulfilment, but when you realise it doesn't quite match up to your ideals or expectations or you start to feel bored by the familiarity of it all, off you go to try something new.

To discuss Sun-Neptune aspects with you, I'd like to use the chart of a man we'll call "Paul." (See Chart 2 on page 150.) In fact, we are now going to delve into a fairly extensive case history, because not only do I have Paul's chart, but I also have the chart of his father, "Bill," and Paul's own son, whom we'll call "Max." We will focus on Paul's chart now, and later on (see pp. 167–193) Liz and I will discuss Paul's chart in relation to the charts of his father and his son. Studying a lineage like this one is a good way to learn about the kinds of issues that can come up between fathers and sons. And when I tell you their stories, you'll see how early complexes and other unfinished business from the past are passed on from one generation to the next, and how accurately these are reflected in the three charts concerned. Astrology is a superb tool for detecting and unravelling the intricacies of family dynamics.

When looking for father in the chart, I would begin by examining the Sun by sign, house and aspect. In particular, I would focus first on the closest aspects to the Sun, whether these are major or minor aspects. You know what is meant when we say an aspect is *exact* — it's when the aspect is exact to the degree or with hardly any orb of variance. It's often quite stunning just how powerful an influence on one's psyche and one's life an exact "minor" aspect such as a semisquare or sesquiquadrate can have. So don't ignore a minor aspect if it is exact or very close to being exact. Also you'll need to see what is going on in the natal house associated with father. As does Liz, and for reasons which I won't go into now because most of you are familiar with them, I often find that the 4th house works as a significator for father, but many of you may prefer to keep him in the 10th. I do have more to say on this quandary a little later. For now, however, I want to start with the

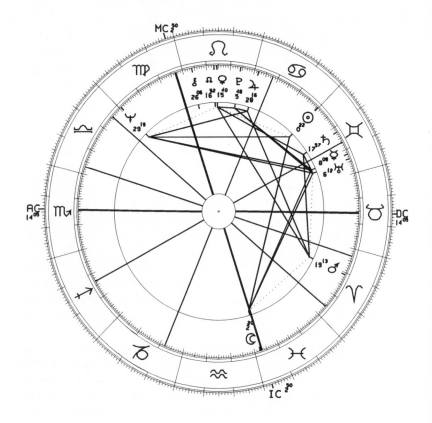

Chart 2. Paul. The birth data has been withheld for confidentiality. Chart calculated by Astrodienst, using the Placidus house system.

placement of the Sun in Paul's chart. You see it in 0 degrees Cancer in the 8th. What planet most closely aspects it?

Audience: Neptune gives a pretty close square.

Howard: Yes, the Sun is in 0 degrees, 22 minutes Cancer and Neptune is 29 degrees, 19 minutes Virgo. It is out of sign, but still only a degree and a bit away from an exact square. Remember your minor aspects as well: in Paul's chart you'll find a very tight semi-square between Venus and the Sun, something we were talking about earlier in terms of the love we crave from father and the high expectations we have of him. Right now I want to focus on the meaning of Sun square Neptune. Before I reveal Paul's history, what do you think about Sun-Neptune aspects in regards to the formation of an ego identity and one's interaction with father?

Audience: Neptune is so nebulous, maybe there is no father around.

Howard: Yes, this is precisely what happened in Paul's case. At the developmental stage when he would naturally be moving away from mother and establishing a separate-self sense there was no father around either to facilitate or deter the process: Paul met Neptune in relation to the Sun, and Neptune can be pretty intangible – it may not offer much to grab onto. More generally, difficult Sun-Neptune aspects can manifest in a variety of ways.

Neptune is a planet associated with sacrifice, and when connected to the Sun it links sacrifice with the father archetype. This can be quite literal – he goes away, dies, or isn't there for some reason and therefore we have to relinquish or let go of him; the basic birthright to have a good father remains an unfulfilled yearning. Even if he is physically present, he might be weak, ill or ailing; he could have an addiction problem such as alcoholism, spending more time at the pub than at home or getting drunk a lot and causing havoc to the family. Or he might be in the navy or merchant marine and away at sea, or working on an oil rig somewhere off the Scottish coast – the sea and oil are associated with Neptune. Two examples from my casework come to mind which further illustrate how Neptune might manifest. Both charts have a close

Sun-Neptune square. The first case is a woman with Sun square Neptune—her father was a world-famous opera singer, and she was deprived of him while growing up because he was performing all over the place. The second example is that of the son of a clergyman: father was so busy tending his flock that he didn't have the time to pay much attention to his own children. You can see how in both cases, father had to be sacrificed: he belonged to the world, not to the child. Obviously, you can get positive expressions of Sun-Neptune aspects. A father who is an artist, a healer, someone who is very imaginative, poetic, inspirational and sensitive, someone it feels healing and soothing to be around. But I've observed over the years that even with a trine or sextile from the Sun to Neptune, especially if it is a close aspect, there is often quite a lot of adjustments to be made when it comes to father. I mentioned before that Sun-Neptune people might idealise the father at first and then be disappointed later on as they get a bit older and wiser and can see him more realistically. There is a sense of a bubble bursting, of father letting you down or failing you for some reason.

Let's focus on Paul's chart. Paul was born in June, 1943, which roughly means that he was conceived nine months before, sometime in late September, 1942, either in late Virgo or early Libra. (Have you heard the joke the American astrologer Michael Lutin tells? He said that if you have sex when the Sun is in Virgo, you are punished nine months later by giving birth to a Gemini!) Paul just made it into early Cancer. One assumes his father was around at the time of conception; but shortly after Paul was conceived, Bill joined the Royal Air Force, took off for Canada and didn't return to England for four years. Paul spent the first four years of his life fatherless, which fits with Sun square Neptune. Paul also has the Sun in Cancer trine to the Moon in Pisces, and in some cases with a Sun-Moon contact, mother (the Moon) ends up having to play father (the Sun) as well. Don't take that as a hard and fast rule, though. In addition, Paul was born with the Sun in the 8th house, Scorpio's natural domain, another clue that there could be complex issues, negative undercurrents or something dark or mysterious going on between Paul and his father.

Freud and Jung both assumed that father wasn't that important until a child was at least 3 or 4 years old. However, more recent investigation has shown that paternal deprivation in the *first* four years of life has a more disruptive effect on a child's development than father's absence after the fourth year. In one study I read about, college men whose fathers had been away at war or in the army during the first three to four years of their lives were compared to other college men whose fathers were around from birth.[16] As children, the paternally-deprived men had enormous difficulty adjusting to father's return when he eventually did come back. Some of them found it impossible to bond with their fathers at all; the newly returned father was viewed as an invader or intruder, a stranger who upset the life they had with mother. This study fits exactly with Paul's experience. I'm not making this up.

I interviewed Paul in June, 1989, specifically to explore the relationship he had with his father and to see how this might be affecting him as a father. I had the three charts in front of me and I listened to his story and asked various questions. One of the first things he said was, "I didn't meet my father until I was 4, and I remember almost nothing about him until I was 6 or 7." I thought that strange. Bill (Paul's father) reappeared when Paul was four, and yet there is this two- or three-year memory gap. I don't want to sound heavy-handed here, but that statement made me highly suspicious; I just couldn't take it at face value. It seemed more likely that Paul had found his newly returned father's presence very difficult to accept; there was something so painful or uncomfortable about it that he *chose* to forget as much as possible about the first few years that Bill was back. So if anyone says to you "I don't remember very much about my early childhood," you can be pretty sure it wasn't an easy time and that there is an awful lot of buried feeling still to be dug up. Of course, you should be prepared to honour what people are ready to hear—don't use the insight the chart gives you as you would a sledgehammer . . . but don't be fooled either.

I gently probed Paul. He had said he remembered "almost nothing," so I asked him to try to recall what little he could remember. He then went on: "I do remember feeling, who is this guy and what is he coming in with? Maybe I felt a little betrayed by my mother for letting him in. I have a tendency now to cut off from

---

[16]Anthony Stevens, *Archetypes* (New York: Quill, 1983), p. 105.

others." The ball was rolling, and Paul himself immediately began to make connections between the havoc generated by his father's return and his "adult" self. He continued, "You know, emotionally I'm a loner. I don't have close male friends. I don't like anyone getting too near to me. Maybe it comes from this period. The person I thought I could trust, my mother, went off with this other guy. Until just before he died I never really got close to my father, and even then there was still a great distance." Paul's story turned out to be a good example of some of the father-son studies I've been sharing with you, the way he couldn't accept his father after a four-year absence. And, in line with Herzog's research into "father hunger," Paul confessed to having problems getting close to people. When we got around to discussing his relationship with his own son Max, he said something else which I found quite moving: "I sometimes look at Max when he is sleeping and I feel a kind of scarlet ribbons thing—you know, how much I love my child and how much I want to give to him. But when Max is actually awake and I am relating to him, we often have great difficulty connecting. I sometimes unleash thunderbolts at him that surprise me." I commented on this earlier today. A father may sincerely wish to give his son the kind of love he himself never received; but if he didn't get that love from his own father, he doesn't have the pictures or images in his mind which would naturally equip him to be that way. In Paul's case, his father was absent for the first four years; when Bill did return, he was the enemy, an intruder. The atmosphere between Paul and his father had been extremely murky—love was scarce, they didn't share much except a rivalry for the mother. And now, although Paul really cares for Max (his first child, his only son), he finds that fathering doesn't come too easily.

Yesterday we discussed how early transits and progressions involving the Moon can give insight into what passed between mother and child. The same rationale applies to the Sun. Take a look at Paul's Sun in relation to his Saturn—the Sun at 0 degrees Cancer and Saturn at 17 degrees Gemini. By most astrologers' standards this is too wide to be a conjunction. But if Saturn is slightly earlier than the Sun, what does this mean in terms of Saturn transits to the Paul's Sun in these crucial, formative years?

Audience: Saturn will transit over his Sun while he is still quite young.

Howard: Yes, in Paul's case Saturn takes about a year to get there. And you remember that from six months onward there is an innate developmental urge to separate your "I," your identity, from that of mother, a process that usually takes three years to accomplish and which father can facilitate. Just when Paul needs "the otherness" of father to help him along the path of individuation, he has Saturn moving up to and over his Sun—an astrological indication of the deprivation he suffered in this respect. In a sense, Paul's Sun was stifled and held back around age 1; he missed out on an early chance to do some ego building. This doesn't condemn him to lifelong nebulousness or indirection, but he'll have to work a little harder later on to achieve self-definition. This may not be an entirely bad thing, because (as Saturn often teaches us) the more effort you put into achieving something, the longer you have to sweat, "slog" and wait, the more you'll value it in the end. At least that's how it is in most cases. Paul's solar force and power may have been retarded or disturbed in its development, but it isn't denied to him forever.

A few other major transits which occurred in Paul's formative years are also noteworthy. Paul was born in 1943 and his father came back when he was 4, which brings us to 1947. During our interview, I became curious to see what transits were happening to Paul's chart the year of his father's return. Is there anyone here born in 1947? I bet you can guess what I'm about to launch into. By that year, Saturn had made it to Leo (one of the signs naturally associated with the father-hero principle). If you check the ephemeris, you'll see that transiting Saturn conjuncted Paul's natal Pluto in June, 1947, and then conjuncted his Venus in August (two months later). Meanwhile, transiting Pluto was moving further along in Leo, slowly but inexorably creeping up to his Venus, getting within one degree of it in 1947, making a first direct hit in 1948, but continuing its harassment of the goddess of love until June, 1950. With both Saturn and Pluto moving over his Venus, no wonder Paul initially said he didn't recall much about the first two years his father was back. It must have been very painful for him— his whole love life in shreds. Remember, transits and progressions show the *inner* meaning of events which occur under them. When Saturn and Pluto landed on his Venus, Paul faced a dual challenge: he had to come to terms with a bossy stranger in the house who happened to be his father, and he had to deal with the cataclysmic shake-up of the relationship with his mother now that there was a serious rival on the scene. Has anyone here today been "fortunate" enough to have experienced transiting Pluto over his or her Venus yet? Think about what happened to you when this occurred. As a general rule, Pluto transits to Venus—and this includes transiting trines and sextiles as well—herald a period of time when you are tested, challenged, torn down and (with luck and effort) rebuilt or transformed in a positive way through what you have to face in the arena of relationships. As with any major Pluto transit, its effects can feel quite devastating—at least until you're pretty well through it and better able to see that the change and disruption Pluto brings has meaning and purpose in terms of further self-unfoldment and psychological growth.

In Freudian terms, we are heading straight for Paul's Oedipal complex. Some psychologists question the validity of the Oedipal theory, but I'm inclined to think Freud was on to something. In the Greek myth, Oedipus kills his father and marries his mother; in real life, most children go through a stage of wanting to have mother or father all to themselves, and seeing the other parent as a rival. Freud's central thesis was that a boy desires mother for himself and therefore would like to get rid of father, and a girl falls in love with her father and wants to erase mother from the picture. Such longings carry quite a lot of guilt with them. What if the rival parent discovers what you're thinking about or plotting? From the point of view of your unconscious, these "forbidden" desires are bound to lead to some form of punishment. Also, you may still feel love or a need in your life for your rival as well, so if you destroy that person you are wiping out someone you actually love and need. Messy stuff.

We'll use the example of a male child who wants mother to himself and sees his father as a rival to examine in a little more detail the usual course of the Oedipal struggle. What happens is that the boy feels guilty (unconsciously) about his forbidden longings, and fears reprisals on the part of the father. Nevertheless, he endeavours to compete with his father in an attempt to prove to mother that he (the boy) is the better of the two. He wants to impress upon his mother-lover that he can do just as good a job as the father in fulfilling her needs, if not better. But in actual fact, he isn't up to scratch. After all, he is only a small boy of 3 or 4. Father is bigger and stronger, father can go out into the world unattended by an adult and earn money for food and shelter—in short, father is better equipped in most ways to "keep" and satisfy mother. Typically, the boy resolves the dilemma by giving up the contest, although I doubt if we ever fully let go of it—the desire to prove the self, to score over competitors, coupled with the hidden fear, the nagging doubts, that we may not be good enough or that we'll bring punishment on ourselves if we actually do succeed haunts most of us to some degree for the rest of our lives. When the little boy relinquishes his desire to have mother all to himself and forfeits the contest, he then (according to Freud's idea of a successful resolution of the Oedipal dilemma) concludes that it makes sense to model himself on the father who seems to have the kinds of qualities that are needed to achieve what one wants in life. So the father is no longer a rival but an ally, someone who has something to teach you. Obviously, this isn't going to work so well if the father is a real *schlep*, which is a Yiddish word that means a mess, a failure, a wimp or a slob. But that's another story, which we don't have time to discuss right now. (You can read what I've written on this in greater detail in "The Stages of Childhood" chapter in *The Development of the Personality*.) The situation for the little girl is reversed but follows pretty much the same pattern: she wants to marry daddy and get rid of mother, she fears mother will punish her if she finds out what is going on, and then having compared herself with mother decides to give up the fight and model herself on her mother instead—provided, of course, the mother isn't a real *schlep*. I wonder what happens when both parents are *schleps*? I do love that word.

Freud's view of the Oedipal complex centred mainly on the fact that Oedipus killed his father Laius and then married Jocasta, his own mother. Oedipus is viewed as the guilty party. Arthur and Libby Colman, in their book *The Father*, interpret the myth from a different perspective.[17] I want to take a little time to examine their

---

[17]Arthur and Libby Colman, *The Father*, p. 96.

interpretation because it illuminates something which fathers need to look at in themselves, and it casts light on an issue which relates directly to the case study I'm presenting. The Oedipus myth does not begin with Oedipus killing his father: it actually starts with Laius (the father) attempting to do away with Oedipus. Laius has been warned by an oracle that he would die at the hands of his son because of a curse cast on him for a past wrongdoing. When Laius's wife Jocasta bears a son, Laius (fearing the prophecy) decides to kill the newborn baby by leaving him exposed in the mountains. The nasty ploy doesn't work; Oedipus is rescued by a shepherd, survives and grows to manhood. One day while travelling he arrives at a crossroads where his way is obstructed by a "stroppy" old man in a chariot who has the gall to hit him over the head with a goad. Oedipus is angered by this unprovoked attack and strikes back in self-defence by hitting the old man with his walking staff and accidently killing him in the process. He then carries on with his journey, unaware that it is his father he has slain, unaware that he has committed patricide; in his mind he had just taken revenge on some grumpy old sod who was standing in his way.

You see what I'm getting at—it is Laius who first tries to do away with Oedipus by leaving him to die in the cold mountain air. His justification is that he was warned by an oracle that he would be killed at the hands of his own son. The Colmans make an interesting point when they write that to the ancient Greeks, "the oracle was an outside voice of prophecy, although it is easier for most moderns to understand the oracle as something that resides within us, giving voice to our own unconscious hopes and fears."[18] In other words, a father may unconsciously fear that one day his son is going to kill him. The Oedipus complex focusses on the son doing away with father in order to bed mother; but looking at the myth from a slightly different angle, we come up with a "Laius complex"—the father who is afraid (unconsciously) that he will be ousted or destroyed by his son, and who therefore wants to kill the child or, at the very least, block his progress and development (just as Laius obstructed Oedipus from moving ahead at the crossroads). You may find this hard to digest—I'm pretty certain not

[18]Arthur and Libby Colman, *The Father*, p. 96.

many fathers would freely admit to such unsavoury urges and feelings. And yet, it's not too hard to see why these fears could exist somewhere in the father's psyche: in the majority of cases, the son will be growing into his full power and potency around the same time his father's prowess is on the wane due to aging.

Father-son rivalry is not only about the son's jealousy of the father for having mother; it is also about the father feeling threatened that his son will eventually outshine and overtake him, usurping his position and power. You see how complex the father-son relationship can be: a father may see his son as someone who will ensure his immortality by carrying on his name and lineage, and yet the birth of a son also can make him more aware of his own aging and mortality. The sense of an offspring as a rival can begin as soon as the wife is pregnant—especially if it is the couple's first child. Think about it, much of the pregnant woman's focus will now be on the new life growing inside her; she is no longer primarily concerned with her partner or husband. Most newborns become the centre of attention, and a man's wife is then as much the baby's mother as she is the spouse. The breast will have to be shared. In line with what the father may have dreaded unconsciously, the baby has indeed supplanted him.

No wonder that some fathers and sons find it easier to be angry and hostile with one another rather than close and loving. I said it earlier and I'll say it again—a father may truly want to nurture and care for his children in the best possible fashion, but before he can do this he will have to come to terms with the undercurrents and unconscious hostility and rivalry that could be getting in the way. We'll eventually be looking at the synastry between Paul and his father, Bill, and you'll be seeing that Pluto figures prominently in their interaspects, highlighting the various forms of unconscious rivalry that can exist between a father and his son. Bill and Paul are good examples of what I've just been discussing. And when we bring in the chart of Paul's son, Max, you'll be able to detect a similar pattern or dynamic at work, although to a slightly lesser extent.

We've dwelt mainly on the Sun as the significator of father, but we also should talk about the 4th and 10th houses in this respect. Now we have the problem whether to assign father to the 4th or the 10th. This is a sticky point for many astrologers, and there may be no clear-cut rule we can make, but let's explore this issue for a few minutes. Earlier in this lecture, we learned that one of father's principle roles is to serve as an attractive outside who draws the infant away from a too-intense bond or symbiosis with mother. Traditionally, father also can be useful to a child's growth and development by acting as a bridge to the outside world. In the conventional setup (and we must remember there are a lot of exceptions to this and every family is a little different from every other), the mother is at home with the small child and the father goes out to work—this is the typical earth mother–sky father coupling. Nowadays of course, we have the phenomena of dual-career families and an increasing occurrence of single-parent families, and in some cases (often due to an economic recession, layoffs and high unemployment) the father may be out of work and at home looking after a child, while the mother is the breadwinner—the one who is out in the world. But let's stick to the traditional arrangement.

Because the father is the one who is at work and away from you (the infant) for much of the day, when he returns each evening he brings a "whiff" of the outside world back into the nest. He may even have stories to tell you about his day, and what the world outside the home is like. You've been around mother all day, so you know what she has been up to. What father has been doing, however, is more of a mystery, and something about which you may be curious. It is in this way that father can act as a bridge between family life and society at large, enabling the small child to see that there are other concerns in life besides what is happening at home. Carrying on from this, the father then serves as a model for how to be in the world, for how to tackle the world—the one who might lay down rules of behaviour for dealing with people outside the sphere of the immediate family. From this perspective, he can be associated with Jupiter (the one who broadens your vision) and he also is very much like Saturn (the lawgiver, the one who sets rules, the one who teaches you about fitting into society). If father is linked with Saturn in this way, he then fits nicely with the 10th house (which has Saturn as its natural ruler).

But I ask you, does it always work like this in real life, even within a traditional family? If we spend so much more time in range of mother, it stands to reason that *she* is the one who ends up teaching us the most about how to behave, the one who actually lays down the rules. Therefore, mother takes up the cloak of Saturn, and for this reason, perhaps the 10th house should be assigned to her. Have you ever heard of Robert Bly? He is quite well known in America as a poet and New Age philosopher. He made one comment which has stuck in my head: he believes that the love unit most damaged by the Industrial Revolution was the father-son relationship.[19] In theory at least, before the sweeping changes effected by the Industrial Revolution, the son usually took on the father's work—the son was an apprentice to the father. This arrangement is no longer so common in the 20th century. It probably was the case last century that father worked fairly near home—mother could drop by with the child to see the father, and the small child then has a chance to observe him in action. If father is a carpenter in a workshop close by, it's pretty obvious what he's up to when you visit him. But if he is employed in a huge office building miles away in the city, his work and what he does during the day is much more obscure and abstract. It may be quite hard for a father to get across to his young son what his work entails if his job involves sitting at a computer all day or shuffling papers around. He therefore may have less of an influence than your mother on how you behave in the world later in life.

I normally attribute the 10th house to the parent who shapes us the most, who had the dominant influence on us. The parent who is less known, who is more of mystery is then assigned to the 4th. In practice, I usually discuss with my clients something about how they saw each parent, and this helps me to decide which house fits best with mother or father. And I'll make a confession to you— sometimes I read both houses for each parent. I know in my own chart, and you might check this out in yours as well, that if I take the 10th house as mother I glean a great deal of interesting information about my mother and myself. If I then read the 4th as father, I can make connections and learn more about my perception of father and my issues with him by assessing the placements there. But if the mood grabs me, I sometimes switch the houses around, looking at the 10th as my father and the 4th as my mother,

---

[19]Robert Bly and Keith Thompson, "What Men Really Want," in *Challenge of the Heart*, edited by J. Welwood (Boston: Shambhala Publications, 1985), pp. 100–116.

and I gain additional insights which make a lot of sense to me. Am I copping out and being a wimp by not taking a stand? I prefer to call it flexibility. There could be a psychological reason why the 10th and 4th are interchangeable: these houses form a polarity, and in any polarity or opposition, one side has a way of changing into the other and vice versa. Mother and father can be seen as a polarity. Perhaps the parents originally were attracted to each other because one lives out what is latent or denied in the other, and together they make a whole. This kind of emotional division of labour is not uncommon in couples. What is hidden or latent in one parent is expressed or lived out more obviously in the other, but in actual fact they each possess both traits. In this sense they are interchangeable, and may even take turns playing out each role—hence, the reversibility of the parental houses. All this is something you can think about. As you can see, I don't have a definite answer to the quandary of which parent goes with which house. It may bother some people, but it doesn't bother me to leave it somewhat open-ended.

Paul's chart is an exceptionally good example of how confusing it can be to decide which house is which parent. I took the 4th to be father in his case, and I'll explain my reasons in due course. But can you see why his chart makes the 4th-10th house question confusing to begin with?

Audience: The ruler of the 4th (Neptune) is in the 10th.

Howard: Yes, that's it. When you find the ruler of one of the parental houses placed in the other parental house, it may be the case that one parent had to be both mother and father. This is true for Paul up to age 4 and well beyond that. One reason I put Paul's mother with his 10th is that she was much more obvious and present than the father and had the most direct influence on him in his early formative years. She shaped him, she set the rules for how he should behave in the world. She actually educated him at home for a while, and she influenced his choice of career. Let me explain the situation in greater detail.

As we know, Bill reappeared when Paul was 4, but Paul never really accepted him. He continued to use his mother as a model for how to be and act in the world, and spent much more time with her than with his father. This inclined me to read the 10th house for her. Therefore, the 4th is father, and we find the Moon in Pisces right on the cusp. The Moon rules Cancer on the cusp of Paul's 9th, which fits with the father being abroad for so many years, and also fits with the fact that the father was a fantasy figure. Paul knew he existed somewhere but he wasn't there to be seen, he wasn't concrete. I know you can argue that this could also apply to Neptune in the 10th if you wanted to make a case for associating the 10th house with Bill. But other factors still lead me to associate the 10th with his mother. The ruler of the 10th is Mercury, and we find that Mercury is conjunct Uranus in Paul's chart—this brings something Uranian into the 10th. His mother is an Aquarius (coruled by Uranus) with the Moon in Mercury-ruled Gemini, so the rulers of her Sun and Moon figure with Paul's 10th house. Also, if mother is associated with the 10th, we find Neptune there, an indication of Paul's fusion with her—although this also could be explained by the Moon in Pisces on the IC, if you wanted to make a case for attributing the 4th house to mother. I'll tell you what really decided it for me though. I asked Paul to describe his father and this was his reply:

> My father was the youngest of eight children and he was always the baby in his family [Moon on the IC]. Everyone always looked after him, everyone was always doing things for him. He stayed like that his whole life. We didn't do a lot with each other, but one of the few things we did do occasionally was to go fishing [Pisces on the 4th]. But even when we went fishing, I had to tie his hooks for him. He couldn't even tackle up himself!

I associate his father being a baby with Paul's Moon on the cusp of the 4th. And fishing was one of the few things they did together—that slayed me, it's so Piscean. The phrase "to tackle up" is a fishing term for putting hook and bait onto a fishing pole. Remember that archetypally father is meant to show you how to tackle the world, but here is the son literally "tackling up" for his father! I wasn't sure of whether Paul was aware of it or not, but he reported all this to me with a great deal of condescension. If we don't get what we need from father, we may (as in Paul's case) be left very angry with him. Are you angry (or hurt, or sad) about the quality of fathering you received? Think about it.

We have to leave things here for right now. In the next session both Liz and I will carry on with the case study bringing in the charts of Bill and Max. I'm sure Liz will have pertinent comments to add to all this.

PART THREE

THE CONIUNCTIO

THE SUN AND MOON IN THE HOROSCOPE

A DISCUSSION USING EXAMPLE HOROSCOPES

BY LIZ GREENE AND HOWARD SASPORTAS

Howard: We'll begin tonight's talk by carrying on with Paul's case history, bringing in the charts of Bill (his father) and Max (his son) (see Charts 3 and 5 on pp. 170 and 180). We will also take some time to discuss the lunar aspects we haven't yet covered.

I have a few more general points to make on the issue of father-son rivalry. We have analysed this conflict from two angles: the son in the Oedipal stage wanting to get rid of father, and the father feeling threatened that eventually his son will outshine and overtake him in terms of power, authority, status or prowess—thereby inclining the father to cut off from his son, compete with him, or stand in the way of his growth and development. While it's natural and quite human for fathers and sons to have these kinds of negative undercurrents with one another, I also find it a little sad. Every son craves to be loved, appreciated and admired by his father, and yet so many factors can obstruct this happening. A son needs his father's blessing, but how often does he succeed in getting it? I'm reminded of Greek mythology again. The early Greek myths are mostly stories about families, and some of the things that fathers and children do to one another are pretty hair-raising. Consider the case of Ouranus shoving his newly born children back into his wife's womb, not wishing they should exist. Kronos (Saturn), one of his sons, then plots with his mother to castrate his father. I mean this is juicy Sunday tabloid stuff. Kronos, however, is not much better as a father. He fears one of his progeny will topple him from his position of power, so he swallows them alive. He doesn't want them to see the light, he won't allow them to be and grow (which also might signify the kind of father who doesn't want his sons or daughters to ever separate from him, who can't let go of them or accept that they may think differently from him—an issue which is rampant when an offspring reaches puberty). Zeus showed some improvement in terms of fathering; he hated a number of his children, but he did foster and encourage some of his many others. Dionysus is an example of the latter. Semele was pregnant with Dionysus when she was killed by one of the revengeful Hera's nasty tricks. Zeus freed the foetus from its dead mother's womb and sewed it into his own thigh, later giving birth to Dionysus himself. So we see some progression in Greek mythology; compared with Ouranus and Kronos, Zeus shows more fairness—at least to some of his children. Jean Shinoda Bolen in her book, *Gods in Everyman*, suggests that Zeus' active participation in the birth of Dionysus foreshadows the modern father who wants to be present during the birth of his children and play a more active role in nurturing and caring for them.[1]

Let's get on with Paul's story. Before his father returned from Canada, Paul and his mother cohabitated in a cosy little bungalow outside a town in the north of England. His mother, faced with having to earn a living to augment what his father was receiving from the RAF, ran a smallholding—a plot where vegetables are grown and then sold to local shops. Paul loved living alone with his mother in the countryside, and she was coping surprisingly well without her husband there. Then as transiting Saturn and Pluto hit Paul's Venus, his father returned and their lives changed dramatically. Paul suspects that Bill (a proud Leo, by the way) didn't like what he found when he got back, that he resented how independent his wife had become and how well she seemed to have managed without him. Whatever his motivation, Bill decided that they should sell the bungalow and smallholding, and move into the neighbouring town to start a grocery shop. You can imagine how much this pleased Paul. No longer alone with his mother, no longer living in the countryside, the three of them ended up in a flat above the shop in the middle of an industrial town. And yet it was mother who was the driving force in building up the shop; even though father was back, she remained Paul's prominent model for dealing with the world. He told me:

---

[1]Jean Shinoda Bolen, *Gods in Everyman* (San Francisco: HarperCollins, 1989), p. 295.

Mother worked hard and Dad would just go out drinking at night. The thing I remember most about my late childhood is in the evenings, sitting in front of the television with my mother. He is at the pub, drinking with his mates. He is never, never there at home. [Paul's Sun square Neptune, and Pisces on the 4th.]

If we are not getting what we need from father, we may search for father substitutes to fill that gap. Paul found a few — a neighbour who not only first taught him to fish, but also introduced him to a lifelong love of music. There is no doubt that Neptune and Pisces are strong in Paul's chart. In fact, by the time he was a teenager, Paul displayed a talent for drawing, and a teacher encouraged him to put it to practical use by training as an architect. His artistic flair is further shown by Mars in Aries in the 5th trine to a Venus–North Node conjunction in Leo. It was the 1950's, and men were expected to be "men" in that part of England, which ruled out something so unmanly as Paul going into the fine arts — although the internationally acclaimed painter, David Hockney, originated from this region and managed to rebel against such constrictions. It also turns out that Paul's mother's first sweetheart (before she met Bill) had become a thriving and wealthy architect, and Paul theorises that she still carried a torch for him. Perhaps choosing to pursue this profession was one way of exacting revenge on his father. (Paul, after all, does have Scorpio rising — a sign which usually knows exactly where to stick the knife.)

Paul left formal schooling in his midteens to work as an apprentice in an architect's office. His mother continued to tutor him at home so that he would acquire the necessary qualifications. Since he worked during the day, Paul would often spend his nights studying or drawing in his room. Listen to what Paul has to say about his father's reaction to the path he was following:

While I was studying at home, my bedroom was my office. Particularly in the winter, I used to draw into the small hours and my father resented this because he said I was using too much electricity. The only power socket for our home was outside the house. My father would stagger back from the pub, and before coming inside, he would turn off the power socket so that my heat and light would go out. Then we

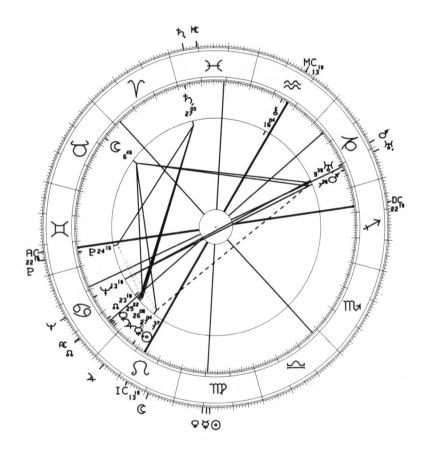

Chart 3. Bill, Paul's father. The birth data has been withheld for confidentiality. Chart calculated by Astrodienst, using the Placidus house system.

would have a big argument. It happened a lot—he thought I was effeminate in pursuing architecture. Later when I did get into architecture school, he once threw a fit, screaming, "I'll take you out of that nancy art college and get you a real job!"

So much for a son receiving his father's blessing. You won't find a much more concrete example than this of a father literally trying to undermine his son's *power*. There is no doubt that Paul's Oedipal complex was still raging, but when we hear how his father obstructed his progress and blocked his path of individuation, I can only conclude that Bill suffered from a whopping great "Laius complex."

It's definitely time to turn to Bill's chart (see Chart 3, page 170). The outer circle shows the progressions happening on the first of August, 1943, shortly after Paul's birth. Also please bear in mind that the transits to Bill's chart at the time of his son's birth are the natal placements in Paul's chart (see Chart 2, page 150). Initially, I was surprised by some of the progressions and transits in Bill's chart which correlated with Paul's birth. If we look at them more closely, you'll see what I mean. There is a progressed stellium in Virgo; the progressed Sun is 12 Virgo, progressed Mercury is 11 Virgo, and progressed Venus is in 9 Virgo. What house is this hitting in Bill's chart?

Audience: It's around the cusp of the 5th house.

Howard: Yes, the house of children. Focus on progressed Venus on the cusp of the 5th. Is it making any aspects to Bill's chart?

Audience: It is in exact trine with Bill's 8th house Uranus.

Howard: How might you interpret this progressed trine?

Audience: Something new is happening in Bill's life which is stimulating and positive. Because it's Venus entering the 5th house of children and making a trine to Uranus, it suggests that Bill is pleased or excited about Paul's birth.

Howard: I agree, although it could also have been a new, hot affair. Who knows what Bill got up to in Canada? Maybe he met someone who couldn't resist that RAF uniform. But that's not the point I wish to make. Progressions show the inner meaning of an event, and this is a very nice one to have at the time of the birth of one's first child – a son to boot. Bill's progressed Sun in the 5th house of children is also coming up to sextile his Neptune in the 2nd, which leads me to conject that Bill felt more worthy now that he had a son. And look at Bill's progressed ascendant at 22 degrees Cancer; it's smack on his North Node to the degree. The sign of the North Node shows qualities that we should strive to develop in the name of growth and evolution. The progressed ascendant is activating his Cancer North Node. I would interpret this as a chance for Bill to get more in touch with his capacity to care and nurture. I wouldn't label that a "bad" progression; it's an opportunity for Bill's feelings to open up and expand. Knowing the difficulties Bill and Paul experienced with one another later, I was surprised to see such "good" progressions around for Bill at the time of Paul's birth.

Turn your attention to the transits to Bill's chart when Paul was born, which also show the synastry between them. There are a number of contacts which I would see as positive. Paul has Jupiter at 28 Cancer, quite close to Bill's natal Venus, Jupiter, and Mercury, trining his Saturn, and, in terms of transits, only six weeks or so away from his Sun. So Paul was born during Bill's Jupiter return in Cancer. These transits and interaspects make me think that some part of Bill's psyche felt joyful and expansive about becoming a father, and indicate the possibility of a good relationship between father and son. I explained all this to Paul and he filled me in on more detail. It turns out that his parents had been trying to conceive a child for fifteen years before they scored a goal with him. Also, as I said earlier, Bill was the youngest of eight children (the 3rd house of siblings is packed in his chart), but none of his brothers and sisters had yet produced any offspring. Bill, at 36, was the first to do so. The fact that his seven siblings (all older than he) hadn't yet parented is curious in itself – I wonder what their parenting was like to have put them off it. In any case, think of the kudos for leonine Bill to beat them at something and produce the first grandchild for his mother and father. Paul then told me something very interesting. After Bill's death, he had gotten hold of a diary his father had been keeping at the time Paul was born. In it were drawings Bill had done—what Paul called "smiling, sentimental pictures" of a father with his baby son. My mind was full of questions. Why, if the birth meant so much to Bill, did it take him four years to finally return to England? Surely he could have swung something with the RAF to arrange this. And the $64,000 question: Why, when he did get back, was he unable to show the love and positive feelings engendered by Paul's birth?

Bill's other transits at the time of Paul's birth do provide some answers to these questions. Take a look at Paul's Saturn in 17 degrees of Gemini—is it close to anything in Bill's chart?

Audience: The Ascendant.

Howard: Yes, Paul's Saturn is 4 degrees from Bill's Ascendant and 7 degrees from his Pluto—orbs I would consider in synastry. The house Saturn is transiting is where we have "work" to do, and this often involves being made aware of our vulnerability or weak spots and doing what is necessary to deepen or strengthen ourselves in that area. The fact that transiting Saturn was going through Bill's 12th suggests that unconscious feelings left over from Bill's past were stirred by Paul's birth; and in some way these have a Gemini slant to them. Similarly, transiting Saturn (Paul's natal Saturn) is heading toward Bill's Pluto, another indication that what is hidden or dark in Bill's psyche is somehow asking for attention. I decided to play astrological detective. My main clue was that all this was occurring in the sign of Gemini, which always makes me think of sibling relationships. I was wondering about a possible connection between the arrival of Paul and unfinished business Bill had with one or more of his brothers or sisters. Paul had already told me that Bill was very pleased about being the first of them to father. I asked Paul if he knew more about how Bill had gotten along with his siblings, and he described an intense rivalry between Bill and one particular brother. The two brothers were jealous and competitive; they had even played on rival cricket teams (note that Bill's 3rd house Leo Sun is inconjunct Mars in Capricorn, another indication of battles with a sibling). As you know, Bill ran a small grocery shop, but the brother in question was involved with a very large and very successful chain of grocery shops. Because of the Gemini contacts between the charts of Paul and Bill, I suspected that Paul could be a catalyst to stir Bill's sibling issues; Paul's birth meant there was another male in the family, and it could reactivate the competitive feelings Bill had with his brother.

You may think that the transference of sibling rivalry onto a son is farfetched, but I'm sure it happens. And even if that doesn't seem a good enough source for some of Bill's trouble with Paul, all you need to do is to look at Paul's natal Pluto, which is the transit Pluto was making to Bill's chart when he was born. Can you see it?

Audience: Yes, Paul's Pluto is 5 degrees Leo, very close to Bill's Sun in 7 Leo, which means that transiting Pluto was very close to Bill's Sun when Paul was born.

Howard: Yes, well spotted. When a father has his first son, he dies as the son and is reborn a father, which is one way we can interpret the Pluto transit to Bill's Sun. But Pluto transits to the Sun also arouse feelings and issues to do with one's own father—not surprising if you consider that Bill has just become a father himself. Paul wasn't clear about Bill's relationship with his father (Paul's grandfather), but I had some suspicions. There were eight children in Bill's family, which can only mean there must have been quite a bit of competition for the father's attention. Bill could be suffering from father hunger, and all the hurt and anger that entails. Since Paul's Pluto is on Bill's Sun (the significator for father), it is not unlikely that Paul somehow reawakened negative feelings that Bill had toward his father. These feelings could have obstructed Bill's bonding with Paul, in spite of the fact that the "smiling, sentimental" pictures of father and son found in Bill's diary indicate that he had hoped for a good relationship with the newly born, long-awaited son.

Bill's Pluto is 24 degrees Gemini and Paul's Sun is 0 Cancer. It's out of sign, but I would still consider it a conjunction. So not only is Paul's Pluto on Bill's Sun, but Bill's Pluto is close to Paul's Sun. You just can't get away from Pluto with these two. We have talked about the Sun in terms of individuation and the urge to develop one's identity, power and authority—to shine in some way. If Paul's Sun activates Bill's Pluto, it indicates that Paul's attempt to individuate and grow triggers off complexes in Bill—complexes related to Bill's sibling rivalry or Bill's father hunger. So any move Paul makes to realise his solar potential will not feel comfortable to Bill, who sees him as a rival or threat — not to mention the fact that Paul reconnects Bill to the hurt and pain he felt toward his father.

Liz: These charts are certainly terribly interesting, and there are a few points I would like to pick up on in relation to the Sun and Moon. One thing which keeps striking me as you talk about Bill and Paul is the mythic background of the solar hero myth, enacted as is so often the case through an envious father (an unlived Sun in Leo) who tried to block the son's potential because he could not fulfil his own.

There are other cross-aspects between these charts which haven't been mentioned yet, but which I think are very important. Bill's Saturn is in an out-of-sign square to Paul's Sun. I have been thinking about Paul's Sun in Cancer, and about what kind of individual he is — someone who is ruled by the Moon and who obviously possesses a rich creative imagination as well as great sensitivity and depth of feeling. This aspect seems to be the focal point for the envy Bill feels toward Paul. I have found that a parent's Saturn in conjunction or hard aspect to a child's Sun almost always suggests envy on the part of the parent, because Saturn has a way of choking up the life force of the sign in which it is placed. Destructive envy usually springs from what we have most difficulty in living in ourselves. Bill's Saturn in Pisces implies that he finds it very difficult to express his dependency on others, and his child's naturally emotional and dependent Cancerian nature must have made him feel shy, awkward and resentful. Also, Bill has probably had trouble giving sufficient value to his own inner imaginal world, and would probably be horrified to know that Paul saw his "smiling, sentimental pictures." Saturn in Pisces is extremely sentimental, but would prefer that no one knew it — not even oneself. And Paul's readiness to pursue an imaginative vocation must also have hurt Bill and mirrored back to him his own feelings of inadequacy. It is very sad about those "sentimental" drawings, because Bill obviously has some artistic talent. He is a true Neptunian.

Howard: And it comes out in his drinking.

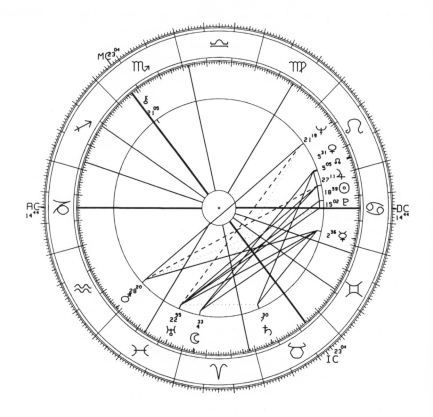

Chart 4. *Composite chart for Paul and his father, Bill. Chart calculated by Astrodienst, using the Placidus house system.*

Liz: It usually does, if there are no other outlets for Neptune's fantasy world. So all the frustrated imaginal life in Bill reacts to Paul's open expression of the very thing that causes Bill the most pain—albeit unconsciously. From one point of view, Bill is the "bad guy" in this drama. But if we look at it from another perspective, it is not so simple. A parent's Saturn, even though it may thwart and criticise, can have a powerfully positive effect on the child's Sun as well, even though the method is painful. Nothing makes us aware of what we are as strongly as someone telling us we are not supposed to be it. I would guess that Bill's attempts to obstruct his son have a lot to do with Paul's determination to develop himself, even though it has cost him a lot. He finds out what he really values, what he truly wants to become, by virtue of the fact that such a fuss is made about it. There is the myth again—the solar hero becomes a hero because he is obstructed, not because he is cosseted. The Sun needs an external father-authority against which to pit itself, in order to grow. If someone keeps telling us we should not do something, it begins to dawn on us that perhaps it is really worth doing. No doubt Adam and Eve would not have touched the fruit if they had not been told to stay away from it.

There are other cross-aspects which interest me between these charts, which support the happy aspects occurring in Bill's chart when Paul was born. I have the feeling that there is very deep, albeit unconscious, love between Bill and Paul. It is very sad that they care about each other so intensely and deeply, and also idealise each other, but cannot express anything other than envy and resentment. Paul's Venus conjuncts Bill's Sun and IC, another aspect between the charts which hasn't yet been talked about. This suggests a deep identification and affection. No matter what he says, Paul appreciates who his father is at core, and secretly admires and values that proud Leonine nature, regardless of the unpleasantness of Bill's behaviour. But the Sun-Saturn cross-aspect, as well as the Sun-Pluto conjunctions between the charts, have made this loving bond inexpressible.

I would also like to look at the composite chart for the relationship between Bill and Paul (See Chart 4 on p. 176). The Sun and Moon in the composite, and the aspects of the composite chart to Bill's and Paul's Sun and Moon placements, are very interesting as well. There is a Sun-Pluto conjunction in the composite. As you say, Howard, these two cannot get away from Pluto. This conjunction suggests a terrific emotional intensity and passion, as well as the likelihood of a power battle, with each of them trying to change or annihilate the other one. They are obsessed with each other. We can look at the composite Sun in exactly the same way as we look at the Sun in a birth chart—it is the essential identity of the relationship. And we can apply the whole of the hero myth to it, and understand the composite Sun as a process of becoming which never really finishes. On the most basic level, the composite Sun in Cancer describes a relationship rooted in deep emotional need and a shared creative talent.

There is also a Venus-Node conjunction in the composite, virtually exact (only 4 minutes of arc between them), and this pair is in turn trine the composite Moon in Aries. Once again I get the feeling of intense love and admiration buried underneath the layers of envy and resentment.

Howard: The potential for it is there. What do you think gets in the way of it?

Liz: Envy, with all its complicated roots. And fear of the vulnerability and dependency which intense love inevitably brings. But I think this love is more than a potential. It is a given. When people go on and on *ad nauseam* about what a dreadful parent they had, you can be pretty certain that there is deeply injured love underneath. Otherwise it would not be necessary to slag off the offending parent quite so vehemently. People can only really hurt us if we care about them, and the composite Venus-Node trine Moon, as well as the cross-conjunction between Paul's Venus and Bill's Sun, reflects that love.

It is also interesting to note that the transit of Pluto over Bill's Sun at Paul's birth (which is also Paul's natal Pluto) was at the same time transiting right over the Venus-Node conjunction in the composite, and forming a trine to the composite Moon. Transits over composite planets are always very revealing, because they reflect a time when that particular quality in the relationship is activated. The deep love between these two came to birth at the time Paul came to birth. There is not much more one can say about this transit in the composite chart, except to stare at it and mutter, "Oh, look, composite charts work."

The composite Saturn is 7 Taurus. Composite Saturn reflects that area where a relationship is uncomfortable, painful and restricted, and here it is in the 3rd house of communication. So these two have considerable difficulty in saying what they really feel to each other. There is a dishonesty between them, springing from Saturnian pride and fear and defensiveness. Both will cut off their noses to spite their faces, and cannot admit any vulnerability or need to each other. This is also part of the problem between them. If Bill could have said, "I really admire your talent. I always wished I could do something artistic but life let me down, and I envy you . . ." Or if Paul could have said, "I really need your appreciation and love, and it hurts me when you're critical . . ." But nothing of the sort could happen with this 3rd house composite Saturn. Saturn is also in square to composite Venus, so there are powerful feelings of rejection and a walling off of love and need, which both are party to.

This composite Saturn in 7 Taurus is in very tight conjunction with Bill's natal Moon. Now we are in the lunar domain. What do any of you in the group think might be reflected by Bill's 12th House Moon in Taurus? What are his essential emotional needs?

Audience: Security.

Liz: Yes, he needs security and material stability. He also needs a lot of physical affection, whether he is aware of this or not. The Moon in Taurus loves to be touched and fussed over and held. Being the last of eight children must have been a little rough for Bill on this count, because he had to wait in the queue. And the Moon is rather lost in the 12th, suggesting that the need for physical affection and closeness was a problem throughout the family background. Planets in the 12th often represent needs which cannot find expression through the family psyche, and which lie beneath the surface in the individual, creating deep unconscious hungers which always threaten to erupt and disturb outer life. I get the impression of a family where no one touched or hugged each other, or admitted the need for physical contact.

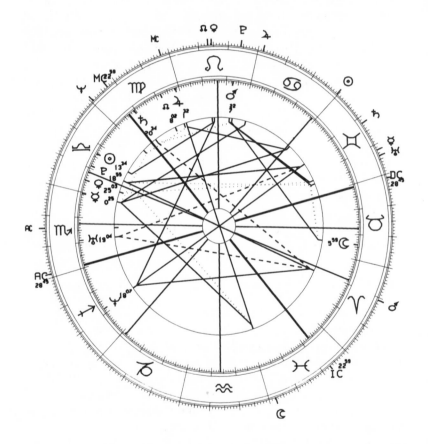

Chart 5. Paul's son, Max. The birth data has been withheld for confidentiality. Chart calculated by Astrodienst, using the Placidus house system.

Howard: Liz, can I come in here? Take a look at Max's chart (see Chart 5 page 180), which has Paul's natal placements in the outer rim. It touched me to hear Liz speak about the love Bill and Paul had for one another, although neither was able to easily express these feelings. Paul told me that he has become much more emotional since Max was born. One astrological factor for this is that Max's Uranus is conjunct Paul's Scorpio Ascendant—in other words, around the time Max was conceived and born, transiting Uranus was waking up Paul's watery Ascendant. Remember what Paul said about Max? I told it to you earlier, but I'll read it to you in full this time:

> Since Max was born everything is more heightened, more scary and yet more valuable. And I worry about being a good father to him. I want to care for Max in the best way, but it doesn't come instinctively, it's not what is built in. I look at him when he is asleep, and I feel a rush—you know, scarlet ribbons—but I can't always get through to him on a daily basis when he is awake. I sometimes unleash thunderbolts at him that surprise me.

I imagine that Bill could have said something very similar about Paul. This is a good example of how patterns are repeated or passed on from one generation to the next.

Bill was 35 years and 11 months old when he had Paul. Paul was 36 when Max was born. It may be sheer coincidence, but somehow it seems curious that Bill and Paul both had their first child at the same age. Now, here is something I find very interesting. Paul's progressed Sun was 5 Leo when Max came along, which means that his progressed Sun was on his natal Pluto in Leo at that time. This afternoon I said that Pluto in Leo suggests father issues because Pluto has to do with depth, darkness and complexity, and Leo is one sign associated with father. Progressed Sun over natal Pluto in Leo is a sure indication that father stuff was "up" for Paul when Max was born. Bill's natal Sun is 7 Leo, so for the first two years that Paul fathered Max, his progressed Sun was coming up to the same place as his own father's natal Sun. There has got to be a connection between their issues around fathers and fathering. Also, Max's natal Mars is 7 Leo, the exact degree of his grandfather's Sun, and only two degrees away from Paul's Pluto and the position of Paul's progressed Sun during Max's early, formative years. To top it all, this is happening on the Venus-Node conjunction in 5 Leo we found in the composite for Bill and Paul. Something just hit me—it's fairly obvious but I hadn't thought of it before. When Bill returned to England in 1947, his presence disrupted the cosy twosome that Paul and his mother had become. Likewise, Max was Paul's first child, and though he was very welcome, he invariably would have disturbed whatever peace and routine Paul and his wife had established living on their own together. Now Paul had to share his wife with Max, just as he once had to learn to share his mother with Bill.

I've one more point to add here. I interviewed Paul on the 23rd of June, 1989, the day after his 46th birthday. When Paul arrived he commented that it was interesting to be meeting with me today to discuss the relationships with his father and son, because the night before he had this enormous row with Max. I listened carefully to the story he had to tell—it reminded me of the way some therapists begin their first session with a new client by asking what he or she dreamt last night. When you know you are going to see an astrologer or any form of counsellor, important issues very often come to the surface in the immediate week or so prior to the appointment. Anyway, Paul told me that Max wanted to go out to the local shops on his own, and that he refused this request because it was already dark and perhaps a little dangerous considering the neighbourhood in which they lived. Max was angry at not getting his way and shouted, "You goddamn bastard!" to his father's face. Paul reacted angrily, yelling, "Nobody calls me a goddamn bastard on my birthday," and the evening's celebrations were ruined. I checked the ephemeris and noted Mars nearly in 4 Leo when the argument took place. There was Mars, so close to Paul's Pluto, and not far from Max's natal Mars and the ghost of Bill's Sun. Surely, it's not just coincidence. I can only feel awe and admiration for whoever (or whatever) has the task of organising who gets what birthchart so that things match up like this! Anyone who studies astrology in depth will see an awesome higher intelligence at work.

Liz: Do you know what makes it even more awesomely intelligent? Guess where Saturn is placed in Paul's and Max's composite. It is in 4 Leo, with transiting Mars dead on it on the night of the quarrel. Where else could it possibly be? (See Chart 6 on page 184.)

Howard: Not every single case is astrologically as clear as this one, although I must admit I've seen many that are. What is also striking about the interconnections between Bill, Paul and Max is the prominence of Pluto and Scorpio. Bill was born with Pluto rising; Paul has a Scorpio Ascendant and Pluto on his father's Sun and Max's Mars. Max has Sun conjunct Pluto with Scorpio rising. The composite for Bill and Paul has Sun conjunct Pluto in Cancer, and the composite for Paul and Max shows Scorpio rising yet again. With Pluto and Scorpio on the rampage in this male lineage, it's not surprising we are talking about heavy undercurrents, unconscious rivalries, anger, and deeply felt love which is not easy to express. Paul's case history highlights these issues, but I believe you'll find similar difficulties and frustrations to varying degrees in many father-son relationships.

Liz: The difficulties are part of the archetypal background, and I agree that they are usually to be found between father and son. In this case history the mythic themes seem to revolve around Pluto's underworld symbolism. There is also a heavy weight in Leo, so the issues of individual creative expression and heroic battle with the underworld demons is also very pronounced as a male family myth. In Bill's chart, the Sun is in Leo at the IC. Even though it is technically in the 3rd house, it is within orb of conjunction of the cusp of the 4th, and it makes no major aspects except a square to the Moon and a few inconjuncts. This Sun at the IC point, symbolic of the relationship with father and father's line, makes me think of the story of Parsifal, who is the most leonine of mythic heroes.

In this story we find the theme of redemption of the father's wound, and transformation of his failed life force. Parsifal is not heroic in the usual sense, since he is not a fighter. He stumbles upon a mystery, where the Grail King is old and sick and has a wound which will not heal, and the kingdom is a wasteland. Here is an image of the failed life force, where faith and hope and growth have vanished. Parsifal is a holy fool. He has no idea what he has stumbled upon, and fails to ask the right question—what is

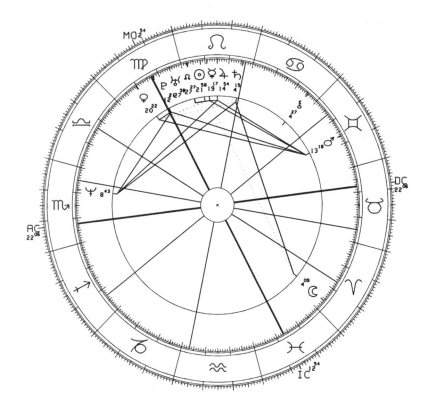

Chart 6. *Composite chart for Paul and his son, Max. Chart calculated by Astrodienst, using the Placidus house system.*

the Grail, and whom does it serve? Ultimately it is his compassion for the wounded Grail King, the injured father, which allows him to redeem himself, the king, and the kingdom. He cannot find the right question until he has sufficient identification with his father, which can only come through recognising that he is wounded in the same way.

It seems to me that this theme is stated twice in Bill's chart—once by the fact that the Sun is in Leo, and again by its conjunction with the IC, suggesting that the dilemma is an inherited one.

Howard: I'm dying to come in here.

Liz: All right, as soon as I finish nattering about Parsifal. You don't by any chance have Bill's father's chart?

Howard: No, I'm sorry. Based on what we know about Bill, Paul and Max, we probably wouldn't have too much trouble making it up right now.

Liz: Yes, I'm sure we could. There would inevitably be something in 5 Leo.

Howard: But I've got something good here once you're done.

Liz: All right. The theme of the redemption of the lost or wounded father is a family theme which runs through all three generations. Although Paul is not a Leo, he has a stellium of Pluto, Venus, Node and Chiron in the sign. In the composite between Bill and Paul, Venus and the Node are in Leo. Max arrives and the composite Sun between Paul and Max is of course in Leo. It goes on and on. These poor men are all holy fools blundering about seeking the Grail, yet not understanding that it can only be recognised if they can find compassion for the wounds of their fathers. Over to you.

Howard: I'd like to add something I'm just seeing now. Liz mentioned Bill's Moon in 6 Taurus, and the fact that his Taurean needs for physical touch and closeness in order to feel safe and secure were probably unrequited because of the size of his family of origin. Do you see anything around 6 Taurus in Max's chart? Yes, his

Moon is 5 degrees 59 minutes of Taurus—very close to Bill's Moon. The same kinds of needs that were there in Bill are there in Max, and Paul is the mediator. If he can help to fulfil Max's Taurean Moon in this way, he is making up for what his father craved and didn't get. It's interesting that Max's Moon is within orb of a conjunction to Chiron—the planet that shows woundedness. The Leo stuff we were talking about before (Bill's Sun, Paul's Pluto and Max's Mars) all square the Taurus placements, creating more tension, bringing issues to do with pride, specialness and other ego-related needs and problems into the bargain. Liz also noted that the composite between Bill and Paul shows Saturn in 7 Taurus.

Liz: I think that is very important, because the composite Saturn between Bill and Paul sits on Bill's Moon. Composite planets which make close aspects to the natal planets in one individual's chart indicate an area where the relationship as an entity impinges powerfully on the individual. There is something in this relationship— the communication block—which constricts Bill and makes him uncomfortably aware of those unfulfilled Taurus needs which he has always been so good at hiding. Maybe he didn't even know how much he needed touch and affection until he had a son who activated the need. And the dilemma of all this frustrated physical contact will also involve Max in some way.

Howard: Exactly, Max brings up unfinished business between Bill and Paul.

Liz: Can we have a brief interval until Max has a son?

Howard: Yes, come back in fifteen years.

Liz: There is a very strange way in which unresolved issues come back over and over again through each succeeding generation. Are you sure you didn't make up these charts?

Howard: I honestly didn't, but sometimes I think I did because of how much I discovered by delving this deeply into them. You can learn an enormous amount if you take the time to set up the charts of as many family members as you can get hold of, even if these are only solar charts. We haven't even looked at the charts of Paul's mother, Paul's wife, or Max's younger sister. Paul's wife has an interesting chart (see Chart 7 on page 188) because she has Mars at 5 Taurus conjunct Venus at 11 Taurus square Pluto at 8 Leo.

Liz: Of course she does. What did he do, find her by mail order? We can see the dominant mythic themes in this family very clearly. The Leo emphasis suggests the motif of redemption of the father's wounded spirit. The Taurus emphasis suggests issues concerned with withholding and possessiveness (think of the story of the Minotaur). The Pluto emphasis suggests the need for an underworld journey, and a confrontation with the darkest dimensions of the personality. Both Taurus and Scorpio tend to be rather unforgiving, and there is a long backlog of resentment and withholding of affection because of wounded dignity. And there is also a Cancer emphasis between Bill and Paul, which seems to talk about midwifing the images of the inner world and anchoring them in some creative form.

Howard: One more thing, Liz

Liz: What have you got?

Howard: Paul and Max both have the same sign on the IC. Paul's father image is coloured by Pisces, and Max's image of father is also Piscean if you take his 4th house to be the father.

Liz: Recurrent family themes can appear even through factors like missing elements. In this case, it is specific signs and planets, even specific degrees, which repeat themselves. But sometimes the inherited myths can be reflected in other ways.

Howard: Because Bill and Max share the same Moon, the composite charts for Bill and Paul, and for Max and Paul, both yield the same Moon—4 degrees Aries. When Paul and I arranged to meet last year in order to begin exploring all of this, transiting Uranus was retrograding back over 4 Capricorn squaring that shared composite Moon. Uranus is the planet commonly associated with astrology, and its transits are famous for waking people up and heralding

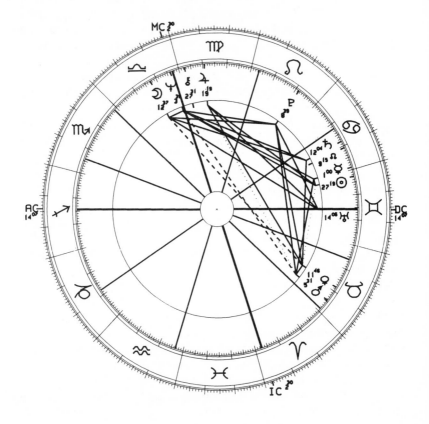

Chart 7. Paul's wife. The birth data has been withheld for confidentiality. Chart calculated by Astrodienst, using the Placidus house system.

breakthrough. The square of transiting Uranus to 4 Aries was an apt time for Paul, through the insight and self-understanding generated by astrological symbolism, to awaken more fully to the unresolved feelings and complexes stemming from his experience of his own father, and to connect these with some of the difficulties he is meeting in the relationship with his own son.

I'd like to take a few minutes to make some concluding remarks on fathers and sons, and then we can move on to other topics. It is important to face and deal with the external concerns or problems that exist or existed between you and father; it is even more essential to do work on healing the *internal image* or inner picture of father you carry inside. In other words – and this is true for both men and women – we need to make peace with and heal "the wounded father" within ourselves.[2] One step in this process is to explore the past and start cleaning that up, but I don't think it ends there. We also need to create fresh, positive images of what a father could be, a more complete picture of a man as a nurturer and carer. Earlier today I talked about the significance of Uranus and Neptune moving through Capricorn in this respect: the time is right for new images of fathering. I would like to conclude my bit here with the picture I have of positive fathering, which is an image I just can't shake off. William Sloan Coffin (ironically the former dean of a bastion of the patriarchy, Yale University in America) once remarked that "the woman who most needs to be liberated is the woman inside every man."[3] I would agree with him, although I would probably phrase it a little differently and say that a man needs to integrate or make a relationship with his *anima*, or that a man can grow through honouring and accepting the feeling side of his nature rather than solely identifying with rationality or the intellect. And I have a picture of a father who is comfortable with his feelings, who isn't afraid of his anima. If a man hasn't accepted "the feminine," he will devalue it, which is what the typical 1950's man did. Many of us here probably had fathers who fit this description. Let me create a scenario and compare how a 1950's type father would handle it with the way "the new man" would deal with the same situation. Imagine a little boy who is

---

[2]See Samuel Osherson, *Finding Our Fathers* (New York: Fawcett, 1987), chapter 7.
[3]William Sloan Coffin, cited in Bolen, *Gods in Everyman*, p. 159.

frightened to go to school for the first time, and he is crying and throwing fits. The 1950's style of father is likely to harass him, "Stop being such a baby, stop being a sissy. Men don't cry and have tantrums. I'm really embarrassed by your behaviour. Grow up, face it like a real man." In doing this, he is discounting or devaluing the boy's instinctive responses and legitimate fears brought up by having to venture into the new and the unknown. Now, let's say this little boy has a 90's type father—a man who is more accepting of feeling, a man who is willing to face emotions rather than immediately deny or run away from them. The boy is terrified of going to school, he is crying and carrying on. His new style father could comfort him, "Yes, I understand, I've been afraid too. It is not wrong to have such feelings. You are not bad because you have them." Because he is familiar with the feeling side of his own nature, he doesn't devalue or ridicule his son's emotional reactions. Such a father could then say, "I understand, it is scary to go out there in the world and face the unknown, *but there is still a tiger to be shot*, there are challenges you need to meet and things to overcome in order to grow and develop." The father is actually teaching the boy that it is all right for him to have these fears but he doesn't have to be completely overtaken or overshadowed by them. He is letting the boy know that he has choices, that there are alternatives, that he can admit to being frightened without losing face, and yet still choose to go out there and confront what he dreads. Do you follow me?

The "new father" has learned to accept and be with his feelings, but he hasn't lost sight of the value of the solar or "masculine" principle, the animus image of the hero or the warrior. He shows the boy that even with his fears and apprehensions, it is still possible to be heroic or courageous, to go out there and take risks with dignity. His son hasn't been put down in the process, as in the scenario of the typical 1950's father. The boy is then well on his way to achieving a better balance between his "masculine" and "feminine" sides. (Women, too, should strive for a better balance between the anima and the inner male. A woman compromises her wholeness if she identifies solely with her animus at the expense of her feeling nature.) So this is my image of positive fathering: it is about nurturing and caring for children without keeping them small. This kind of father doesn't just commiserate with his son and let him stay home from school; he reminds him that there is still a tiger to be shot. Or as Samuel Osherson writes in *Finding Our Fathers*, he can shelter and guide his child without keeping him an infant, and transmit "the sure, quiet knowledge that men as well as women are life-giving forces on earth."[4]

Probably the best way for you to start working through your paternal issues is to set up your father's chart—even if you don't have an accurate birth time, even if it is only a solar chart. By studying your father's birth map, you will gain a sense of what he was like *inside* as a person, what was going on for him as a fellow human being. It will help you to accept and understand him better.

Liz: Do your mother's as well. What you are really talking about, Howard, is what alchemy describes as the conjunction of Sun and Moon. I would like to take up your theme and use the alchemical images to amplify it. I wanted to mention alchemy because its central image is the *coniunctio* of Sol and Luna, the mystical marriage or *hierosgamos*, and I thought that would be an appropriate rounding off of our material on Sun and Moon.

For each individual the optimum balance of Sun and Moon will inevitably be different. There is no one normal or best balance of masculine and feminine, and moreover the balance may need to shift within one person at different junctures in life. Probably the appropriate balance is connected in some way with the Sun and Moon signs in the birth chart, and with the entire shape and blend of chart factors. Whatever our own alchemical *opus* might be about, no one else can tell us how to do it. The alchemical gold which was the goal of the work, and which the alchemists were forever insisting was not "common gold," is an image of the combination of Sun and Moon, representing the whole person. Inevitably, the question will arise, after the work we have been doing on Sun and Moon symbolism in astrology: "Fine, but how do we put these two together? Where do we begin?"

We have seen how both Sun and Moon need conscious validation and expression if a person is to feel real and fulfilled. But what if they fight? What happens if they are in square or opposition, or if

---

[4]Samuel Osherson, *Finding Our Fathers*, p. 229.

their respective signs don't mix very well? At some point they will inevitably fight, even if they are in trine, because the instincts and the conscious goals will sooner or later collide when the hero within us strives to break free of the safe world of his childhood and his past, and the child within us tries to stay with what is safe and known. This might be reflected in the chart by movements such as the progressed Moon coming into square or opposition to the natal Sun, or vice versa. Sometimes it is appropriate to give priority to one rather than the other, while continuing to value both. This might be reflected by transits and progressed aspects; if your progressed Sun has arrived in conjunction with Mars, for example, and both are being opposed by transiting Uranus, your priorities will have to go with the Sun, because it is that sort of time.

I have found the *alembic*, or alchemical flask, a helpful image, because it portrays the container within which the process of conjoining the Sun and Moon takes place. In alchemical literature, this work is described as full of crisis and conflict, and I think that you will have seen in the last two days of our seminar how this crisis and conflict are typical of the process in our own lives. The alchemical work and the hero's journey are two different images for the same process, which moves along in stages, some of action and movement and some of gestation and waiting. But all these stages—these important steps in our lives when we are more than usually aware of being both spirit and body, mind and heart, and when we are more acutely conscious of how difficult it is to get them to dialogue together—occur within the safe framework of the alembic. So what might this be within us, and what might it be in the horoscope?

In one sense, the alembic is the ego itself, the sense of "me" which is the sum total of our individual values and which provides a sense of consistency and continuity that can contain our conflicts. In another sense, the alembic is the feeling of a unified meaning, an Ariadne's thread running through all the various chapters of life, a repeating life theme which, although it may wear different costumes, always serves to mobilise our deepest resources. This dimension of the alembic I associate with the Ascendant in the birth chart. There is something very profound about the way in which the Ascendant works to bring together the dichotomy of

Sun and Moon. This sign seems to embody a set of values or a range of life experiences which always rise up to challenge us, and to which we must respond through both the instinctive wisdom of the Moon and the conscious goals of the Sun. Life keeps hitting us over the head with Ascendant issues, and through developing the values of the rising sign, inwardly as well as in our behaviour, we gradually strengthen the Sun and Moon, and discover that they can operate together with the Ascendant as the unifying link.

If we look at Paul's chart, we might consider his Scorpio Ascendant as a pointer to how he could combine his Cancer Sun and his Pisces Moon. In Paul's case, the Sun and Moon are in trine. But this does not necessarily mean they will function together in the deeper sense of an alchemical union. Both luminaries are in water, so the ground of his instinctual responses and his conscious goals will be the realm of the feelings and the imagination. But that Sun-Moon trine does not automatically tell us that Paul will be able to express as a whole person whose instinctual needs and conscious goals work in harmony. We have seen that he has had a lot of trouble expressing his feelings and his imagination, and has had to contend with considerable difficulty in his family background and in his relationship with his own son.

Howard: You know, I've been studying and practising astrology for twenty years, and I still wonder if I fully understand the significance of the Ascendant. I agree with you, though – the Ascendant-Descendant axis says something about the path you need to follow to alchemise the Sun and Moon. But I also believe that Mercury, the planet Jung would associate with the transcendant function, has a role to play in this process.

Audience: What about when the Sun is unaspected?

Liz: I will give you my usual overused metaphor for any unaspected planet. It is rather like owning a large house where a lot of people live together. Each of them knows the others, and everyone knows where their bedroom is, and they all meet in the sitting room and exchange gossip and quarrel and so on. But there is someone who lives in the basement unbeknownst to the others. This is the unaspected planet. This unknown person is a tenant in the house, but all of their movements and activities and motives and needs are not being communicated to the others. No one has bothered to explore the house to find out whether there are hidden dimensions to it, and the lonely tenant in the basement remains isolated and locked into their own fantasy world.

Have any of you seen the film, *The Enigma of Kaspar Hauser*? It is about a young man who from babyhood has been kept in total isolation, with no human contact. When he finally emerges and is brought into the civilised world, his behaviour and appearance are a shock to everyone else, and everybody else is in turn a shock to him. An unaspected planet lives in total isolation, and has not had the benefit of interchange with other chart factors to modify and integrate its nature. If something remains so unconscious, it tends to stay archaic and primitive in nature. It is the contact with consciousness and the outside world which "civilise" the various drives within the psyche, and humanise what Freud called the id. An unaspected planet is raw and archetypal in nature; it has not yet been humanised. One day an important transit or progressed aspect comes along, or another person comes along with a planet in their chart which lands on the unaspected planet, and then the unknown tenant in the basement suddenly puts a grenade under the floorboards and bursts through into the upper floors of the house. Then everyone rushes about shouting, "Good God, where did that come from?" and there is a period of chaos while one must come to terms with a new and important piece of oneself.

If the Sun is unaspected, we need to think about the myth of the solar hero, to get a sense of what this energy looks like in its most primitive form. The most creative dimension is the raw, powerful creative force, which if it can be channelled is immensely fertile and potent. The darkest dimension is the sense of messianic specialness and inflation, because the archetypal hero has not been humanised into an ordinary person. There are also other levels. The early relationship with the father is often a poor one, and usually very unconscious. There may be a sense of complete disconnection from him, resulting in the lack of a sound inner image of father to mediate the godlike power of the Sun. Then there are likely to be many problems with authority, with fathering, and with one's perception of masculinity in general. The Sun is also the sense of individual reality, and this may also be very unconscious.

Then the person may not feel real unless there are other people around mirroring him or her. The self-generating power of the Sun is not easily expressed when it is unaspected, so one wanders about asking everybody, "Tell me who I am."

Audience: Is there a chance for this to get better?

Liz: Certainly. Every month the transiting Moon will conjunct that unaspected natal Sun. And sooner or later the big boys will come along and make strong aspects. Saturn will make a hard aspect roughly every seven years. There are many chances.

Howard: Or, as Liz said, you meet someone with a placement that brings out your Sun. I've done charts for a number of people with an unaspected Sun, and in many cases they never knew their father—he died when they were young, or he disappeared for whatever reason in their early years. I've also observed the phenomenon of an unmediated solar archetype in certain cases of the Sun in hard aspect or conjunction with Neptune. Paul has Sun square Neptune and I wish you could see a photo of him—he looks like a living statue of Poseidon, a physical embodiment of that particular male archetype.

Liz: Is he covered in seaweed?

Howard: Seriously, Liz.

Audience: What about the problem of double binds, which could be created by the Sun and Moon? Father with one message, mother with another one. And the client starts turning in circles, because he or she gets stuck, and doesn't know what to do.

Liz: There is an innate double bind with the Sun and Moon, and it is in us all. There is a level where the impetus toward consciousness and individuality inevitably collides with the pull toward security and belonging. But sometimes it is more acute. In fact Bill has this problem, which is suggested by his Sun square the Moon. Hard aspects between these two—even the conjunction—imply that the basic human conflict between ego and instinct is sharpened and made more acute in that particular individual. This sharp conflict is usually reflected in the parents' marriage.

Howard: With difficult aspects between the Sun and Moon, there is a good chance that the parents had trouble getting along, and the child was caught in the cross fire. This reminds me of something I meant to comment on earlier. It can show up with difficult Sun-Moon aspects, or in a variety of other ways; it's the case where a mother does not want her son to bond with his father, as if she is claiming sole rights to the child. Her own need to be loved and feel special could be at the root of this. So a mother might try to undermine father and son getting closer. She could repeatedly say nasty things about the father to the son in an attempt to alienate him from his father. She might be intrusive, and butt in every time father and son are beginning to relate more closely. Triangles often give rise to these kinds of problems.

Liz: Another thing I think you all ought to do, as well as setting up your father's and mother's chart, is to look at the composite chart between your father and mother (you can do this even with a solar chart, although you will of course have only composite planets and aspects, and no composite Ascendant or house placements). Look at the interchange between this composite and your own birth chart, since this will say a great deal about how their relationship has affected you. Also, you might explore the composite between you and your father, and see what this does to your mother's chart; and then check the composite between you and your mother, and see what this does to your father's chart. This kind of investigation reveals great insight into your family dynamics.

Howard: You're up all night, of course.

Liz: Well, you're up for weeks, actually.

Howard: I didn't finish Moon-Neptune and Moon-Pluto aspects with the group yesterday. Why don't you do it now?

Liz: Me? Was it something I said?

Howard: Well, we'll do it together, but why don't you start? We were examining lunar aspects in light of the early love affair with mother.

Liz: All right. Off we go with Moon-Neptune. Since the Moon describes the substance you and your mother share, the qualities which your mother seemed to possess and which had the greatest impact on you in childhood, then this aspect will describe her as Neptunian. That suggests that, on some level, she was lacking in boundaries. Her identity was perhaps not sufficiently formed, and she may have needed to fuse emotionally with those around her. The most creative dimension of this "porousness" is its natural empathy and imagination. The difficult side of it is that Moon-Neptune may represent a mother who could not bear loneliness or separateness, and who may have allowed herself to be victimised because of her fear of being an independent entity. All the arche-typal themes of sacrifice and suffering and powerlessness may permeate the image of mother, because Neptune is that aspect of us which wanders through life seeking redemption. It is our long-ing to return to Eden, to have the sin of a separate existence washed away. So a Neptunian mother may look to her child for redemption, and the child is cast in the role of redeemer, while the mother is really the emotional child. There is sometimes a very deep unconscious state of fusion between mother and child, wrapped around with images of victimisation and redemption. Also, the mother may in her craving for emotional unity virtually vampirise the child, and unconsciously undermine through guilt all the child's nascent efforts at self-expression. I have seen this aspect very frequently in the situation you described earlier, Howard, where the mother claims the child for herself and excludes the father—as though the child were a divine child, immaculately conceived for the sole purpose of its mother's redemption. Making a relationship with the father (the Sun) then means giving up identification with the archetypal redeemer, which is a hard act to follow by being just an ordinary mortal. The experience of first love with Moon-Neptune is therefore a state of paradisical fusion between mother and child, which is both deeply addictive and suffocating at the same time.

Howard: I've often seen people with Moon-Neptune aspects who, as children, were made to feel guilty for wanting to separate from mother. I mentioned the practising stage that children reach at about nine months old, a phase when they start to have a love affair with the world and not just with mother. With Moon-Neptune, you may want to explore the environment, you may want to venture away from mother to some extent, but you are made to feel guilty or bad for leaving her side. It's as if she is asking that you sacrifice yourself and your needs for her sake. Or your own urge to stay fused with mother overrides your natural drive to grow through achieving greater independence from her, or a self-definition distinct from hers. A pattern is set up, and later in life you may still be seeking a kind of divine fusion with a loved one, or you are prepared to twist yourself out of shape in order to win love by adapting to what you think other people would like you to be. Inevitably you lose yourself in the process, which on some level will make you very resentful or angry toward the other person.

Liz: There is generally a boundary problem with Moon-Neptune. Rather than attempting to change the nature of the aspect (which is impossible anyway), it is perhaps more helpful to recognise the positive side – the empathy and capacity to "enter into" another person's feeling states – and to work to develop better boundaries in the small areas of everyday life. Otherwise, the nastiest feature of this aspect is its penchant for emotional blackmail. "I've sacrificed so much for you, and given up my chances for an independent life. Now you owe me nothing less than your soul." That is sometimes the unspoken and unconscious message from the mother, and one tends to repeat it as an adult oneself. Neptune has a congenital abhorrence of ordinary everyday 6th house Virgo boundaries. Something simple, like, "No, I don't really want to go to that party, but I'm perfectly happy for you to go on your own," is incredibly difficult for the Neptunian. There isn't really any "I" – there is only a "we." But effacing oneself for the sake of fusion tends to generate considerable resentment inside, because even if you have an exact Moon-Neptune conjunction, you also have eight other planets plus Chiron, and they have no intention of fusing. The Sun and Mars in particular begin to give off sulphurous odours, usually unconscious but quite unmistakeable, and known in the trade as "atmosphere." So it is necessary to be able to create some boundaries, without attempting to turn oneself into a triple Virgo. Learning how to say no occasionally is a great help. One discovers that one hasn't died afterward.

Howard: Or the other person doesn't die because of it, or hate you for it.

Liz: Quite. Nor are they necessarily going to punish you by throwing you out of Eden permanently. Temporarily, perhaps—but then, if we cannot cope with a temporary spell outside the gates, we are not fit to cope with life at all. The more confidence we develop in a relationship's capacity to encompass boundaries as well as fusion, the more we heal the Neptunian wounds of guilt and resentment around the mother.

Howard: With Moon-Pluto aspects, you meet Pluto through the mother—which can manifest in a variety of scenarios. Something in you instinctively picks up on her darker or hidden feelings, any frustration, destructiveness or rage she is sitting on. You thus feel threatened by her, as if the one you love is also the one who could destroy you, who might turn around one day and kill you or abandon you. Later in life, you unconsciously attract or set up relationships which repeat this pattern, because this has been the experience with mother—the first role model of what love and being close to others is going to be like for you. You may gravitate to a partner with a festering nature or strong destructive urges, which you unwittingly trigger off, or you simply equate love with trouble. You (consciously or unconsciously) believe that love will lead to your downfall. You can't relax easily in a relationship if you are waiting for the day your partner is going to turn ugly, or abandon or betray you. You might then become extremely devious, controlling or manipulative as a means of trying to prevent your worst fears from happening.

Sometimes the reverse is true; you are afraid that *you* will destroy what you love. As infants, we all had times when we wanted to kill our mothers for frustrating us in some way. Naturally this is not a comfortable feeling, because if you were to act on these urges, you would be destroying the same person you also love, you would be wiping out the person you need to ensure your survival. Moon-Pluto people have to come to terms with the tension inherent in such ambivalence. I believe that love and hate go hand in hand in a close relationship. There are a number of reasons for this. Perhaps one part of you starts to feel smothered by the relationship and therefore resents the other person for denying you the space or freedom to be yourself more fully. Also, the more you love somebody, the more your happiness and fulfilment depend on that person. Therefore, if they let you down, you could turn very angry, or you'll simply resent the fact that someone has so much power over you. The best relationships are those that can contain the negative emotions you'll feel from time to time toward your partner, along with the positive, loving, cooing stuff. In most cases, Moon-Pluto people are quite intense, and they seem to thrive on intensity, drama and intrigue in relationship, no matter how adamantly they deny this to be true. Unconsciously, they equate intimacy and closeness with transformation, as if relationships are meant to be catalysts through which one is torn down and rebuilt.

Liz: Intensity of emotion, or compulsive emotion, inevitably has a transformative effect, because its impetus will burn through whatever conscious rules and agreements have been made between two people, and suffering inevitably ensues. The word that I tend to associate most often with Pluto is *passion*, and passion can run the whole range from passionate hatred to passionate love and desire and erotic feeling. But the operative word with Pluto is always passion. This word has a Latin root which means "to suffer" — hence the Passion of Christ. Moon-Pluto aspects make a statement about the mother's passion. I have heard many people with Moon-Pluto say, "My mother was very cold and repressed, she never showed any feelings." I look at the Moon-Pluto contact in the birth chart and think to myself, "Yes, I am sure that is how she learned to behave in order to protect herself, as all good Plutonians do with their ferocious Luciferian pride, but there must have been a proper volcano building up pressure inside." This constant smouldering of emotion in the mother can breed rage and jealousy and an unconscious desire to kill the child who may by its very existence seem to be responsible for the frustration of her life dreams. Or it can reflect an obsessive albeit unconscious sexual fascination with the child, if the real object — the husband — has left or is inaccessible.

Howard: The love affair you have with mother becomes the proto-type for what you expect in closeness and intimacy later on, the inner image of what you expect to meet when you are trying to fulfil basic emotional needs. So later on you go for those people who are complex, deep or passionate, people with whom you are bound to have a complicated, intense relationship. You'll simply not be attracted to someone who doesn't fit the bill. Or if you do marry a person who is too safe, too easy, or too uncomplicated for you, it probably won't last forever, or you'll have affairs on the side which are full of intrigue and intensity so that your Plutonic image of closeness is satisfied.

THE RHYTHM OF LIFE

A DISCUSSION OF THE LUNATION CYCLE

BY LIZ GREENE

I thought it might be appropriate to close our structured sessions with some material on what is known as the lunation cycle. This is an approach to the Sun and Moon which concerns their mutual cyclical interaction rather than their natal signs, house placements and aspects; and it can offer considerable insight from a number of different perspectives. One viewpoint is taken by Dane Rudhyar in his book *The Lunation Cycle*,[1] and it is chiefly concerned with the phase of the Moon under which an individual was born, and the psychological characteristics of that phase. I do not want to spend time on this approach because Rudhyar does it so well, and I have little to add. You should simply read his book. However, there are other ways of looking at the interaction between Sun and Moon which can give additional perspectives.

One important approach is the cycle of the progressed Moon in the individual horoscope. For those of you who might be unfamiliar with the movement of the progressed Moon, this is roughly a 28-year cycle, using the symbolic analogy of one day of planetary motion equalling one year of life. The Moon moves roughly 13 degrees a day through the zodiacal signs, or, symbolically, 13 degrees a year; and by progressed motion it will therefore cover the whole 360-degree round of the zodiac in more or less 28 years (you must calculate this exactly for the individual chart, as there is variation in the Moon's motion each day). As the progressed Moon moves around the chart, covering each 30-degree sign in roughly 2½ years, it will make major aspects both to the natal Sun and the

---

[1]Dane Rudhyar, *The Lunation Cycle: A Key to the Understanding of Personality* (Santa Fe, NM: Aurora, 1986).

progressed Sun, which in its turn moves along at approximately 1 degree of actual motion per day, or, symbolically, 1 degree per year by progression. These progressed lunar aspects to the natal and progressed Sun are cyclical—they occur at regular intervals, and most important are the progressed new and full Moons, when the progressed Moon reaches the conjunction or opposition of the natal and then the progressed Sun. This progressed lunation cycle is most interesting to track, and we can have a look at it later on. The years in which the progressed lunations occur are invariably extremely important, especially if the progressed Moon and progressed Sun conjunct or oppose and hit a natal planet by strong aspect at the same time.

We can also look at the lunation cycle as an ordinary transit cycle, because every month the Moon returns to its own place in the birth chart. This is the basis of the lunar return chart, on which many astrologers place great emphasis for the trends of the following month. As the Moon transits around the zodiac, it produces a series of conjunctions and oppositions with the transiting Sun—these are, astronomically, the new and full Moons—and if such a lunation happens to fall within a degree of a natal planet or angle, it can be a very powerful trigger to activate slower-moving transits and progressed aspects. But even if a transiting new or full Moon does not hit anything directly in the birth chart, it is still very interesting to look at the house in which it falls. The lunations follow each other through the houses during the course of the year, with a new Moon, for example, falling in the 4th house and the subsequent full Moon straddling the 4th/10th axis; then the next new Moon might land in the 5th, with the following full Moon landing across the 5th/11th axis; and so on, all the way through the houses during the course of the Sun's 365-day cycle around the zodiac. So every house in the birth chart is triggered in consecutive order by a new and full Moon during the yearly cycle. Many astrologers who write predictive newspaper columns use these lunations as the basis for their monthly forecasts, depending upon which house of the solar chart they land in, and what aspects they make to other transiting planets.

During the course of the year, the most powerful lunations are the eclipses, which can be tracked in the ephemeris by the lunation conjuncting one of the Nodes. This means that the transiting Sun and Moon are aligned not only in degree of longitude but in degree of latitude as well. There is a lot of argument about just what eclipses mean, and how long their effects last; but there is no argument about their power as triggers for natal placements and for slower-moving transits and progressed aspects, which may hang about within orb for a long time but which usually "come ripe" if an eclipse sets them off. There are generally two pairs of eclipses a year, two solar (new Moon) and two lunar (full Moon), each pair falling around six months apart. These are the high energy points of the year's cycle, with the lesser lunations forming a low-key rhythm in between; and in very ancient astrology, before the individual birth chart was understood as having any significance, eclipses were the main predictive tool for world events.[2]

Finally, another approach to the lunation cycle, or the moving relationship between Sun and Moon, is the axis of the Moon's Nodes. The nodal axis has its own cycle of approximately 18 years, and it is a juncture point where the Moon's orbit crosses the Sun's. The Nodes move backward through the signs, and their axis is extremely powerful in transits and progressions, as many of you know. There seem to be many different ways of interpreting the Moon's Nodes, ranging from the fatalistic Hindu approach (Rahu, the North Node, and Ketu, the South Node, are understood as demonic energies which always bring disaster) to the "past life" reading of them (where you messed up in your last incarnation and have to work to get it right in this one). This morning I would like to explore a more psychological approach to the Nodes as a reflection of the relationship between Sun and Moon.

In order to find our feet in the midst of these different dimensions of the lunation cycle, I think it is important to be as clear as possible about the basic meanings of the Sun and Moon. Howard

---

[2]A good example of this is the Gulf War of 1991. The stage was set for this war when Saddam Hussein invaded Kuwait immediately after the solar eclipse at the end of July, 1990; this eclipse fell in 29 degrees Cancer, within 4 degrees of Iraq's Ascendant. The deadline given by the Allies to leave Kuwait was January 15, 1991, on the day of the next solar eclipse in 25 Capricorn — which fell exactly on Iraq's Descendant. Any competent Babylonian astrologer would have warned Saddam that it was not a good idea to invade another country under such auspices, and one wonders whether he was given astrological advice in January, since he tried to shift the deadline date — without success, and with subsequent disaster.

and I have both spoken about the Moon in relation to change, material life, and the cycles of the body and the instinctual nature. The Moon is our vessel of physical embodiment and our instrument of reception; it is our connection to the temporal world. Through the Moon we respond to life through the body, the feelings and the instincts; and most importantly, through the Moon we are plugged into the changing rhythms of the larger physical world of which we are a part.

Whereas the Moon reflects a changing principle within us, the Sun — although it evolves — is a constant. The Sun symbolises the essential self, which hopefully grows in consciousness during the course of a lifetime (like the mythic hero), but which preserves a core of "me-ness" which is unchanging and gives us our sense of continuity and permanent identity. While we experience ourselves as fated by time and change through the Moon, we experience ourselves as potent creators through the Sun. Because of its constancy, the Sun gives us a sense of eternity — we feel this indestructible "me-ness" as the divine child, the spark of spirit incarnated in the lunar physical form. Through the Moon, we experience ourselves as "merely" flesh, and therefore bound to the fluctuations of mortal life. Through the Sun, we experience ourselves as essentially greater than, or capable of transcending, that endless lunar cycle which the Tarot portrays as the Wheel of Fortune.

So the Moon, our antenna for life's perennially changing drama, goes out and soaks up a little taste of experience, and then comes back to offer its responses to the Sun for processing. Then the Moon ventures forth again, and another chunk of life is absorbed and brought back home. Lunar encounters with life, as the Moon progresses through the twelve houses of the horoscope, eventually build up a reservoir of experience which the Sun can gradually transform into "my" vision of life, "my" worldview and "my" identity. There is a constant interaction between a changing, receptive principle and a constant, radiant principle. The solar inner self depends upon the Moon for experience, precipitated by emotional need; without the Moon, there would be no connection with life or other people. There would, in effect, be no relationship and therefore no growth, for the Sun is not a relating principle.

The Sun develops through this lunar adventure of going out into life and coming back again filled with emotional responses to experience. The Moon in turn depends upon the Sun because, without it, the Moon is utterly at the mercy of the body and of nature. It remains driven by blind instinct, and there is no sense of meaning to life, nor any feeling of individual worth and potency. This basic interpretation of the relationship of the solar and lunar principles is, I feel, very important if we wish to understand any of the different facets of the lunation cycle. For example, when we look at the individual progressed Moon's cycle, we are getting an intensely focussed view of the Moon's forays out into life, by sign, house and aspects to other natal and progressed planets. As the Moon progresses through a particular house, it picks up experiences in that domain of life. As it touches other planets, it encounters people or situations who embody those planets. When the progressed Moon returns to its conjunction with the progressed Sun (at intervals of 30 years), the Moon has returned home with all its hard-won booty, and a new cycle of experience is about to begin.

On a more global level, the Moon's cyclical journeying is reflected by the transiting New and Full Moons, peaking at the time of the eclipses. Thus, the collective world of which we are a part undergoes the same rhythm as we ourselves do in our own personal lives. During the course of a month, events happen "out there" which are the stuff of news broadcasts, and anyone who keeps an eye on these things will notice that they tend to happen in batches. There may be a solar eclipse conjuncting Saturn, for example, or a New Moon square transiting Mars and transiting Uranus, and there is a train crash followed by an earthquake in Armenia followed by a mass murderer running amok in Paris.

This is really what I feel to be the essential relationship between the Sun and Moon: change, mortality, and the lunar cycle of birth, fruition and decay which always draws its meaning from and serves the purposes of something constant and eternal standing beyond. The Sun incarnates through the Moon, which is perhaps one of the reasons why, in traditional symbolism, the Sun and Moon represent male and female, and the masculine incarnates in life through the feminine, while the feminine draws its meaning from the masculine. Obviously I am not talking about men and women, but about a pair of principles within all of us. In archetypal terms, the masculine principle depends upon the feminine to actually inhabit the earth and relate to it. I am reminded of a passage in Mary Renault's novel, *The Bull from the Sea*,[3] where Theseus is being told by his mother, a priestess of the goddess, that while it is fitting for Theseus to pray to Apollo for knowledge, she (the goddess) is what the Sun god ultimately knows. Solar consciousness is thus not built upon abstract concepts about life, but upon life itself, and experience of life depends upon lunar instinct and emotional contact. The quest for meaning comes from the Sun, but meaning can be found only through the authenticity of the Moon's immersion in human form.

Audience: Can you just mention briefly Rudhyar's definition of the lunation cycle?

Liz: All right, but only very briefly. Do you understand what I mean by the phase of the Moon you were born under?

Audience: Not really.

Liz: I think astrologers should really have some basic astronomy as part of their studies. I am not terribly good on astronomy, but a series of visits to a planetarium can demonstrate a three-dimensional solar system to even the least concrete of thinkers. I fear that in astrological circles we have become too accustomed to looking at two-dimensional maps.

Let's say, for the sake of simplicity, that you have the Sun in 0 degrees Aries. If you were also born with the Moon anywhere between 0 and 10 degrees Aries, you were born under a New Moon, because they were conjuncting at your birth. In the following days, the Moon shows its crescent in the sky as it moves away from the Sun and begins to reflect the Sun's light. Eventually it reaches a square, a 90-degree angle, away from the Sun, which is the Moon's first quarter. With the Sun in 0 Aries, you would be born under a first quarter Moon if you had the Moon in 0 to 10 degrees Cancer. If you were born with the Sun in 15 Taurus, you would be born under a New Moon if the Moon were in 0 to 10

---

[3]Mary Renault, *The Bull From the Sea* (New York: Random House, 1975).

Taurus, and under a first quarter Moon if the Moon were in 0 to 10 Leo. Are you all right so far?

The Moon then keeps increasing in light until it reaches the opposition to the Sun, which is the Full Moon. If you have the Sun in 0 Aries, you would be born under the Full Moon phase if the Moon were in 0 to 10 Libra. In other words, everyone with the Sun in opposition to the Moon is born under a Full Moon. The Moon then begins to wane, to decrease in light, as it travels back toward the Sun, and reaches its second quarter, which is also a 90-degree angle from the Sun, but *applying toward the conjunction*. Remember that the first quarter Moon *applies toward the opposition*. These two squares of Sun and Moon are very different in nature. Try to imagine that the Moon is an intelligent principle, a person if you like. It moves away from the security of its conjunction with the Sun and voyages out into life, reaching its maximum power and intensity at the Full Moon, and then packing its bags and checking out of its hotel and making the return journey home again toward the next New Moon. There is an excitement and naive enthusiasm about the first quarter square, while the second quarter square has a reflective, philosophical quality because it is on its way home.

When the Moon is moving from its second quarter back toward the conjunction with the Sun, it often looks a little seedy in the heavens. Rudhyar calls this a balsamic Moon. You can imagine what it is like by remembering the times you have come to the end of a trip or holiday. Your suitcase is full of clothes that need laundering, and you have run out of spare cash, and you are a bit sick of eating foreign food all the time, and you are beginning to think that all that travel was lovely but it will be nice to be back home and see familiar faces and speak your own language again. The balsamic Moon has begun to unload its parcel of experience, and there is a melancholy, sacrificial, almost weary quality to this lunar phase.

You can see from this short description that the lunar phase can supercede the signs in which the Sun and Moon are placed. A New Moon in Pisces, for example, can have tremendous energy and creative life, and can sometimes behave more like a Moon in Aries than a second quarter Moon in Aries does, because the lunar receptivity under a New Moon is obscured by the bright light of the solar drive. A person born under a Full Moon, regardless of the sign, will be highly sensitive to other people, just as though he or she had the

Moon in Libra, because the lunar principle of relationship is at its height under this phase. The first quarter Moon, with its adventurousness alternating with timidity, can behave very like a Moon in Cancer, because the Moon is exploring new terrain and craves new sensations while at the same time worrying about whether it was such a good idea after all. The second quarter Moon can behave a lot like the Moon in Capricorn, world-weary and experienced and reflective and a bit cynical, because the Moon has passed its full stage and is digesting all that experience and making it concrete.

Well, that is enough on the traditional lunation cycle, and you can now go out and buy Rudhyar's book. It is very useful material, although I would not say it is the first thing I consider when I look at a horoscope. I am more interested in the movement of the progressed Moon, because of the way in which it faithfully reflects the ebbs and flows of life. The progressed Moon gives us a chance to experience and feel the energy of every house and sign of the zodiac, because it completes its round in 28 years. Also, we experience every planet at cyclical intervals, because the Moon will make some kind of aspect to all of them in the course of only 30 months; and we experience every midpoint, because it will cover all these in only 45 months. It is fascinating to watch the way people reflect the progressed Moon's shift in signs. They start dressing in different colours, and gain or lose weight, and begin to meet others who have that sign prominent in their charts, and find that their interests change and gravitate toward the concerns of the sign. In a person who is strongly lunar (prominent Cancer in the chart, or an angular Moon) these shifts of the progressed Moon by sign every couple of years can be very striking indeed.

It is most interesting to look at where your progressed Moon was at a particular period, and what kind of people and events came into your life at that time. The relationship function of the Moon will usually attract people who embody the qualities the Moon is "learning" as it moves through a particular sign. And the house is equally important, since the Moon's movement through that sphere seems to highlight issues in the outer world which must be dealt with or experienced at that time. The houses, however, are of unequal size if you are working with a quadrant system, so the Moon will not spend the same interval of time in each house as it does in each sign. It may spend several years in a house where there is an intercepted sign, and skip through another house which contains only 15 degrees of a sign which straddles two cusps. Nevertheless this irregular rhythm is still a rhythm, because the houses alternate from active (fiery and airy houses) to receptive (earthy and watery houses) and this is a kind of breathing out and breathing in rhythm. There is a distinctly extraverted feeling about the fiery and airy houses, and a distinctly introverted feeling about the earthy and watery ones. The progressed Moon moving through the 12th, for example, almost invariably describes a withdrawn and deeply introverted time, when the individual may feel very lost and confused. This is a period of gestation, and if one is attuned to one's natural lunar rhythm, one will accept the quiet waiting and working on internal (usually family) issues that arise, and will not go rushing about trying to force things which are not yet ripe. Then, when the Moon arrives at the Ascendant, it is time to act and to move out into life, and it often feels like a kind of new birth. Major changes often occur when the Moon crosses the angles, and the shift from the 12th to the 1st is particularly marked by decisions which assert the self and alter the person's environment.

Then the Moon moves into the 2nd house, and there is an introverted movement again, with security and stability and the formulation of personal values emphasised. The 3rd is once again an extraverted house, where one wants to make new contacts and study new things. You can see what I am getting at here. The Moon plunges into the affairs of a particular house, especially if it conjuncts a planet there, and gathers experience through its emotional encounters with others. The Moon also aspects itself by hard angle (conjunction, square, opposition) every seven years, so it has a cycle in relation to its natal placement just like transiting Saturn does. In youth, there is a rough overlap between the hard angles of transiting to natal Saturn, and the hard angles of progressed to natal Moon, although this overlap ceases as one gets older since the Saturn cycle is roughly a year and a half longer. We could spend another week talking about the relationship between the Saturn and progressed Moon cycles, but I fear it will range too far away from our theme of the inner planets.

As the progressed Moon moves along, so does the progressed Sun. The year in which these two conjunct varies from one individual to another, depending on how many degrees apart they are in the birth chart (the lunar phase). If you have the Sun in 0 Aries and the Moon in 5 Pisces, the progressed Moon will reach the natal Sun for the first time at around 2 years old, and then for the second time at around 30. The progressed Sun at 2 years old will have reached 2 Aries, so the progressed New Moon would occur 2 months after the progressed Moon reached the natal Sun. This interval between the progressed Moon conjuncting first the natal and then the progressed Sun increases as we get older and the progressed Sun moves along at 1 degree a year in progressed motion. The same person at 30 would have the progressed Sun in around 0 Taurus, so the progressed Moon would take 2 1/2 years to move from the natal Sun to the progressed Sun. And so on.

These progressed lunations are terribly important timers in life. I have found that the progressed Moon conjuncting the progressed Sun is especially marked in outer terms, because the progressed chart is who we are now, and what is happening in our world at this moment. Usually the important events, outer and inner, occur in the *progressed* house in which the lunation falls, although if it strongly aspects a natal planet then it will of course activate the issues of the natal house in which that planet is placed. Often there is a radical change in life seeded at the time of the progressed New Moon.

Is there anyone here who can remember what happened to them under a progressed New Moon?

Audience: I experienced a physical crisis. The progressed New Moon was opposite my natal Saturn.

Audience: I had a progressed New Moon at the Descendant, and it was a terrible time. My marriage broke up.

Liz: There is nothing innately negative about a progressed New Moon. But we must look carefully at what natal planets are aspected, and also what transits are hitting the lunation as well. A progressed New Moon conjuncting transiting Pluto at the Descendant and square natal Venus, for example, might well give you a terrible time with your marriage. But it will also mark a new phase of life, which may begin with difficulty but which will unfold more creatively as the lunar cycle moves along.

Eclipses are also not inherently negative. They reflect an intense focus of energy, and serve as triggers for whatever has been building up to a state of ripeness. If there is an aspect of progressed Mars in square to Saturn, and transiting Pluto has been hovering around within a degree or two, and then an eclipse lands on the progressed Mars, one might well expect some kind of crisis to come to a head within a fortnight of the eclipse; but it is not the eclipse which carries the negative energy. Even if an eclipse does not aspect a natal planet directly, it can stir up matters in the house in which it lands. And it can also trigger a progressed planet, even if there is no strong aspect from that progressed planet to a natal planet at the time. I think we pay too little attention to eclipses, but if there is anything which is obviously building up and has not yet come out into the open, you can be sure that an eclipse will do the job of helping it along. This is particularly true of the lunar eclipses which, because the Full Moon represents the Moon's maximum power, tend to manifest in terms of physical events and emotional encounters with others.

I believe it is very valuable to spend some time with your own chart, tracking these cyclical movements at important junctures in your life. This is not in order to predict events, which have an unpleasant way of surprising us anyway; it is in order to understand your own rhythms better, so that the continuity of life begins to make more sense. You will see, if you put this effort into the Sun and Moon cycles, that nothing in life is random. The things which happen to us are faithful reflections of what we are in process of becoming inside, and occur as part of an ongoing cyclical movement which turns back on itself and returns us over and over again to the same characters in the drama, dressed up in different costumes. T. S. Eliot puts this beautifully in *Little Gidding*:

> We shall not cease from exploration
> And the end of all our exploring
> Will be to arrive where we started
> And know the place for the first time.[4]

---

[4]T.S. Eliot, "Little Gidding," from *The Complete Poems and Plays of T.S. Eliot* (London: Faber & Faber, 1969 [p. 97]; and San Francisco: HarperCollins, 1952).

The affairs of life do not "happen" without an intelligent pattern, nor are we as much at the mercy of some impersonal external "fate" as we might sometimes think. All our experiences have a connecting thread of meaning, and this is what emerges when we study the ongoing movements of the Sun-Moon cycle.

Audience: Which is more important for the progressed lunation, the natal house in which it falls or the progressed house?

Liz: I think I mentioned that a progressed lunation tends to manifest outwardly according to the progressed house in which it falls, and the progressed planets which it aspects. Do you all understand that a progressed horoscope includes not only progressed planetary placements, but progressed house cusps as well? The deeper meaning of the lunation, however, with its implications of fruition (Full Moon) or ending and beginning (New Moon), can be seen from the natal house in which it falls, and the natal planets which it aspects. Both are important, and sometimes both are triggered in terms of worldly events. Although it may seem a bit complicated, you will get the hang of it if you examine the progressed lunations in your own chart, in both the natal and progressed houses.

Perhaps we could move on to the Moon's Nodes now. I would like to spend the rest of this session on these, because I believe the nodal axis crystallises the relationship between Sun and Moon and reflects that sphere of life in which the *coniunctio*—the inner blending of the two principles—is most likely to manifest. I can see that some of you are looking rather shell-shocked after all that technical information about progressed New and Full Moons. It requires a little homework. But you will have an easier time with the Moon's Nodes, since you no doubt all know where these are located in your own birth charts.

I believe I mentioned that in traditional Hindu astrology, the Nodes of the Moon have a rather nasty reputation. They are understood as malevolent demons because they "swallow" the Sun or Moon at the time of a solar or lunar eclipse, and they are associated with fate. This is all very well if you are a Hindu, since the philosophy is deeply fatalistic, but we do not view astrology in this way in the West. There is a different archetypal background to the psychology of the Western person, and it tends to reflect our emphasis on free will and individual value. That is neither better nor worse than the Hindu approach; it is merely different, and it is the one which is deeply rooted in the Western psyche. So we must work with what we are.

I have not found that the nodal axis is in any way inherently malefic, any more than eclipses are. But it seems to reflect a point of manifestation, where what we are inside is distilled and incarnated outside us and comes to meet us like a "fate." Because the nodal axis is the point of intersection between the orbits of the Sun and Moon, it is a kind of gateway into incarnation, a point of meeting between the solar principle of consciousness and meaning and the lunar principle of embodiment. I have not found that there is any difference between the North and South Nodes in terms of their effects by transit or progression; they move as an axis, and anything aspecting one end will automatically aspect the other. I would say the same about the natal nodal placements. You must work with a pair of houses, and the issues of both those houses – where they oppose and where they complement – will always be activated together. Sometimes one seems more troublesome than the other, but the trick with any polarity is to achieve a workable balance. If one end receives too much emphasis then the other will inevitably act up. We need to think in terms of a polarity here, rather than in terms of the North Node being "better" or "worse" than the South Node.

As I have said, the Sun's function of meaning and the Moon's function of embodiment occur together in the nodal axis, and I believe this is why experiences tend to occur here which are both concrete and also resonate on a profound inner level. I have often heard people say, "This was *meant!*" when something important transits the Nodes, or when the transiting nodal axis strikes an important point in the birth chart. If I had to give a keyword to the nodal axis, I would call it "manifestation," and when it is involved by progressed or transiting motion with natal placements, external issues usually arise which have a deep meaning for our development (Sun) as well as an emotional and physical expression (Moon).

I am often surprised at how many astrologers neglect the transiting nodal axis, even when they are picking through the biquintiles of transiting Ceres to natal Vesta. The most powerful transit is of course the conjunction of the transiting nodal axis to a natal planet. The "fated" or "meant" feeling which so often accompanies these transits is understood by many people to reflect some kind of karma coming due. But I am not happy about making assumptions of this kind to a client, even if one believes in it personally. Fate or karma can also be understood psychologically, and this more neutral approach frees the client from the burden of moral judgment which inevitably accompanies our interpretations of reincarnation. I am deeply suspicious of this kind of moral judgment, since values change according to cultures and epochs of history; and no individual is in a position to really know why another person has acted in a certain way, nor what ultimate repercussions the act might have. We need to have our own personal morality by which we make our choices in life, but I do not feel it should be imposed on a client, whose inner values might be very different and just as sound.

So I prefer to interpret the manifesting action of the nodal axis as a reflection of a purposeful inner impetus to combine the Sun and Moon principles in the birth chart, rather than as the reflection of past life karma. They are not mutually exclusive viewpoints anyway; they are merely different ways of saying it. If something happens on a concrete level (the Moon) but the event does not invoke any inner feeling of meaning or growth (the Sun), then it seems like chance—an encounter with external reality which may be pleasant or nasty at the time, but which does not leave any profound change in its wake. Equally, we can have a deep insight, or a feeling of "me-ness" which is very intense, without an external trigger. But the nodal axis combines both levels of experience. For example, at the moment Saturn is transiting around 22 Capricorn, and if any of you have the nodal axis in 22 degrees of the cardinal signs, you will be receiving a Saturn transit to the nodes, which is likely to activate events and inner realisations in the two houses in which the nodes are placed. The trigger may be typically Saturnian—worldly pressures, money problems, issues of separation, work challenges, a permanent commitment of some kind—but the impact will be felt where the nodal axis is placed.

Audience: Do all the planets progress at the same rate of speed?

Liz: Only if you use what are called solar arc progressions, where every point in the chart, the angles and house cusps included, symbolically move at the same rate of speed per year as the actual daily motion of the Sun. But in what are called secondary progressions, each planet symbolically moves per year at the speed it moves in actuality per day. That varies enormously, especially when a planet is retrograde at birth, or is slowing up to go direct. I think both methods of progression are valid, and as is usual in astrology, there is often a coincidence of strong aspects between the two during the important junctures in life.

So do have a look at the important transits that have moved across your natal nodal axis, as well as the transits of the nodal axis to your natal planets. Some astrologers associate the nodal axis with relationship issues, particularly Ebertin. In *COSI* [5] he refers to the nodal axis as "a tie-up, association or alliance," and I have found his interpretations of midpoint pictures involving the Nodes to be extremely accurate. This interpretation of the Nodes is in accord with the idea of the *coniunctio* or blending of Sun and Moon, which combines relationship (Moon) with individual development (Sun). When the nodal axis is involved, one has "fated" or deeply meaningful encounters. Other people are usually part of the package involved with nodal activity, and because of the solar component, these people are often very important for our growth as individuals. They are connected in some mysterious way with our meaning and purpose in life. (The same may be said of synastry cross-aspects between one person's nodal axis and the other's natal planets.) The progressed Moon may bring us relationships which are interesting, passionate, fun and exciting; but when we look back at our lives and consider who had a truly important impact on the unfoldment of our real selves (even if the relationship was short-lived), we will usually find that the nodal axis was involved at the time of meeting, by its transit to a natal planet or a transiting or progressed planetary aspect to its natal position.

If you can remember our material on the solar hero's journey, you might recall the different characters whom the hero meets— the envious dark twin, the dragon at the threshold, the damsel in

---

[5]COSI is the abbreviation for Reinhold Ebertin's *The Combination of Stellar Influences* (Aalen, Germany: Ebertin Verlag, 1960).

distress, the helpful animal, and so on. These symbolic characters, who belong to the unfoldment of the Sun in the chart, tend to enter our lives when the nodal axis is active by transit or progression. We may meet more than one person during the course of a lifetime who embodies a similar mythic role for us. The dark twin, for example, may first appear as one's parent or sibling, and later as one's work colleague or one's best friend. This is why it is worth looking at the periods in life when a repeating transit (such as Jupiter's 12-year cyclical conjunction) hits the Nodes—for even if new people arrive in our lives, their meaning for us may be connected with an earlier experience with someone entirely different, whom we do not at first recognise as the same mythic character.

Audience: Do you think the Nodes are more important than other things in the chart?

Liz: No, I don't feel anything is "more important" than anything else. It simply depends upon which lens will give you the most helpful focus at the time. When you look at a landscape, it is an integrated whole; you cannot say that tree is the most important feature, or that wall, or that cloud. But if you focus on the tree for a while, and then the cloud formation, and then the wall, you deepen your understanding of the components which make up the landscape. Then when you look at its overall appearance again, it is enriched and touches you on many more levels, because you realise you are looking at a clump of birches rather than a clump of oaks, and the clouds are a cumulonimbus formation, and the wall is made of local slate.

We have been focussing during the week on the development of the personality through the functions of the Sun and Moon. The nodal axis is a very important part of this particular focus, because it distills the Sun-Moon relationship and represents it as a specific sphere of life where individual growth is most likely to occur through the agency of meaningful external relationships. Because the Nodes are not planets, they do not reflect urges or needs within us, and in that sense they are not "personal." But they indicate where our most important personal urges—the lunar need for relationship and the solar need for self-realisation—merge and manifest.

Audience: What sort of orb do you allow for transits of the Nodes?

Liz: The same as I would use for planetary transits. I think there is something like a 10-degree orb on either side with a slow transit over a natal placement, just as there is with a strong natal aspect. Transiting planets take time to make their approach; we do not suddenly wake up on Thursday morning with transiting Saturn conjunct the Sun. A transit represents a process, and there are stages of buildup, release and integration that must be passed through. Of course, a transit is most powerful when it is within a degree of orb, but even when it is three or four degrees away, a minor transit or a lunation may release its effect. This is especially true of the slow-moving outer planets with their endless retrograde cycles, which may have several "peak" times during a two-year period when smaller transits and lunations activate them. And more importantly, a transit, from the nodal axis or anything else, will trigger more than one thing in the birth chart, since most natal placements form configurations of aspects.

As an example, perhaps we could think about someone with a natal T-cross, such as the Sun in 3 Aries, Neptune in 7 Libra, and Mars in 4 Cancer. The progressed Moon will come along into Aries one day, and when it arrives around 1 or 2 Aries, it is beginning to trigger the natal Sun. Then it will square Mars a month after it makes its exact conjunction to the natal Sun, and it will oppose Neptune three months after that. And it will still reverberate until it moves a degree or two off the opposition to Neptune, two months later still. So we have a time frame of around eight or nine months when the progressed Moon is triggering the entire natal T-cross. Rather than saying, "Ah, it will be on the Sun exact to the minute on 27 July, and then it will square Mars on 31 August, and so on," it is more accurate to read the configuration as a whole – Sun-Mars-Neptune – and *all* the issues involved (the need for self-assertion, the longing for fusion with others, the quest for individual meaning) will be activated at the same time, over that 9-month period.

I would work this way with the transiting nodal axis as well. Like the progressed Moon, it will begin to show its maximum effect when it reached 0 Aries/Libra (but even earlier for the initial seeding), and would not finish its main process of bringing the T-cross into manifestation until it had passed around 10 or 11 Aries/ Libra. We must learn to think in terms of triads when we work with midpoints, and there are usually at least three if not more factors involved in a major birth chart configuration.

Audience: Can you say something about aspects from the natal planets to the natal nodes?

Liz: If we understand the natal nodal axis as a point where the Sun and Moon principles merge and manifest in life, then the natal planets will help or hinder that process according to their aspects. If Saturn, for example, were conjunct one of the nodes, then the major encounters in life which foster growth will very likely be accompanied by issues of separation, restriction, and the necessity to come to terms with the limits of the material world. If Venus were trine/sextile the nodal axis, then the individual's values and sense of what is beautiful and worthwhile in life would harmonise with and facilitate those relationships which fostered growth. I think you can work this out for yourself, if you understand the principles involved.

I have an example chart which I would like you to look at in relation to the nodal axis. Are there any other questions before we do this?

Audience: Do you allow the same orb for a progressed planet as you do for a transit?

Liz: I thought I had made that clear with the example of the progressed Moon. Yes, I would always allow an orb of a few degrees on either side—perhaps as much as 10 degrees—with all major aspects of transiting and progressed planets as well as the transiting nodal axis. The process is the same. Experiences are seeded in our lives without our realising it at the time, and usually when we come to notice the thing it has already had a long time to set down roots. When you are involved in depth psychotherapeutic work, you can see that personal issues first formulate in a person's dreams many months, sometimes even years, before they ripen and reach consciousness. Some of these issues are more transient—they might reflect the movement of the progressed

Moon, or the transits of Mars, and they deal with the "top" layers of the personality. A dream formulating such an issue might have a three-month period of integration into consciousness and into life. Other issues are deeper life themes which reach down to the central core of the personality, and might correspond with the movement of the progressed Sun over a natal configuration (usually several years in duration), or a transit of Pluto (which can hang about on a natal planet for up to three or four years); and then the person's dreams will begin to herald a deep process at work years before the actual life changes occur in outer reality. Jung thought that the first dreams of early childhood often encapsulated the entire life myth, and in a way that reflects the birth-chart mapping, which depends upon time and the chain of choice and consequence to flesh itself out as an individual life.

However, we tend to notice these profound changes only when they hit us on the head, not when they are seeding or gestating. That is when the astrological triggers—eclipses, lesser lunations, transits of energetic planets such as Mars, stations of transiting inner planets such as Mercury or Venus—bring into focus what has really been brewing in the psyche for a long time. Mars is well known for its trigger effect on slower-moving configurations, and so are eclipses, as I have said. But I have always liked the Stoics' idea of *Heimarmene*, the invisible thread which weaves itself through choices based on the effects of other choices based on the effects of other choices, and so on, back into the impenetrable past of our parents and our parents' parents' parents. If we cast light on this thread at any point when a critical event occurs, it may seem as though the event has just sprung into being from nowhere; but in fact nothing comes from nothing, it is always built upon the residue of what has come before. This idea of the Stoics is not dissimilar to the Eastern idea of karma, but does not require belief in reincarnation. A single human mind cannot possibly grasp the entirety of the thread of *Heimarmene*, which encompasses the whole of life; but we can keep the idea in mind when we look at the meaning of transits and progressions, which build upon all the preceding transits and progressions and how the individual dealt with those at the time. Events are like the tips of icebergs. They are not isolated and independent, but have deep, interconnected roots.

Aspects of the transiting heavy planets always have a far longer seeding and gestation period than those of the inner planets, and involve deeper and broader family and collective issues. But they must be processed through the inner planets, which are the organs of the individual personality. This takes time, which is what I understand an orb to really mean—it reflects the duration of the process with all its stages, from seeding at the unconscious level to integration on the level of the conscious personality.

Audience: I would like to know more about the effect of Chiron in relation to the Moon's Nodes, both natally and when they combine in a transit or progression.

Liz: Chiron seems to reflect that area where the individual feels wounded or inadequate in some way. It is similar to Saturn, as we have said, but unlike Saturn, Chiron seems to require an increase in understanding and tolerance, because there is a sense of the wound never really healing or totally going away. If we put this principle together with the nodal principle, which is the gateway through which others affect our growth and self-development, then a relationship which comes into being when Chiron and the nodal axis are involved will very likely have elements of irreconcilable conflict, ongoing pain, and a potential increase of understanding and compassion. In short, there is likely to be a therapeutic element in the relationship, even if it is a passionate love affair and not an analyst-patient bond.

When a natal planet aspects the nodal axis, important relationships usually include the component reflected by that planet. A natal Chiron-Node tieup will reflect an ongoing tendency to become involved in relationships which bring the person's deeper hurts and fears and pain to the surface so that they may be understood and integrated. Our attitudes toward relationship are profoundly coloured by planets aspecting the Nodes, because this is where a pattern tends to repeat itself. A person with Chiron conjunct the Node may ultimately come to believe that all deep encounters involve pain and the exposure of one's most vulnerable side; and that all deep encounters equally contribute to one's deepening worldview (the philosophical dimension of Chiron, which emerges out of trying to deal with the wound). A Chiron transit to the Nodes may bring one such encounter; a natal configuration will reflect a pattern.

We all have our own particular vision of what life is really about, and when we are younger it is very difficult to comprehend that others see something quite different. One assumes that everyone sees the same world and evaluates it in the same way—or ought to. Because the nodal axis brings together experience with meaning, it is a very important influence on a person's worldview, and a worldview coloured by Chiron will have as its archetypal background the theme of wisdom acquired from ongoing suffering, or learning to accommodate an insoluble conflict. Because we tend to create outside what is inside, Chiron involved with the Nodes tends to expect and seek complicated relationships which bring suffering as well as pleasure; and if a relationship is too pleasurable and superficial, there may be a tendency either to create crises, or to break it up. There is some of this same quality about Chiron in the 7th house or in Libra or in strong aspect to Venus; but I feel it is extremely powerful as an influence on the individual vision of life when it is aligned with the Nodes.

Now I would like to spend some time on this example chart. (See Chart 8 on p. 224). I didn't actually make the chart up specially for our session on the nodal axis; Nigel really was born under a total solar eclipse, with the Sun and Moon both conjuncting the Moon's North Node. This is an extremely powerful personality, with such an emphasis in Leo in the 1st house. Pluto is closely conjunct Jupiter, which in turn conjuncts the Sun and Moon and the North Node; then there is Mercury conjuncting Chiron, which has just moved into the beginning of Virgo. This Sun-Moon conjunction is of course a New Moon, which is also a solar eclipse because they are parallel in latitude as well as conjunct in longitude.

I can remember reading long ago in some ancient astrological text that children born under a solar eclipse tend to die. Nigel did not; I have met few people with as much vital energy as he has. I don't know where this sort of rubbish about eclipses comes from, but I think it is our inheritance from medieval astrology, which picked up the Hindu idea that the nodal axis is demonic. This man is anything but a feeble and debilitated character, although as you

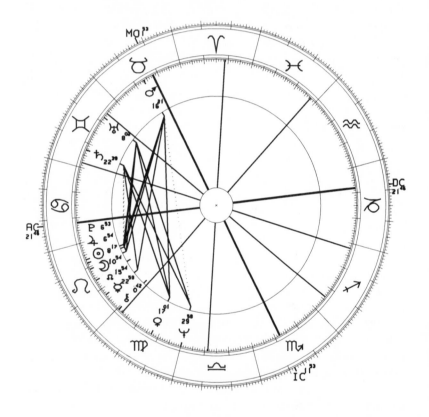

Chart 8. Nigel. The birth data has been withheld for confidentiality. Chart calculated by Astrodienst, using the Placidus house system.

will see he has certain problems around his emotional life because of that New Moon.

Perhaps we might look at Rudhyar's interpretation of the New Moon phase, because it would be applicable regardless of the sign in which the New Moon is placed. Obviously with such a fiery conjunction in a fiery house, Nigel is extremely intense and very preoccupied with expressing his own creative gifts. But the New Moon has some of these attributes anyway, because the lunar receptivity to others is overshadowed by the burning solar need to realise the self. Nothing and no one gets in the way of a New Moon, even if it is in Pisces, never mind in Leo. The Jupiter-Pluto conjunction is likely to exaggerate Nigel's intensity and concentrated need to constantly find new vehicles to express his imagination. Pluto loves to tear the old down in order to build anew, and a Sun-Pluto may be deeply restless and discontented for this reason, although not in the same fidgety way that the mutable signs are. And we also need to remember the mythology of the solar hero, which is particularly relevant because of the emphasis on Leo in this chart.

I will give you a little background on Nigel's family. His father was an alcoholic whom he rarely spoke to, all family negotiations being performed by his rather overbearing and martyred mother. I think this is interesting in terms of Leo's characteristic mythic theme of Parsifal's quest for the Grail and the redemption of the spiritually sick father. A good deal of Nigel's perennial quest for creating an inner ideal in the outer world springs from this archetypal Leonine need to find a sense of meaning, a Holy Grail which can nourish and father him in the spiritual wasteland into which he was born. Having worked his way up from an obscure and difficult background, Nigel managed, at the age of around 28 or 29 (the time of his progressed lunar return and also his Saturn return), to produce a film which won numerous awards at international film festivals, and which went on to be highly successful at the box office. He made a considerable fortune from this film, and used the money to set up his own production company, earning a reputation not only for producing fine marketable films, but also for using unknown actors whose potential talent had previously remained undiscovered.

This particular gift of intuitively recognising potential talent in others, and drawing it out to full flowering, is, I feel, a reflection of the Sun-Moon-Jupiter-Pluto combination, which makes an excellent Pygmalion. Nigel first built his reputation on hiring drunken down-and-out unknowns and making celebrities of them, creating enduring careers and of course keeping his own film budgets low by avoiding highly paid stars. This is the manner in which his creative gifts manifested themselves. One could of course speculate on the fact that Nigel, with his New Moon in the 1st house in Leo, should have been in front of the camera himself; and I do not doubt that, if he had had more self-confidence (or perhaps an Ascendant other than shy and diffident Cancer), he might have done so.

Nevertheless, successful film producers are stars in their own right. This first burst of success occurred, as I have said, around the time of Nigel's progressed lunar and Saturn returns; and it also occurred when the transiting nodal axis happened to be transiting through Leo/Aquarius and moved over all those 1st house planets. So here we meet the Nodes in action, and one could hardly call all that success malefic or demonic. We might say that the nodal axis crystallised all of Nigel's creative urges and brought them into manifestation through the agency of others—his actors and their audiences. What the people around him thought of as luck, Nigel himself recognised as a kind of inner destiny working itself out—he could not put a foot wrong as long as he acted on his intuition and instinct about people. He felt that it was all "meant."

One of the interesting features about Nigel's life is that he is a kind of walking progressed lunar cycle. This is perhaps because of the Moon being his chart ruler (with Cancer on the Ascendant), and because of its prominent position with the Sun and the North Node in the 1st house. His initial great spate of achievement occurred under the progressed lunar return and the transit of the nodal axis to the natal New Moon; but once this had passed, and the transiting Nodes had aligned on the Ascendant/Descendant axis, things began to go wrong. Nigel had some extremely difficult encounters with business partners, and in the end he lost his production company and most of his money, and vanished into obscurity for a time. Everyone thought he was finished, and would turn up waiting on tables somewhere. For the next fourteen years no one knew where he had gone; he simply disappeared, as people tend to do in the film industry, which is said to be ruled by Neptune.

Then Nigel's progressed Moon reached the cusp of the 7th house moving toward the opposition to its natal place and at the same time, the opposition to the natal Sun (a progressed Full Moon). Suddenly Nigel surfaced again. It seems he had spent those fourteen years, while the progressed Moon moved along below the horizon, breeding sheep somewhere in Scotland, and dabbling in property development which had reestablished his financial solidity. When the progressed Moon finally moved into Aquarius and formed the oppositions to the natal Sun, Moon and nodal axis, Nigel formed a new film production company, and returned to his original field of creative work. And as the transiting nodal axis returned to Leo/Aquarius (in reverse this time) and aligned once again with the natal New Moon in the 1st house, the first film he made with his new production company hit the cinemas and was, to the astonishment and envy of his colleagues, wildly successful. Phoenixes are rare in the film world, for once a person has slipped, they usually vanish forever. But perhaps people underestimated that Sun-Moon-Pluto-Jupiter, which has the power to rise from the ashes to play Pygmalion once again.

You can see why I described Nigel as a walking progressed lunar cycle. He is also an excellent example of the way in which fiery people turn their own lives into myths. The close orbs of the natal eclipse are reflected by the deeply cyclical nature of his life, because when a recurrent transit hits, it hits everything at once. With most people the lunar and nodal cycles are not so obvious. Of course, there are many other things we can look at in this chart, but I thought it was a particularly vivid example of both the progressed Moon and the nodal axis at work. It is also a good example of the attributes of the lunar phase of the New Moon, where the Moon is hidden by the light of the Sun. There is an interesting quality about Nigel which a number of people who know him have described to me in almost identical terms. When they are in his company, he seems very attractive and powerful and magnetic (as we might expect); but they go away feeling that they have no idea who he really is on an ordinary personal level. The lunar level of the personality, which is the function that connects us with others, is somehow hidden or obscured in Nigel; one is in the presence of a personality of mythic stature, but one cannot easily approach the human being through ordinary emotions and instincts.

The Moon placed in the 1st or 10th houses has always been traditionally interpreted as reflecting a gift at "handling" people because of the sensitivity to others' feelings and needs. I have found this to be the case most of the time, and the Moon in the 10th may even make a career of it in such fields as acting, public relations and the helping professions. But in Nigel's case, the 1st house Moon is a dark Moon, Hekate's Moon, and he expresses the curiously paradoxical combination of being remarkably gifted in intuiting others' undeveloped gifts while withholding his own emotional life from them at the same time. Nigel makes a tremendous solar impact on those around him, and on the larger world as well through his films. Yet he is inaccessible and difficult to know as a person, although this is hidden from less perceptive eyes by the glamour that surrounds him, and the natural charm that one might expect from all that 1st house Leo and the Moon-Jupiter conjunction. All one is left with is the vague uncomfortable feeling that the real man has not shown himself; and yet, in another sense, he has, in terms of solar expression and a highly individual creative contribution to the world.

We might also look at Nigel's Mars, which is prominent because of its squares to both Sun and Moon and nodal axis, and its placement at the MC.

Audience: He has to get somewhere in life.

Liz: Yes, that is quite right. This culminating Mars reflects Nigel's restless ambition and need for conquest. He has got to "make it," to be first and best in the broader arena of the marketplace. Mars placed here also suggests that he has inherited these qualities from his mother, who certainly sounds a rather Martial type of personality, but who did not achieve anything herself in worldly terms. She wanted her son to succeed, and so he has. Some of his worldly striving springs from the need to fulfil his mother's expectations, although they are his own expectations as well. Nigel has used his Mars consciously and well, and his success and professional stature reflect this. What about Mars in Taurus?

Audience: It's very slow and persistent.

Liz: Yes, it is the grind-the-opposition-down principle. Mars in Taurus may be a slow starter, but once it gets rolling, nothing can stop it. And it needs practical achievement; the competitive instinct is expressed through earthy forms, such as making money and acquiring professional status. Nigel does not do things because he thinks they will be good for his soul's evolution. He wants concrete results. I also feel this Mars says something about his capacity to work long and hard. He is not merely "lucky" or intuitively opportunistic, as it might appear from the sudden successes he has had. He has worked for every bit of it, patiently and carefully, although his Leonine need to present a larger-than-life personality might make him play down this dogged, hard-working side of his nature because it lacks glamour.

Audience: Mars in Taurus is also very sensual. There is a strong sex drive.

Liz: Yes, it reflects a powerful physical drive. Nigel's romantic career is, to put it euphemistically, rather colourful. As we might expect, he has had a great number of women in his life. A man with Mars in Taurus tends to identify his sense of power and potency with sexual pleasure and conquest, which is very different from an airy Mars which might identify power with intellectual acumen or organisational abilities.

Audience: I would like to know more about his mother. You said that Nigel needed to fulfil his mother's expectations for success which she did not achieve herself. Does Mars at the MC always mean this?

Liz: No, it does not always mean that the mother ruthlessly drives her child toward achievement. Any planet at the MC reflects a shared substance between mother and child, which can be expressed creatively by both. I have known many people with Mars at the MC whose mothers were successful in the world, and embodied positive models of achievement and energy for their children. We cannot tell from the chart alone whether the mother has been able to express these qualities herself, or whether she is even conscious of them. If they remain unconscious, then problems are likely to occur between mother and child, for there is a powerful unspoken pressure on the child to live the planet out for both. In Nigel's case we can make some educated guesses from his family history. We know that his mother had to "look after" an alcoholic husband, and that she was possessive, domineering and did her best to keep her son from forming any relationship with his father. She never worked, but expressed her Martial qualities in an indirect and unconscious way, for martyrdom is often a form of covert aggression and control; and I would guess that she contributed to or colluded with her husband's drinking problem because this gave her a justification for the "self-sacrifice" which disguised her inability to make anything of her own life. A husband with a "problem" – be it alcohol, womanising, financial failure or whatever – can be a very useful whipping-boy upon whom to heap one's rage that life has not fulfilled all the dreams for free.

To be fair, we must also take into account the generation into which Nigel's mother was born, for there was far less encouragement and support for a Martial woman than there is now. So the difficulty between Nigel and his mother, suggested by Mars at the MC, would probably reflect a combination of the collective values of her time (which expected every woman to be a devoted wife and mother), her own character (which opted for a dishonest rather than a clean way of living Mars), and her parental background, which might through no fault of hers have destroyed her confidence at an early age and made it even more difficult for her to express Mars in an open, positive way.

If we put all these factors together – and some are not described by the chart – then we can guess that there was a ferocious push from his mother for Nigel to "become" somebody. But it is also Nigel's push, and we must remember this before we indulge in too much parent-bashing. One of the important issues which Nigel would have to confront is that of distinguishing between what he wants for himself, and what he wants in order to placate his mother. It is the difference between compulsion and choice. If Nigel owns his own Mars, then he can pursue his own goals and desires. If he is unconsciously identified with his mother's unlived life, he will try to become something which is more her dream than his, and he will feel that he is working for somebody else all the time, and will not be able to relax and enjoy the fruits of his labours. There has been some of this element in the story of Nigel's relationships with women, for he had a tendency when younger to become involved with women who idolised him and wanted to be looked after, contributing nothing to the relationship themselves either financially or creatively. This is a repeat of the pattern of Nigel's relationship with his mother.

Audience: Is it possible for a woman not to express the Moon, or a man not to express the Sun?

Liz: Certainly. I am very wary of sweeping generalisations about men living the Sun and women living the Moon. The Sun and Moon are archetypal significators for male and female, but people vary enormously in their modes of expression of these qualities. Very often I have found that the Moon is quite unconscious in a particular woman's chart. She may try to find it through a lunar man, just as a man who is not well-connected with his Sun may try to find its creative fire through a solar woman. There is nothing inherently "wrong" or pathological in this, although I think that sooner or later we are pushed by our own psyches to live out as best we can what we have within us, which includes all the planets. But chart placements are highly individual, and a woman with an angular Sun and the Moon tucked away in the 12th house with few aspects will at first relate more easily to the solar principle. Sometimes it is family complexes, rather than chart significators, that disconnect a woman from the Moon or a man from the Sun. Then there is usually more pain around the issue, for one is reacting compulsively rather than expressing what comes most naturally. Once upon a time, the clearly defined roles of men and women were inevitable and natural and dictated by biology and the demands of the environment. But as we have increased in complexity, sophistication and individuality over the centuries, these archetypal roles have become much less rigid on the outer level. However, disconnection from any planet poses a problem sooner or later, because what is unconscious in us is compulsive and leads us into being victimised by our complexes and therefore by life.

I would also like to look at the squares between Mars and the Sun-Moon conjunction. We have seen a fair amount of these squares during the course of the week. Do any of you have any comments on these aspects in Nigel's chart?

Audience: He must be very angry and irritable a lot of the time.

Liz: Actually, the odd thing is that he never gets angry. This is a good example of what often happens with squares—one end gets pushed into the unconscious, and the person meets it outside. If Nigel finds himself in a situation which might invoke rage in less controlled folk, he just makes a subtle, Cancerian inference and goes quietly away, and the person never sees him again. If he must dismiss someone who works for him, he invariably has another employee do it for him, and vanishes for a couple of weeks, because he loathes direct confrontation. Despite his ambition and drive toward achievement, you could not imagine anyone less Mars-like in personal encounters. The result of all this evasion and avoidance is that a great many people wind up very angry with Nigel. He has a lot of enemies who are still waiting to corner him and "have it out" with him.

So one manifestation of these squares is that Nigel's Mars—the dimension of it which reflects directness, confrontation with others, defence of one's own position, healthy aggression—is quite unconscious, and is therefore projected outward and comes to meet him through other people, usually involved with his work. I have seen this a great deal with Sun square Mars, because the sense of self (which includes the self-image) is in conflict with the aggressive impulse, and the person becomes frightened of his or her own anger and cannot bear to be seen by others as brutal or forceful. I also think that this Sun-Mars square has something to do with why Nigel fosters the talents of others but has not put himself on stage, although one might expect it with all the planets in Leo in the 1st house.

Audience: It sounds as though he has not really separated his Mars from his mother.

Liz: Exactly. That is what I think as well. Nigel can express certain attributes of Mars—ambition, competitive spirit in work—but these attributes are the ones his mother wanted him to express on her behalf. What he was not allowed to express in childhood was his own aggression, his direct expression of his own wishes. Nigel's will collided with his mother's will (both being exceedingly self-willed), and in this sense his mother has taken possession of his Mars. To put it more brutally, she has performed a kind of psychological castration of him. You would not think this from his career with women, or from his worldly success, but it may account in part for the compulsive quality which drives him to keep reasserting his potency. And it may also account in part for his real inability to be direct with other people in a personal context.

Audience: Is there any significance to the fact that Leo is intercepted in the 1st house?

Liz: When a sign is intercepted, it is not directly connected with a house cusp, and therefore does not have a direct channel out into the world. Each house governs a particular sphere of concrete life, and has a planetary ruler which is its conduit. But an intercepted sign in a house is like a tenant who must answer to the landlord—the planet which rules the sign on the cusp, which in Nigel's case is the Moon, the ruler of Cancer. So the Leo energy, in order to express itself, must be directed through the Moon, which means that Nigel's great sensitivity to others—albeit unconscious—makes it difficult for him to "shine" overtly. This may also have something to do with why he fosters others' talents rather than his own need to be seen and recognised.

Audience: Does he have children?

Liz: Yes, and he seems to get on extremely well with them. I think he is a very generous and attentive father, which one might expect from the combination of Cancer and Leo; and also because he knows what it is like to be utterly ignored by his own father. He has a number of children by different women, which seems to reflect a bit of that Sun-Jupiter conjunction—the profligate Zeus who fathers demigods on many mortal women. Zeus had a problem with his father, too.

Audience: Can you say more about the feeling of a New Moon in the birth chart?

Liz: It has a strong flavour of Aries about it. In Nigel's case this could be explained by the New Moon falling in Aries' natural house, the 1st; but I have seen this same quality even if the New Moon is in a more obscure house. There is great sensitivity about oneself, but not very much sensitivity to the feelings of others as separate people. That is the gift of a Full Moon, which can be so preoccupied with others that it generates indecision and tension. A New Moon tends to be so preoccupied with its own creative goals that the lunar function usually gets put second. Yet anything unconscious is always enormously potent in a covert way—hence the hypersensitivity about one's own feelings being hurt. One sometimes needs to shout, "Hello, I'm here!" three times at New Moon people, whereas with the Full Moon you need merely to blink inadvertently and they are immediately worried about whether they have offended you.

Despite Nigel's powerful intuition and ability to manipulate people, he often really puts his foot in it with regard to their emotions—in spite of that Cancer Ascendant. He is sensitive, as one might expect, but primarily about himself. He is easily hurt by others, but genuinely does not recognise when he has completely flattened another person. He can see the creative potentials in others without recognising how they feel, unless they spell it out in no uncertain terms. This can sometimes be true of the fire signs in general—there may be a great sense of the potential in others, but little capacity to respond to the nuances of others' timing and needs. That is why many people feel pressured and pushed about by fiery types, who are astonished by such an accusation because they were genuinely and selflessly trying to nurture the other person's abilities, without noticing that it needed more time or a gentler method of handling. Of course Nigel's typically fiery attitude is that it is up to the other person to complain, and if he or she doesn't, Nigel shrugs and says, "How was I supposed to know? I'm not a telepath."

Now shall we look at Nigel's Venus? It is a rather difficult Venus, I think, because although it has a nice trine to Mars, it is in the sign of its fall, and square both Saturn and Uranus, as well as being on their midpoint. Ebertin describes Venus = Saturn/Uranus[6] as "Tensions and stresses in love-relationship." Also, Venus turned retrograde when Nigel was around fourteen years old, which suggests a lot of frustration in the sphere of love and sexuality at a particularly sensitive age. If we take Venus as a symbol of Nigel's sense of self-worth, this is being challenged or hurt by the isolated feeling of Saturn in Gemini in the 11th house of the group, the collective. The 11th house is our experience of belonging to the larger human family, and Saturn in the 11th can suggest someone who is very much a "loner," who feels painfully different in some way. In Gemini, Saturn brings out fears of being misunderstood and thought stupid, and it can reflect not only the early childhood—Nigel was the only child, with no siblings to talk to— but also a quality of intellectual depth and seriousness which can create communication problems on the ordinary "social chit-chat" level.

Saturn in Gemini often has a problem with "small talk" (over-compensation notwithstanding), and can be very shy and experience discomfort in ordinary social situations such as parties. So the strong Saturnian feelings of isolation and differentness interfere with Nigel's sense of his own value, especially his feeling of being worthwhile and attractive on the physical level (Venus in the 2nd in Virgo). He will need to work to find a sense of worth about his own body, and may also need to confront the issue of inner integrity and not being "for sale" in order to win the love of others. Saturn in square keeps telling him, "But other people won't like you." Nigel certainly does not give an initial impression of being underconfident and shy, because he has developed excellent camouflages (Cancer Ascendant); and his capacity for self-mythologising tends also to throw people off the scent.

---

[6]This is the accepted format of designating a planet on a midpoint. Venus = Saturn/ Uranus could mean Venus square, conjunct, oppose, semisquare, or sesquiquadrate the midpoint.

Audience: But his feelings of inadequacy would be much more obvious in close relationships. Saturn rules the 7th house.

Liz: Yes, it is more obvious, and I am sure it is through his close encounters that he experiences most of the fear and diffidence of the Venus-Saturn square. But Venus-Saturn people often unconsciously choose "safe" partners—people who are emotionally, intellectually or socially not up to their level of competence—because they feel less threatened, and so the women Nigel chooses may not notice his unexpressed fear of being unloved. They will simply think he is hard and insensitive.

Another thing I have found about Venus in the earthy signs is that one needs to be able to live the quiet, inarticulate dimension of earth. I have heard many people with Venus in earth express the fear of being boring, because the element of earth reflects the mute, serene world of nature. Earth does not sit chattering away at you, being clever. It just *is*. The positive qualities of stillness and serenity and harmony with natural rhythms are often underrated or overlooked if there is a chart emphasis in fire, or if one's parents were hoping for a lifetime's entertainment; but if this happens when Venus is in earth, one loses one's sense of self-worth through trying to shine and be exciting all the time. Nigel is no doubt frightened that if the performance stops, and he is anything less than mythic and charismatic and brilliant, that people will find him stupid and boring. I remember reading an interview with John Malkovich, who said that he defined an exciting weekend as staying home and staining a table. I don't know if he has Venus in an earth sign, but I suspect something similar might be said about Nigel. Nigel, however, would probably find it much more difficult to admit.

There may also be a fear, when Venus is in earth but undervalued, that the body itself is lumpish, boring and uninteresting. I would guess that Nigel's square of Saturn to Venus in Virgo in the 2nd house reflects many deep unexpressed fears about being physically unattractive and boring—despite the erotic conquests. The trine from Mars at the MC is a great help, because worldly success and sexual prowess help to compensate for the more vulnerable feelings. The more success Nigel has, the more he can forget about those other, uncomfortable issues. But I think he will need to bring more consciousness into the Venusian realm, which may serve as a kind of bridge to opening up more of that obscured Moon.

I am aware that we are running out of time, so perhaps we can move on now and deal with any other questions or issues around the Sun and Moon cycles and the nodal axis.

Audience: If something is projected, like Nigel's Mars, does this mean he is not living it at all?

Liz: I don't think it is quite so stark a division as that. Every planet has different facets, and we may be conscious of some of them, and able to express them in adequate enough ways, while experiencing difficulty or even great unconsciousness around other facets. Nigel certainly expresses Mars at the MC in Taurus in many recognisable ways—he is wealthy and successful, he has carved a highly individual place for himself in an extremely competitive profession, and he can be very aggressive in business dealings with others. In worldly terms, he is a winner. So he is "living" many facets of Mars. But he has difficulty in expressing Mars in one-to-one encounters, and his aggression on this level is covert and unconscious. Rather than responding to another person's anger, he backs away and disappears and doesn't answer the telephone. It is very annoying to try to speak your mind to someone directly and then find that they are just never available. That is a way of saying, "I can't be bothered," and it is why people become so infuriated with Nigel.

It is very unusual to find a planet totally unconscious and blanked out in the personality. There are usually bits of it which are owned and lived, and bits which are not. A planet is like a person in a way, complex and multifaceted, and we develop and deepen the expression of each planet over the course of a lifetime. When we are dealing with psychological issues such as projection, we need to be careful not to be too literal and sharp-edged about it, for it is usually a question of a mixture of things. The Sun square Mars may have no problem at all owning an image of macho sexuality, yet may find great difficulty in being direct in emotional encounters. Also, Nigel's positive expression of Mars—his worldly achievement—provides him with an outlet for the anger which he cannot articulate at the personal level. He can bash the competition where he cannot shout at his mother, and this keeps him healthy because he has some outlet, however contaminated it might be with unconscious family issues. No factor in a chart is ever totally conscious and expressed to the point where there is nothing left to discover.

Audience: Can you discuss the intercepted signs and planets in greater detail? I think I understand, but not quite enough.

Liz: I will give you one of my crude analogies. The signs can be seen as energy fields, which colour the expression of a planet's basic drive or impulse. The house cusps are like lightning conductors, which exteriorise the planetary drives and sign energies and make them manifest in the world. The house cusps of a chart define the concrete reality in which the individual lives, the limits within which the planets must function. If there is a planet in a sign which does not have a house cusp to work through, it is like a tenant renting a flat from the landlord who owns the building (the ruler of the cusp). If you own your own flat, you can do more or less what you like with it; you can paint the walls purple and plant deadly nightshade in the garden and no one will interfere. But if you are a tenant, you must ask the landlord for permission first. The landlord may say, "Sorry, but all flats in Zürich must be white." So your flat stays white. You can of course move out, but a planet in an intercepted sign cannot. All the intercepted Leo planets in Nigel's chart must ask permission of the Moon (which is itself in Leo) before they can express themselves through the 1st house.

Audience: Would you say that all that Leo makes Nigel narcissistic?

Liz: I think we need to be careful in how we use that word. Narcissism is both a clinical term and an expression people use to insult others who are not giving them what they want. Remember Ambrose Bierce's definition of an egotist? We can dispense with this second, more common usage since it is relative to the person making the accusation, and has no objective basis. As for the clinical definition, narcissism is a psychological state wherein the individual self is not yet developed enough to interact with the outer world as a separate organism. Freud used the term "primary narcissism" to describe the perspective of an infant who is aware only of its own overwhelming needs, and who falls into a raging tantrum if those needs are not gratified. The infant is all-powerful, the centre of the universe, and there is no comprehension of "other." The adult who is narcissistic in this sense, however clever and socially adapted he or she may appear to the unfocussed eye, has usually been deeply hurt in childhood, and has not developed enough of a self to recognise the reality of other people. Everything and everyone exists as a "part-object," an extension of oneself, like one's arm or leg. One takes for granted that one will be given what one needs, just as we take for granted the fact that our arms and legs will move when we want them to; and if this assumption is challenged by the boundaries of another person, great rage ensues. We all have our narcissistic pockets, and some people have bigger pockets than others. And some are so terribly stuck in this infantile state that other people are no more than objects to feed oneself, even if the surface behaviour is apparently loving and self-sacrificing.

Now, the fiery signs are focussed more on their inner imaginative world than on the needs of others. But that is not narcissism in the clinical sense. At worst, it is simply insensitivity. Fire is theatrical, and self-mythologising; it is far preferable to live life as grand drama, even if it is difficult, than to live it as an obscure, ordinary mortal. Hence, the fiery signs tend to draw attention to themselves in one way or another—when this is unconscious, it can be highly manipulative and even rather hysterical—but clinical narcissism reflects profound injury to the structure of the identity, and this can happen to anyone, regardless of sign. Each zodiacal sign responds to conflicts and wounds in its own unique way, and a fiery person who has suffered in this fashion may be narcissistic in a particularly flamboyant and obvious way. But an earthy or watery sign may be equally narcissistic in the clinical sense, and express the problem through martyrdom or bodily symptoms.

To some extent I would say that Nigel has narcissistic elements in his personality, but not to the extent that he is truly handicapped in his functioning; and I would not attribute this to his being a Leo, but rather, to his childhood background. As I said, we all have pockets where we have not yet sufficiently formed, and Nigel's parenting was certainly undermining to his will and identity because of his mother's efforts to possess him. However, the form in which this narcissistic wound expresses itself will be Leonine in Nigel's case, which means that he needs the approval of the audience (especially female) to feel real.

Narcissism is a lonely, anxiety-producing state, because one feels empty and unreal inside unless something outside is found which can provide the mirror for one's identity. Do you all remember the myth of Narcissus? He was not permitted to see a reflection of his own face, because his mother forbade it. When he finally encountered it in the mirror of the pool, he fell in love with it, and could not break free, nor recognise another's love (Echo). This is a profound myth, which tells us a good deal about the problem. If the mother does not validate her child's developing "me-ness," but requires her child to mirror *her* needs and unfulfilled life, it is like denying Narcissus a view of his own face. Then the child will grow up seeking mirrors everywhere, and will depend upon the validation of the outside world to fill up the empty hole which is felt inside. Fire may depend upon the outside world's perception of oneself as a larger-than-life symbol; earth may depend upon the show of external wealth and status; air may depend upon validation of one's cleverness; and water may depend upon a family unit through which to live vicariously. But the tragedy of narcissism, when it is severe, is that the individual is really a very young child who cannot adapt to outer reality because it does not exist. The only thing that exists is the empty place inside where the self, the hero's treasure, was robbed by a mother who was herself narcissistically wounded and needed her child to fill up her own emptiness. Narcissism thus runs in families. The only antidote is what we have been talking about all week: the slow building of a sense of independent identity through the developing the functions of the Sun and Moon.

About the Centre
for Psychological Astrology

The Centre for Psychological Astrology provides a unique work-shop and professional training programme designed to foster the cross-fertilisation of the fields of astrology and depth, humanistic and transpersonal psychology. The programme includes two aspects. One is a series of seminars and classes, ranging from beginners' courses in astrology to advanced seminars in psychological interpretation of the horoscope. The seminars included in this volume are representative of the latter, although the same seminar is never given verbatim more than once because the content changes according to the nature of the participating group and the new research and development which is constantly occurring within the field of psychological astrology. All these seminars and classes, both beginners' and advanced, are open to the public. The second aspect of the programme is a structured, in-depth, three-year professional training which awards a Diploma in Psychological Astrology upon successful completion of the course. The main aims and objectives of the three-year professional training are:

- To provide students with a solid and broad base of knowledge both within the realm of traditional astrological symbolism and techniques, and also in the field of psychology, so that the astrological chart can be sensitively understood and interpreted in the light of modern psychological thought.

- To make available to students psychologically qualified case supervision along with training in counselling skills and techniques which would raise the standard and effectiveness of astrological consultation.

- To encourage investigation and research into the links between astrology, psychological models and therapeutic techniques, thereby contributing to and advancing the already existing body of astrological and psychological knowledge.

The in-depth professional training programme cannot be done by correspondence, as case supervision work is an integral part of the course. It will normally take three years to complete, although it is possible for the trainee to extend this period if necessary. The training includes approximately fifty seminars (either one-day or short, ongoing weekly evening classes) as well as fifty hours of case supervision groups. The classes and seminars fall broadly into two main categories: astrological symbolism and technique (history of astrology, psychological understanding of signs, planets, houses, aspects, transits, progressions, synastry, etc.), and psychological theory (history of psychology, psychological maps and pathology, mythological and archetypal symbolism, etc.). Case supervision groups meet on weekday evenings and consist of no more than twelve people in each group. All the supervisors are both trained psychotherapists and astrologers. Each student has the opportunity of presenting for discussion case material from the charts he or she is working on. At the end of the third year, a 15,000–20,000 word paper is required. This may be on any chosen subject — case material, research, etc. — under the general umbrella of psychological astrology. Many of these papers may be of publishable quality, and the Centre will undertake facilitating such material being disseminated in the astrological field.

Completion of the seminar and supervision requirements entitles the trainee to a certificate of completion. Acceptance of the thesis entitles the trainee to the Centre's Diploma in Psychological Astrology and the use of the letters D. Psych. Astrol. The successful graduate will be able to apply the principles and techniques learned during the course to his or her profession activities, either as a consultant astrologer or as a useful adjunct to other forms of psychological counselling. Career prospects are good as there is an ever-increasing demand for the services of capable astrologers and astrologically oriented therapists. In order to complete the professional training, the Centre asks that all students, for a minimum of one year, be involved in a recognized form of psychotherapy with a therapist, analyst or counsellor of his or her choice. The rationale behind this requirement is that we believe no responsible counsellor of any persuasion can hope to deal sensitively and wisely with another person's psyche unless one has some experience of his or her own.

The seminars offered in this book are just six of the fifty or so workshops offered by the Centre. The other volumes in the Seminars in Psychological Astrology Series are *The Development of the Personality*, Volume 1, *Dynamics of the Unconscious*, Volume 2, and *The Inner PLanets: Building Blocks of Personal Reality*, Volume 4. As stated earlier, these seminars are never repeated in precisely the same way, as the contributions and case material from each individual group vary, and as there are constant new developments and insights occurring through the ongoing work of the seminar leaders and others in the field. If the reader is interested in finding out more about either the public seminars or the in-depth professional training offered by the Centre, please write to The Centre for Psychological Astrology, BCM Box 1815, London WC1N 3XX, England. Your request for information should include a stamped, self-addressed envelope (for United Kingdom residents only) or an International Postal coupon to cover postage abroad.

RIGOR
&
IMAGINATION

ESSAYS FROM THE LEGACY OF GREGORY BATESON

edited by
C. Wilder
& John H. Weakland

PRAEGER SPECIAL STUDIES • PRAEGER SCIENTIFIC

P
90
.R53
1981

Published in 1981 (hb) and 1982 (pb) by Praeger Publishers
CBS Educational and Professional Publishing
A Division of CBS, Inc.
521 Fifth Avenue, New York, New York 10017 U.S.A.

© 1981 by Carol Wilder-Mott & John H. Weakland

Library of Congress Catalog Card Number: 81-83995
23456789 145 987654321

Printed in the United States of America